INNOVATE

or

evapora[...]

Test & Improve
Your Organization's

I.Q.

Its
Innovation
Quotient

James M. Higgins

Crummer Graduate School of Business
Rollins College
James M. Higgins & Associates Inc.

THE NEW
MANAGEMENT
PUBLISHING COMPANY
400 North New York Avenue, Suite 215
Winter Park, Florida 32789

DEVELOPMENTAL EDITOR: Carolyn Smith

PRODUCTION EDITOR: Susan Novotny

DESIGNER: Keri Caffrey

ILLUSTRATOR: Keri Caffrey

WORD PROCESSOR: Susan Crabill

New Management Publishing Company, Inc.
400 North New York Avenue, Suite 215
Winter Park, FL 32789

Publisher's Cataloging in Publication Data
(Prepared by Quality Books, Inc.)
Higgins, James M.
Innovate or Evaporate: Test and Improve Your Organization's IQ—Its Innovation Quotient/ James M. Higgins
p. cm.
Includes index.
Preassigned LCCN: 94-065551.
ISBN 1-883629-01-2
1. Organizational change—Management. I. Title.

HD58.8.H54 1994
658.4'063
QBI94-1219

This book is dedicated to
Sally and Sterling Lamp
for their loving support and enthusiasm for my work.

INNOVATE OR EVAPORATE

PREFACE

You can forget saying any eulogies for Japanese and European firms. Their deaths have been greatly exaggerated. Buoyed by recent successes against these firms, by increasing profits, and the fact that both Japan and Europe have only recently emerged from a trying economic period, too many U.S. firms are relaxing their competitive intensity. Doomsdayers are predicting a major loss of economic power for the Japanese, and many experts have written off most European firms because they are still having difficulty becoming globally competitive.

Do not be fooled by these *short term* aberrations. The Japanese are redefining their organizations. Always looking to the long term, they are moving swiftly to make their organizations more innovative, changing their organizational cultures and management styles. Their actions show that they have learned from their mistakes as well as from their successes. European firms are moving perhaps less rapidly, but with increasing momentum to become competitive first by cutting costs, through restructuring, reengineering, and so on; and secondly by increasing their innovation skills. And even if the Japanese and Europeans were suddenly no longer an issue, U.S. firms cannot overlook the burgeoning competitors from Pacific Rim nations, Eastern Europe, and Latin America. Fear not, the global race is still on.

So how does a firm obtain a global competitive advantage in the face of such stiff competition? TQM no longer serves this purpose. Having a successful TQM program simply keeps you in the race, but it doesn't help you pass the competition, because savvy competitors also have TQM programs. Furthermore, these savvy competitors are using speed strategies, reengineering, and flexible manufacturing, and many have begun continuous improvement programs. What's the next source of competitive advantage going to be? **Innovation!** *Innovation is the only long term sustainable competitive advantage.* It's the only competitive advantage that is adaptable to any situation. In fact, while it is not generally recognized, innovation determines competitiveness in most situations. It is, after all, what enables an organization to create its products and services and differentiate them from those of its competitors. Innovation is also where the ideas come from that enable an organization to cut costs. Innovation is the focus of this book, especially in terms of how a firm uses innovation to achieve competitive advantage in a global marketplace.

But global competition is not the only challenge facing businesses and their managers, professional staff, team leaders and other employees as they approach the 21st century. Change is occurring at an accelerating rate. The number of competitors is increasing dramatically. New technology is being introduced at a rapid pace. The workforce is increasingly diverse. There is a scarcity of certain resources, for example, highly skilled workers. There is a transformation occurring from an industrial to a knowledge based society. Economic and market conditions are increasingly unstable, especially on a global basis. Constituents are more demanding. And finally, the entire business environment is becoming more complex.

To meet these ten strategic challenges and take advantage of the opportunities they create, businesses need to embrace creative problem solving and innovation as never before. To achieve effective and efficient levels of creative problem solving and the innovation which results, an organization must improve the creativity of its work groups and individuals, and it must create the right kind of organizational culture which will foster that creativity and turn it into innovation.

This book describes the 49 characteristics that an organization's culture needs to possess to achieve strategic competitive advantage through innovation. These characteristics are based on research and case studies of innovative organizations. Four questionnaires are provided so that a firm may measure its performance on these characteristics relative to four types of innovation-product, process, marketing, and management. Later chapters provide guidance for achieving superior performance on these characteristics in the form of examples of innovation, and through strategic and operational planning guides.

Two other books by this same author discuss the other aspects of achieving organizational innovation-increasing individual and group creativity, and the use of creativity techniques. *Escape from the Maze: Increasing Individual and Group Creativity* focuses on how individuals can increase their intuitive prowess. It briefly reviews how group dynamics can be improved to increase creativity. *101 Creative Problem Solving Techniques: The Handbook of New Ideas for Business* describes 101 creativity techniques that can be used to improve both individual and group creativity levels. Learning such techniques adds a tremendous capacity for creativity in a relatively short time period and for a relatively small amount of energy and resource commitment. These three books form an "innovation trilogy." Order forms for all three books may be found in the final pages of this book.

SPECIAL THANKS

No book is the work of the author alone. I want to thank several people for their critical inputs into this book. First, Keri Caffrey, a really creative talent, has illustrated and designed this book in a masterful way. Susan Novotny managed the project from word processing through final printing in a most professional manner. Susan Crabill word processed much of the original manuscript. Carolyn Smith, my developmental editor on one of my college texts, and on *101 Creative Problem Solving Techniques,* did an outstanding job of making this book user friendly. Several hundred Roy E. Crummer Graduate School of Business MBA students and Crummer Management Program students provided important feedback about the questionnaires, as did employee groups from several companies. My business reviewers provided excellent input. I especially want to thank those who so graciously allowed me to use their comments on the back cover: Buell G. Duncan, Jr., Chairman of the Board, Retired, Sun Banks, Inc.; Napier Collyns, President, Global Business Network; Thomas F. Kirk, Sr. V.P. & CFO, Rhône Poulenc, Inc.; Kendra VanderMeulen, V.P. & General Manager, McCaw Cellular Communications, Inc.

The Roy E. Crummer Graduate School of Business is a special place in the universe. Innovation has been a driving force there for many years, starting with the deanship of Martin Schatz, and continuing through the deanships of Sam Certo, Alan Nagle, and Ed Moses. Working in such an environment with faculty members similarly inclined is a prerequisite to a work such as this book.

Our golden retriever, Macmillan, spent as many hours by my PC as I did in front of it. He helped me keep a sense of balance about life-it can't be serious all the time. You have to take time out for fun.

And finally, my lovely wife Susan has always believed in the innovation trilogy and has provided constant encouragement throughout its writing and publication. With her own career, she still found time to encourage and support mine.

TABLE OF CONTENTS

PART I

TEST

YOUR
ORGANIZATION'S IQ
Its Innovation Quotient[1]

---

[1]A term recently used by Peter J. Neff, CEO of Rhône-Poulenc Inc.

1

INNOVATION: THE KEY TO PRODUCTIVITY

CHAPTER 1

*Every organization—not just businesses—needs one core competence:
innovation. And every organization needs a way to record and appraise
its **innovative** performance..*

Peter F. Drucker, Consultant and Author
"The Information Executives Truly Need"
Harvard Business Review

The 3M Company is famous for its never-ending series of new
products, which have included Scotch brand cellophane tape
and the ubiquitous Post-It note pads.[1] Almost every year, General Electric files more U.S. patents than any other firm headquartered in the United States.[2] Bell Labs has consistently produced a large number of successful new products, among them
the transistor and fiber optics. The company is currently developing an "optical computer" that would revolutionize the
computer industry.[3] Apple Computer gave us the Apple II, followed by the Apple Macintosh. Now it is pursuing a visionary
personal computer, that will incorporate voice command and

permit remote database searches; it will include a video telephone. All of these functions will fit in a unit the size of a notebook.[4] The Power Macintosh and the Newton are first steps towards fulfilling that vision.

Ford Motor Company continues to cut production costs, improve product quality, and utilize new management systems that increase productivity.[5] Toyota's aggressive innovations may someday make it the number one automobile company in the world, profiting handsomely from product successes such as the Lexus and from a relative low cost advantage that virtually no other firm can match.[6] Chrysler continues to amaze the auto world with new products like the Concorde, Chrysler LHS, and Neon, all of which are sold at reasonable prices.[7]

McDonald's is constantly searching for new products and services as well as ways to reduce costs, for example, by reducing the amount of labor required to provide each product or service.[8] Sony is the recognized world leader in consumer electronics, introducing some 1,000 products each year; 800 of those products are new versions of old products but 200 are totally new.[9] Xerox cuts costs, brings out new products at a relentless pace, and has revolutionized its approaches to management.[10] Hewlett-Packard continues to dazzle the industrial world because, despite its size ($24 billion in sales and 96,000 employees), it continues to grow at a staggering pace. It launches successful new products at a rate few competitors can match. Many point to its innovative ways of managing as a major reason for its success.[11]

These firms have all shown a remarkable proclivity for innovation—both in products and in processes. Yet many firms fail to produce much that's new or to improve the processes by which they provide their products or services. Is there something different about organizations that are consistently innovative? Absolutely! Case and research studies have revealed a set of characteristics that are shared by innovative firms, regardless of differences in their organizational cultures. It is these characteristics that will enable a firm to survive and prosper in the coming years. These characteristics create the **profile of the innovative organization**, and are the subject of this book.

INNOVATE OR EVAPORATE

Before we explore these characteristics in detail, let's examine the business environment and the concept of innovation.

Surviving and prospering in business have never been easy. There are always problems to be solved and opportunities to be taken advantage of. But from now through the first decade of the twenty-first century, organizations, managers, and other employees will be confronted with a number of unprecedented strategic challenges. The primary challenges are these:[12]

1. **Accelerating Rates of Change:** In his famous 1970 book *Future Shock*, Alvin Toffler predicted that as the twenty-first century approached, all facets of life, including organizational life, would involve accelerating rates of change.[13] This prediction has certainly been borne out! Not only are changes occuring at an accelerating rate, but the magnitude of their significance is increasing.[14] "Change is the order of the day. Choose it or chase it. Adapt or die," proclaimed Theodore Levitt, former editor of the *Harvard Business Review*.[15]

2. **Increasing Levels of Competition:** The 1990s are proving to be the most competitive decade of the twentieth century. More competitors are entering both domestic and global markets. But the next century, with the expected emergence of more powerful European and Pacific Rim firms, will be even more competitive. Entrepreneurship is increasing throughout the world. Many markets, such as automobiles and steel, offer little hope of future growth, especially in the short term. In those markets, the name of the game is market share. Other markets, such as consumer products, will offer a multitude of growth opportunities, especially in the long term.

3. **The Globalization of Business Competition:** The changes resulting from the Europe 1992 initiative, the high probability that the Pacific Rim will have the world's most significant economy before the middle of the twenty-first century, increased levels of foreign competition in the domestic economies of most countries, and similar trends make it imperative that managers develop and maintain a global

perspective when doing business. It simply isn't enough to consider the domestic market as sufficient to support a firm's future. Even if that is the case today, it won't be long before foreign competitors enter all markets in an effort to gain increased market share in the face of stagnant growth in their own domestic economies.

4. **Rapid Technological Change:** Most firms, even service firms, depend in some way on technology to attain the competitive advantage necessary to survive and prosper. But technology changes rapidly in virtually all industries. **Technological discontinuity**, wherein a firm's technology becomes obsolete due to another firm's new technology, will be pervasive. Competitors will often develop technologies that "leapfrog" another firm's, thus giving the competitor a strategic advantage.

5. **A More Diverse Work Force:** During the 1990s, the work force has become significantly more diverse than those of earlier decades. Greater diversity can be seen in several areas, including demographics, worker expectations, preparedness for work, and the age of the average worker. The white-male-dominated work force is no longer the norm, and the percentages of women and minorities in the work force will continue to increase. A major increase in the number of foreign-born workers entering the U.S. work force is expected to occur, compensating for an expected shortage of workers. Thus cultural diversity in the workplace is becoming the norm, rather than the exception. Workers' expectations in terms of rewards are anticipated to increase, and their values are likely to shift as well, leading them to seek more meaningful work. At the same time, however, workers' average skill levels are expected to decrease because of a deficiency in the overall educational and experience levels of new entrants to the work force. Finally, the work force as a whole is expected to age, primarily owing to the aging of the baby boom generation.[16]

6. **Resource Shortages:** During the next few years, several important resources, notably electrical energy, water, and skilled human resources, and quite probably investment

capital, will be in increasingly short supply in many parts of the world, including the United States. In addition, specific industries may find that certain raw materials may be in short supply, such as hardwood lumber for housing construction.

7. **The Transition from an Industrial to a Knowledge-Based Society:** In the twenty-first century, knowledge management will be pervasive. In some companies, it already is. Information can be used to establish a strategic advantage. For example, the ability to provide information to customers can give a firm an advantage over others. Electronic data interchange (EDI), whereby customers and suppliers share databases, results in closer relationships, which help lock out competitors. But the society of the twenty-first century will be much more than an information society. It will be a society based on knowledge—"patents, processes, management skills, technologies, information about customers and suppliers, and old-fashioned experience."[17] It is knowledge in this sense that firms will use to create a competitive advantage. Of course, knowledge has always been important, but never to the degree that it will be in the next century. So, although until recently we really haven't thought about managing knowledge, we must now make it the central focus of management.[18]

8. **Unstable Market and Economic Conditions:** U.S. firms will face an unparalleled level of instability in market and economic conditions during the remainder of the 1990s. The savings and loan bailout program which is expected to cost at least $500 billion, is just one example.[19] Federal budget deficits have reached disturbing proportions.[20] As if these problems were not enough, the United States has an extremely high trade deficit fueled by several factors. These factors include lack of investment in research and development;[21] Japanese trade practices that U.S. firms consider unfair;[22] and a potential shortage of capital as the world's economy adjusts to expansion in Eastern Europe, Russia, China, and the Pacific Rim. President Clinton's health care proposals offer additional challenges. Consider these and other key issues, such as the effect of the baby boomers as a significant "age wave" in the popula-

tion, and it is easy to understand why firms will have to deal with a wide range of strategic issues in this decade.

9. **Increasing Demands of Constituents:** As the twenty-first century approaches, various constituent groups will continue to make significant demands on businesses. They will be calling for greater attention to environmental protection; for improved employee health and safety; for more attention to employee security during mergers and acquisitions; for higher value for shareholders; for higher quality and better service for customers (including internal customers); for increased efforts to ensure equal employment opportunity; for more corporate philanthropy; and for the application of high ethical standards both to managers and to business as a whole.

10. **Increasing Complexity of the Environment:** As this list of strategic challenges suggests, the environment in which businesses operate is becoming ever more complex. More and more variables must be considered by managers at every level, either when formulating strategy or while implementing it. Hundreds of problems must be solved by companies and managers every week, and many of those problems are themselves increasingly complex. Complex problems demand innovative solutions.

As a consequence of the challenges just described, every facet of business, from overall strategy to daily operations, is full of new problems and opportunities. Nevertheless, the task of just "doing business" remains. This in itself is difficult enough regardless of the other challenges that must be faced. How can a business survive and prosper under these conditions? *By innovating!*

Virtually all leading authorities on business, including Fortune 500 CEOs, researchers, and consultants, agree that there is only one way firms can cope with all the challenges confronting them in the 1990s, not to mention those they'll have to face in the twenty-first century. Firms must be innovative.[23] *3M, General Electric, Apple Computer, Bell Labs, Ford, Toyota, Chrysler, McDonald's, Sony, and Xerox all innovate in order to survive and prosper. They have all recognized that in today's environment they must **innovate or evaporate.***

INNOVATION AND CREATIVITY

Innovation is how a firm or an individual makes money from creativity. Organizations, their managers, and other employees seek to create original ideas and concepts that will end up as innovations, such as new or enhanced products or services, processes that increase efficiency, highly competitive marketing campaigns, or superior management. The process of generating something new is known as **origination.**

Something **original** is something new, something that didn't exist before. **Creativity** is the process of generating something new that has value. There are many original ideas and concepts, but some may not have value and hence may not be considered creative. A **creation** is something original that has value.

Innovation is the process of creating something new that has *significant* value to an individual, a group, an organization, an industry, or a society. **An innovation** is a creation that has significant value.

These distinctions may seem superficial and academic, but they are not. This is so for several reasons, all of which are related to achieving the goal of innovation. First, you need to learn how to tell whether the ideas you generate are creative or merely original. Original ideas just aren't enough. Second, to be innovative you need to go beyond merely being creative. You need to know whether the ideas you generate have the potential for significant value, that is, the potential to become innovations. Finally, firms as well as individuals must learn to turn creations into innovations. Unfortunately, while U.S. firms and their employees are not nearly as creative as they should be, their performance record is even worse when it comes to turning creations into innovations[24]. On average, only one idea in ten developed in a laboratory ever gets to market.[25] As a result, the global competitive positions of many U.S.

Innovation: The Key to Productivity

Chapter 1

firms have eroded significantly in recent years and will continue to do so unless those firms become more innovative.[26]

Moreover, in meeting the other strategic challenges and in "doing business" every day, firms will not be as effective or efficient as they should be if they cannot be innovative. Solving problems and pursuing opportunities require solutions, many of which may be unique to the specific situation. Therefore, creativity and the intended resultant innovation are fundamental to the survival and prosperity of the firm. This chapter's *Innovate or Evaporate 1.1* examines Hitachi, a firm that handles its management challenges well, a firm that innovates.

Creativity, the Springboard to Innovation

Before we can have innovation, we must have creativity.

Expanding on our earlier definition, **creativity** is the skill to originate something new and to make it valuable.[27] The key word here is **skill**. *Creativity is a skill. It is not something mystical, available only to a few. Everyone possesses an innate capacity for creativity.* But in most people the transformation of this capacity into a skill has been thwarted by parents, teachers, and bosses who provide and enforce rules about what behaviors are acceptable. Because only a few behaviors are allowed, creativity, which involves exploring new realms (and thus breaking the rules), is stifled. Therefore, firms must act to develop the skill of creativity in their employees in order to unleash their untapped potential.[28]

Creativity can be incremental, occurring in a series of small progressive steps; an example is the lengthy, painstaking research that led to the development of polio vaccine. Conversely, creativity can involve giant leaps forward in which many links in the evolutionary chain of concepts are hurdled by a single effort. The main workings of Apple Computer's Macintosh personal computer, a highly advanced system at the time, were a giant leap forward in technology.

The product of the creative effort need not be a tangible physical object. It may be an idea, an association of facts, an insight, or a more effective or efficient process as well as a new product or service. Each of these, when fully expressed and functioning, has value.

HITACHI INNOVATES LIKE NOBODY'S BUSINESS

With $62 billion in sales, Hitachi Limited produces nearly 2% of Japan's yearly gross national product. It has 28 factories, 800 subsidiaries, and 320,000 employees. It annually sells $9 billion worth of consumer electronics products, and yet it also sells $20 billion worth of power plants, generators and robots. It also has a computer chip division that annually sells more than Motorola, Intel, and Sun Microsystems combined. It is singly responsible for 6% of Japan's total R&D expenditures. It is Japan's largest patent holder and has been at the top of the U.S. patent list most of the past ten years. Of its rivals in size, General Electric, Matsushita and IBM, only Hitachi has interests in more than three of these business areas: computers, chips, software, consumer electronics, power plants, transportation, medical equipment, and telecommunications. It has interests in all eight areas. Thus it is capable of undertaking huge projects, such as a national maglev transportation system, that literally no one else could undertake.

Hitachi's success story begins with product R&D, but goes beyond new products to include processes in all areas of the firm helping drive costs down, down, down. Facing increased competition and sagging demand in many of its business areas such as mainframe computers, Hitachi has turned to Spartan cost cutting to maintain its market positions. It is advancing its vision of the future through a sophisticated, innovative information network where technology fusion is a frequent result. Sharing information among sister units is seen as paramount to new product development and cost cutting.

INNOVATE OR EVAPORATE 1.1

continued next page

=

HITACHI

Hitachi's 63-year-old president, Tsutomu Kanai, is just the non-conformist to lead this firm. He has a vision for the firm, one that takes advantage of its diversity in an integrated way. Thus the firm is pursuing integrated complex projects with zest. Because it has huge cash reserves and has invested in basic businesses that survive recessions well, Hitachi has been able to protect its product R&D stream more than most firms. "Basic science is something we will never sacrifice," observes Kanai.

Hitachi, unlike other Japanese firms, has a loose, decentralized management structure. Renegades are encouraged by this system. One such renegade is Yasutsugu Takeda, Hitachi's top R&D administrator. He was undaunted by the fact that none of Hitachi's factory managers were interested in making several products his labs had developed. So he created catalogs of these products, lined up customers, and then went to Hitachi factory managers and convinced them that they should make these products after all. Decentralization is the name of the game at Hitachi. The 28 factories are run more as separate businesses than as factories. It's often hard to tell exactly who runs the firm. There are ten managing directors, and clearly, Kanai is President. But the firm moves as a large group of equals might move, more than a pryamidal organization run by a powerful CEO would react.

Hitachi is working on new products at various distances into the future. In 3 to 5 years, they expect to have neural networks and multimedia office products. In 5 to 10 years, they forsee hand-held computers that accept voice commands and exchange data over radio waves. In 10 to 20 years they expect to produce computers with 100 times the power and 10 times the speed of today's models. Over 20 years from now, they expect biocomputers that can organically repair themselves. Innovation is truly the focus at Hitachi.

Source: Takeo Imori, "Hitachi: Too Little, Too Late?" *Tokyo Business Today* (December 1992), pp. 12-13; Neil Gross, "Inside Hitachi," *Business Week* (September 28, 1992), pp. 92-100.

THE "FOUR P'S" OF CREATIVITY AND INNOVATION

Important to raising levels of creativity and innovation is an understanding of the **"four P's"**: **product, personal and group creativity, processes** (techniques), and **possibilities.** The first of the four P's, the product or result, will not occur unless the other three P's are in place.[29] (See Figure 1.1.)

If a firm, group, or organization is not moving to increase its innovativeness—that is, if it is not providing the correct *possibilities* (essentially the right organizational culture) or educating its members in the right individual and group creative *processes*, or developing its members' levels of *personal and group creativity*—it will not be able to cope with the ten strategic challenges identified earlier, nor will it be able to solve its other problems as well as it might otherwise. It won't have the *products* it needs to survive and prosper.

The Innovation Equation: How the 4 P'S Fit Together with Creativity and Innovation

Creativity can be increased both by increasing levels of personal and group creativity and by learning certain techniques (processes). If these occur within the right organizational culture (possibilities), the result is innovation, as shown in Figure 1.1.

FIGURE 1.1 THE INNOVATION EQUATION

CREATIVITY	+	ORGANIZATIONAL CULTURE	=	INNOVATION
Personal & Group Creativity Processes (Techniques)		Possibilities		Product 4 Types of Innovation: Product, Process, Marketing, Management

The Product

The **product** is the result of the creation/innovation process. It can be a physical product, a service, or an enhancement to these; a process for increasing effectiveness and/or efficiency; a more innovative approach to marketing; or a better way to manage. To be a true creative product it must have value and not merely be original. To be innovative, it must have *significant* value.

How do you determine what has potentially significant value? Sometimes by analysis, sometimes by intuition. (Value is relative, both in terms of the value system of the evaluator and in terms of the timing of the creation.) For example, twelve Hollywood studios turned down the "Star Wars" movie concept. Finally, Twentieth Century Fox agreed to take the risk and ended up making the most financially successful movie of all time. Similarly, some inventors and their investors offered to sell a new idea to IBM, General Motors, DuPont, and several other major firms and were turned down by all of them. Finally, they decided to build and market the product themselves and became multimillionaires. The process was photocopying, and the company became Xerox.[30] In both of these examples, a number of idea evaluators' values caused them to reject a new product, yet others intuitively saw its potential.

Even successful entrepreneurs may misjudge the value of a creation and, hence, its potential to become an innovation. Victor Kiam, of Remington Razor fame, was once offered the patent to Velcro for $25,000; he turned it down, believing it had no future.[31] As of 1988, Velcro products had brought in a total of about $6 billion in sales since their inception. Even innovative firms, like Chrysler, can let innovative ideas get caught up in bureaucracy. Ron Zarowitz had the brilliant idea of providing built-in car seats for toddlers in Chrysler minivans. Zarowitz, a Chrysler manager, pushed the idea very hard, but it took the company seven years to finally accept it. Chrysler now sells all the built-in toddler seats it can make.[32]

Personal and Group Creativity

Increasing **personal creativity** involves a three-pronged effort:

1. Increasing the individual's levels of intuition. For most people, this means increasing the use of the right side of the brain and increasing the ability of both sides of the brain to work together.

2. Freeing the individual from any socialization that may have limited his or her creativity. The latter includes not only resocializing the individual but also learning new habits that will help him or her be more creative.

3. Learning creative processes.

Increasing **group creativity** requires the learning of group creativity processes, and also the proper management of group dynamics.

The Processes

Numerous individual and group **processes** (techniques) can be used to increase the amount of creativity applied in solving problems within an organization. Among these processes, some of the more familiar ones are brainstorming, mind mapping, and storyboarding. But they are not the only ones; in fact, over 100 different techniques are available.[33] These processes are directed at increasing creativity in all stages of the problem-solving process. Learning them takes time and effort, but you can master them.

The Possibilities

For innovation to occur, the **possibilities** for creativity and innovation must exist. Regardless of your creative talents, however great your knowledge or skill, you will not be able to create many innovations if you are not functioning in a favorable situation. If the organization's culture, in the broadest sense, does not support and even require innovation, and if the prevailing management style is not appropriate, it is unlikely that innovation will occur. The evidence indicates that organizational innovation results from careful management of the organization's culture and management style.

Innovation: The Key to Productivity

Chapter 1

This issue can be understood most readily in terms of McKinsey & Company's "Seven S's" of organizational success:[34] strategy, structure, systems (management), style (leadership), staffing, skills (sought synergies as an organization not a collection of individual skills), and shared values (organizational culture). The term *shared values* includes values related to the other six S's. These seven S's form the framework for this book. They are discussed in Chapter 4 and in Chapters 5 through 13.

A Trilogy of Books on Creativity and Innovation

The four P's of creativity and innovation—product, possibilities, processes, and personal and group creativity, are the subjects of the three books in this series, which form a trilogy on creativity and innovation.

1. *101 Creative Problem Solving Techniques: The Handbook of New Ideas for Business* reviews the *processes* (techniques) that individuals and groups can use in the creative problem solving process in order to make their problem solving more creative.

2. *Innovate or Evaporate: Test and Improve Your Organization's IQ—Its Innovation Quotient* discusses both the *product* (the four types of innovation), and the *possibilities* for achieving the product.

3. *Escape From the Maze: Increasing Individual and Group Creativity*, discusses how to raise levels of *personal creativity* by working to improve intuition and removing barriers to creativity. A discussion of how to improve group dynamics in order to improve *group creativity* is included.

THE FOUR TYPES OF INNOVATION

As noted earlier, the product or result of the innovation process is an innovation. There are four principal types of innovation: product, process, marketing, and management.[35]

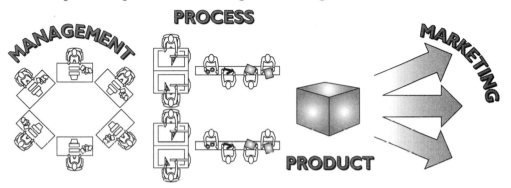

1. **Product innovation** results in new products or services or in enhancements to old products or services. The opening paragraph in this chapter describes product innovations by Apple Computer, Toyota, and Chrysler.

2. **Process innovation** results in improved processes within the organization—for example, in operations, human resources management, or finance. It focuses on improving effectiveness and efficiency. Toyota's cost advantage, discussed at the beginning of the chapter, is a result of process innovation. Cooper Tire Company, the subject of *Innovate or Evaporate 1.3*, focuses its efforts on process innovation. *Innovate or Evaporate 1.2* describes a service firm that has found that innovation is necessary for survival.

3. **Marketing innovation** is related to the marketing functions of promotion, pricing, and distribution, as well as to product functions other than product development (for example, packaging). To cite one example, in advertising its new products, Chrysler uses innovative marketing themes such as those featuring its $1 billion Technology Center.

4. Finally, **management innovation** improves the way the organization is managed. Bell Laboratories uses unique management innovations, such as programs aimed at improving researchers' productivity, to create new products.[36]

INNOVATION AND FIRM SUCCESS

Innovation is the key to productivity. Studies of successful organizations reveal that they design more new products, services, and enhancements; utilize their processes more effectively and efficiently; market their products more innovatively; and manage more innovatively than less successful organizations.[37] Studies also reveal that innovative firms also make more money than non-innovative firms.[38]

It is innovation in managing all of the organization's economic functions—marketing, operations, finance, human resources, research and development, and information management—together with greater innovation in the management process itself, that separates the truly successful companies from the less successful ones. This can be seen in the discussion of Hitachi in *Innovate or Evaporate 1.1*. Note that although Hitachi is a high-tech firm, it operates in several industries, including one that would be considered basic manufacturing. An important lesson to be learned from this reading is that innovation is applicable to most jobs in all kinds of industries.

PART I OF THIS BOOK

Part I of this book contains four chapters that introduce the topic of innovation and test for what can be done to improve a firm's—and its employees'—innovativeness. Chapter 1 discussed the basics of innovation and the relevant terms and concepts. Chapter 2 frames the global competitive situation—the situation that requires strong action by North American and European firms to become more innovative. Chapter 3 reviews the nature of the product that results from the innovation process. That product can be a physical product, a service, a process, or an idea. Four types of innovation are discussed, and examples of each are provided. Chapter 4 contains two questionnaires that will allow you to test your organization's **Innovation Quotient**[1], or IQ. Using these questionnaires, you can compare your firm to the profile of the innovative organization. The characteristics of that profile are discussed in more detail in Part II of this book.

AT NORFOLK GENERAL, PEOPLE DON'T GET LOST IN X-RAY ANY MORE

In Paddy Chayefsky's satirical screenplay, "The Hospital," a killer hides his victim in X-ray, explaining, "People get lost in X-ray. Someone lying unattended there for days would never be noticed."

Well it wasn't quite that bad at Norfolk General Hospital, but it did take 72.5 hours elapsed time between the ordering of an X-ray, CAT scan or other radiological test, and the delivery of the related report to the doctor who ordered it. "We were all embarrassed by that turnaround," comments Chief Radiologist Robert Woolfitt. Using a team of nine employees and managers, that time was reduced to 13.8 hours, an 81 percent improvement. The task force met only 11 times during the year that it took to reduce the time for this process, but informal meetings were frequent, and as soon as a problem was spotted, it was eliminated. As in many firms, for some reason or other, activities had been added to the total X-ray process that really had no utility in retrospect. For example, adding hand stamped physician signatures or adding the word "permanent" to printouts so they weren't thrown out were requirements that were found to be unnecessary, but that at some point in time, someone had requested.

Part of the problem was improving the quality of the work done, for example, assuring that nurses indicated any special requirements for a patient, such as oxygen. And in some cases, extra effort was necessary to speed things along. For example, X-ray

continued next page

NORFOLK GENERAL

technicians began walking developed film to those at the next stage of the process rather than waiting for someone to pick up the film from their temporary storage boxes. And in some cases, improvement meant buying new equipment, such as a CD-ROM storage device, so that information could be processed faster.

The final result was one of careful process innovation, the kind that many firms have been investing in heavily in the 1990s.

Source: Kevin Anderson, "Dramatic Turnaround: X-Ray Processing Time Cut 81%" *USA Today* (April 4, 1992), p. 5B.

AT COOPER TIRE, THE ACCENT IS ON PRODUCTIVITY

Cooper Tire & Rubber Company Inc. focuses on driving its costs lower so it can give its dealers higher margins. Why, because when customers ask what the dealer recommends, Cooper wants to be sure its their tires and not those of some competitor. Cooper focuses on maintaining a down home management style. Its executive offices feature 1960s vintage grey metal desks, and the copmany board room table was actually pieced together from two tables by Cooper carpenters sometime in the 1970s.

Cooper spends just five cents for every dollar of sales to sell its goods, compared to most of its rivals' twenty cents. The annual report is done in black and white, and spots on the Paul Harvey show are its main advertisements. But its no frills approach, and rock bottom prices have allowed it to capture 12 percent of the total U.S. replacement tire market.

Cooper focuses on finding new ways to manufacture that will drive costs down. For example, it invests heavily in advanced systems technology, it modernizes facilities and equipment when such investment cuts costs long term. It uses computerized manufacturing where possible. It intentionally develops equipment rather than contracting for it. And, yes, occasionally, it develops new products especially for niche markets.

Source: Mary Driscoll, "Cooper Tire & Rubber: A Short Course in Value Pricing," *CPO: The Magazine for Senior Financial Executives* (January 1994), p. 24; "Cooper Recycles Waste," company bulletin on waste policies (September 1993), pp. 1-4; Dan Cordtz, "Cooper Tire Rolls Along," *Financial World* (April 27, 1993), p. 63; Albert G. Holzinger, "A Successful Competitor," *Nation's Business* (April 1993), pp. 59-60; Cooper Tire Company, "1992 Annual Report," (Findlay, Ohio: Cooper Tire Company, February 15, 1993), p. 5; Carol Hymowitz and Thomas F. O'Boyle, "A Way that Works: Two Disparate Firms Find Keys to Success in Troubled Industries," *Wall Street Journal* (May 29, 1991), pp. A1, A7; Ivan Gorr, "Cooper Tire: Successful Adaptation in a Changing Industry," *Journal of Business Strategy* (Winter 1987), pp. 83-86.

INNOVATE OR EVAPORATE 1.3

REFERENCES

1. Russell Mitchell, "Masters of Innovation—How 3M Keeps Its New Products Coming," *Business Week* (April 11, 1989), pp. 58-63.

2. Peter Coy, "The Global Patent Race Picks Up Speed," *Business Week* (August 9, 1992), pp. 57-58.

3. Robert Buderi, "American Inventors Are Reinventing Themselves," *Business Week* (January 18, 1993), p. 79; Janet Guyon, "Bell Labs Takes a Small Step Toward an Optical Computer," *Wall Street Journal* (July 18, 1986), p. 23; Natalie Angier, "Folding the Perfect Corner," *Time* (December 3, 1984), p. 63; "Bell Labs: Imagination Inc.," *Time* (January 25, 1982), pp. 56-57.

4. A telephone discussion with Apple's research staff on February 3, 1994 confirms that while the product is visionary, some of its features will begin appearing in other Apple products in the near future. General Magic, a firm partly owned by Apple and staffed with numerous former Apple research gurus, is actively pursuing the concept of the Knowledge Navigator. John Sculley, then CEO of Apple, in his speech at the MacWorld 1988 Convention (February 8, 1988), first brought our attention to the Knowledge Navigator.

5. Raymond Serafin, "Trotman's Tenure May See Ford Seize the Lead," *Advertising Age* (October 11, 1993), pp. 1, 50; Alex Taylor III, "Ford's $6 Billion Baby," *Fortune* (June 28, 1993), pp. 76-81.

6. William Spindle, "Toyota Retooled," *Business Week* (April 4, 1994), pp. 54-57; Karen Lowry Miller, "On a Collision Course with the Future," *Business Week* (October 11, 1993), pp. 16-21; "Toyota Puts It on the Line," *U.S. News & World Report* (August 23, 1993), pp. 47-48; Alex Taylor III, "How Toyota Copes With Hard Times," *Fortune* (January 25, 1993), pp. 78-81; Alex Taylor III, "Why Toyota Keeps Getting Better and Better," *Fortune* (November 19, 1990), pp. 66-79; Kathryn Graven and Bradley A. Stertz, "Gaining Speed: Toyota Is Gearing Up to Expand Output, Extend Global Reach," *Wall Street Journal* (July 20, 1990), pp. A1, A8. Note that the high value of the yen has hurt all Japanese automakers in the 1992-1994 period. This is probably a short-term phenomenon, however.

7. David Woodruff, "Chrysler's Neon," *Business Week* (May 3, 1993), pp. 116-126; "Eaton's Plan: Keep Focused," *U.S.A. Today* (May 10, 1993), p. 3B.

8. Lois Therrien, "McRisky," *Business Week* (October 21, 1993), pp. 114-122.

9. Brenton R. Schlender, "How Sony Keeps the Magic Going," *Fortune* (February 22, 1992), pp. 76-84.

10. Tim Smart, "Can Xerox Duplicate Its Glory Days?" *Business Week* (October 4, 1993), pp. 56-58; Thomas H. Stewart, "The Search for the Organization of Tomorrow," *Fortune* (May 18, 1992), pp. 92-98.

11. Alan Deutschman, "How H-P Continues to Grow and Grow," *Fortune* (May 2, 1994), pp. 90-100; "The Best of 1993: The Best Managers, The Best Entrepreneurs," *Business Week* (January 10, 1994), pp. 122-130; Jennifer Laabs, "Hewlett-Packard's Core Values Drive H-P Strategy," *Personnel Journal* (December 1993), pp. 38-48; Robert D. Hof, "Hewlett-Packard Digs Deep for a Digital Future," *Business Week* (October 18, 1993), pp. 72-75.

12. James M. Higgins, *The Management Challenge: An Introduction to Management*, 2nd ed. (New York: Macmillan, 1994), Chapter 1; James M. Higgins and Julian W. Vincze, *Strategic Management: Text and Cases*, 5th ed. (Fort Worth, TX: Dryden Press, 1993), Chapter 1.

13. Alvin Toffler, *Future Shock*, (New York: Bantam, 1970), Chapter 1.

14. Michael Naylor, Executive Vice-President for Strategic Planning for General Motors, speech to the Academy of Management, Chicago (August 14, 1986).

15. Theodore Levitt, "Editorial," *Harvard Business Review* (January/February 1988), p. 4.

16. For a review of the demographics, see "Needed: Human Capital," *Business Week* (September 19, 1988), pp. 102-103; Robert W. Goddard, "Workforce 2000," *Personnel Journal* (February 1989), pp. 64-71.

17. Thomas A. Stewart, "Brainpower," *Fortune* (June 3, 1991), p. 44; Robert W. Goddard, loc. cit.

18. Ikujiro Nonaka, "The Knowledge Creating Company," *Harvard Business Review* (November-December 1991), pp. 96-104.

19. John Meehan, "Is There any Bottom to the Thrift Quagmire?" *Business Week* (March 4, 1991), pp. 62-63.

20. Edward H. Ladd, "Why the 1990s Will Be Nothing Like the 1980s," *Bottomline* (May 1990), pp. 7-9.

21. Charles W. Hill, Michael A. Hitt, and Robert E. Hoskinson, "Declining U.S. Competitiveness: Reflections on a Crisis," *The Academy of Management Executive* (February 1988), pp. 51-60.

22. Alan Murray and Urban C. Lehner, "Strained Alliances: U.S., Japan Struggle to Redefine Relations as Resentment Grows," *Wall Street Journal* (June 13, 1990), pp. A1, A8; Robert T. Green and Trina L. Larsen, "Only Retaliation Will Open Up Japan," *Harvard Business Review* (November-December 1987), pp. 22-28.

23. For example, see: CEO Lewis Platt of Hewlett-Packard as quoted in Alan Deutschman, "How H-P Continues to Grow and Grow," *Fortune* (May 2, 1994), p. 90. Ed McCracken, CEO of Silicon Graphics as interviewed in Steven E. Prokesch, "Mastering Chaos at the High-Tech Frontier," *Harvard Business Review* (November-December 1993), pp. 135-144; Jack Welch (CEO and chairman of General Electric), who sees innovation driving productivity, which drives competition, as quoted in Thomas A. Stewart, "GE Keeps Those Ideas Coming," *Fortune* (August 12, 1991), pp. 41-49. Michael E. Porter (researcher and consultant) observes in *The Competitive Advantage of Nations* (New York: Free Press, 1990), pp. 578-579, that innovation, continuous improvement, and change are the cornerstones of global competitiveness. Gary Hamel and C. K. Prahalad, "Strategic Intent," *Harvard Business Review* (May-June 1989), pp. 43-76. *Business Week* considered the topic of innovation so critical to U.S. competitiveness that it devoted two special issues to it (June 1989 and 1990). John Sculley (then CEO and chairman of Apple Computer), in "Speech to MacWorld," February 1988, indicated that only the innovative firm would survive in the future. A 1987 survey of 1000 CEOs by consulting firm Arthur D. Little found that 92 percent believed that innovation was critical to the future success of their firm, "Common Sense, Experiences Are Not Enough: It's Time to Get Creative," *Marketing News* (January 18, 1988). Thomas J. Peters (consultant and researcher) indicates in *Thriving on Chaos: Handbook for a Management Revolution* (New York: Knopf, 1987), pp. 191-280, that innovation is one of five prescriptions for chaos (accelerating change, complex environment, global competition, and other challenges). See also William P. Hewlett (chairman and co-founder of Hewlett-Packard), "Graduation Speech," as reported in Helen Pike, "Hewlett Sounds Call for Engineering Creativity in MIT Graduate Speech," *Electronic Engineering Times* (June 23, 1986), p. 78. Richard N. Foster (consultant), in *Innovation: The Attacker's Advantage* (New York:

Summitt Books, 1986), p. 21, indicates that in his thirty years at McKinsey & Company every successful firm he saw was innovative. Michael E. Porter discusses the criticalness of innovation to competitiveness in *Competitive Strategy* (New York: Free Press, 1980), pp. 177-179.

24. Brian Dumaine, "Closing the Innovation Gap," *Fortune* (December 2, 1991), pp. 56-62.

25. Amal Kumar Naj, "Creative Energy: GE's Latest Invention—A Way to Move Ideas From Lab to Market," *Wall Street Journal* (June 14, 1990), pp. A1, A9.

26. Andrew Kupfer, "How American Industry Stacks Up," *Fortune* (March 9, 1992), pp. 30-46.

27. John G. Young, "What is Creativity?" *The Journal of Creative Behavior* (1985, 2nd Quarter), pp. 77-87.

28. James M. Higgins, *Escape From the Maze: Increasing Personal and Group Creativity* (Winter Park, FL: The New Management Publishing Company, 1994).

29. Similar to but not the same as the 4 P's of creativity identified by M. Rhodes—person, press (culture, management style, and resources), process (the creative process, consisting of preparation, incubation, illumination, and verification), and product, in "An Analysis of Creativity," *Phi Delta Kappa* (vol. 42), pp. 305-310.

30. "Chester Carlson—Xerography," Xerox Internal Documents; "A Profile in Entrepreneurship," a special advertising session, *Inc.* (July 1988), pp. 109-110.

31. Victor Kiam, speech to the Roy E. Crummer Graduate School of Business, Rollins College, Winter Park, FL (October 28, 1985).

32. Brian Dumaine, op. cit., pp. 56-57, 62.

33. James M. Higgins, *101 Creative Problem Solving Techniques: The Handbook of New Ideas for Business* (Winter Park, FL: The New Management Publishing Company, 1994).

34. Thomas J. Peters and Robert H. Waterman, Jr., *In Search of Excellence* (New York: Harper & Row, 1982), pp. 9-11. Adapted slightly from their seven S's model—strategy, structure, systems, style, staff, skills, shared values (culture).

35. Ray Statta, "Organizational Learning—The Key to Management Innovation," *Sloan Management Review* (Spring 1989), pp. 63-74; Michael Porter, op. cit., pp. 177-178.

36. Robert Kelley and Janet Caplan, "How Bell Labs Creates Star Performers," *Harvard Business Review* (July-August 1993), pp. 128-139.

37. For example, see Jeff Mauzy, *Succeeding in Innovation: The Synectics Report on Creativity & Innovation in U.S. Corporations* (The Synectics Corporation: Cambridge, MA, 1993); P. Rajan Varadarajan and Vasudevan Ramanujam, "The Corporate Performance Conundrum: A Synthesis of Contemporary Views and an Extension," *Journal of Management Studies* (September 1990), pp. 463-483; Richard N. Foster, loc. cit.; Thomas J. Peters, loc. cit.; Ray Statta, loc. cit.

38. Anton Cozijnsen and Willem Vrakking, "Introduction" in *Anton Cozijnsen and Willem Vrakking's Handbook of Innovation Management* (Oxford, UK: Basil Blackwell, Ltd., editor, 1993), pp. 9-12. They cite the following Dutch study, NEHEM (Stichting Nederlandse Herstructueringsmij) 1987: *Kiezen voor de Jaien Negentig*, Hertogenbosch. Also see Richard N. Foster, loc. cit.; Thomas J. Peters and Robert H. Waterman, Jr., loc. cit.; P. Rajan Varadarajan and Vasudevan Ramaniyam, loc. cit.; Michael E. Porter, loc. cit.

INNOVATION: THE TURNING POINT

CHAPTER 2

The key to success for Sony, and to everything in business, science, and technology for that matter, is never to follow the others.

Masaru Ibuka
Co-founder of Sony

Each of the ten strategic management challenges identified in Chapter 1 and summarized in Table 2.1 poses many problems and opportunities; unfortunately, there isn't room here to discuss each of them in depth. However, most of them deal in one way or another with making the firm more competitive. For example, if a firm doesn't lead the way in technological change or at least keep pace with it, its competitive advantages will erode. Similarly, a less skilled but more demanding work force such as we have in the United States (compared to, for example, the Japanese work force) puts a firm at a global disadvantage. Global competitiveness is such a major issue in the 1990s, that a detailed discussion of this challenge is necessary as a way of showing just how critical innovation is in the business environment. And make no mistake about it, American firms face competitors that are savvy, have financial muscle, and are determined to succeed. Japanese, Korean, Taiwanese and other Pacific Rim competitors are especially forceful in today's global marketplace. European firms are increasingly competitive.

TABLE 2.1

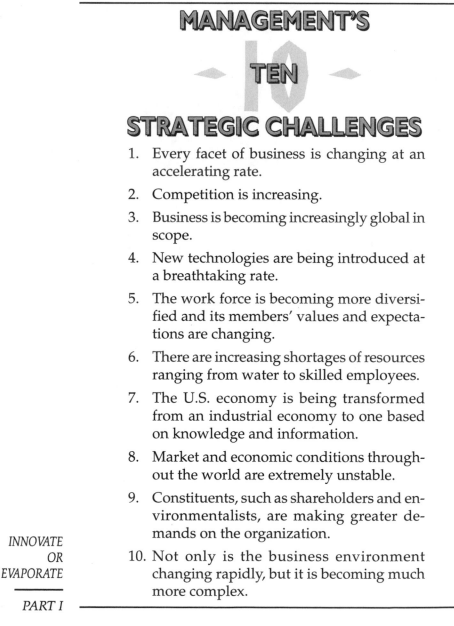

MANAGEMENT'S TEN STRATEGIC CHALLENGES

1. Every facet of business is changing at an accelerating rate.

2. Competition is increasing.

3. Business is becoming increasingly global in scope.

4. New technologies are being introduced at a breathtaking rate.

5. The work force is becoming more diversified and its members' values and expectations are changing.

6. There are increasing shortages of resources ranging from water to skilled employees.

7. The U.S. economy is being transformed from an industrial economy to one based on knowledge and information.

8. Market and economic conditions throughout the world are extremely unstable.

9. Constituents, such as shareholders and environmentalists, are making greater demands on the organization.

10. Not only is the business environment changing rapidly, but it is becoming much more complex.

GLOBAL COMPETITION: THE CRUX OF THE PROBLEM

In 1980 Robert H. Hayes and William J. Abernathy warned American managers that U.S. firms were losing their international competitive edge and were, as they expressed it, "managing [their] way into an economic decline."[1] Their concern was that U.S. firms were not sufficiently innovative. Their analyses of data showed that U.S. firms were not investing enough in research and development. They pointed out that European and Japanese firms were much more concerned with their ability to compete than were U.S. firms. We have learned since that the Japanese have been investing heavily in R&D, and that the Europeans are now beginning to do so also in an effort to catch up.[2]

Echoing Hayes and Abernathy, in 1988 Charles W. L. Hill, Michael A. Hitt, and Robert E. Hoskisson, reflecting their research efforts, also attributed much of the lack of the U.S.'s global competitiveness to an absence of innovation.[3] It is true that U.S. firms have made progress using speed strategies and by emulating the Japanese.[4] American firms have invested record amounts in R&D; however, those amounts represent little or no growth after allowing for inflation.[5] Furthermore, many foreign born scientists, key components of U.S. research success, are returning to help their countries' R&D efforts.[6] Finally, U.S. firms are backing off basic research as Japan is forging ahead in this endeavor.[7] The consequence of these trends is that many foreign firms have been much more innovative than their American counterparts.

Another frustrating aspect of this problem is the inability of U.S. firms to reap as many business applications, such as sellable products, as their Japanese counterparts from the same amount of research. While we invent, they innovate. While we spend time conducting basic research, they spend time developing applications. Their innovation process is aimed at producing products and services. Ours is aimed at producing knowledge, often for its own sake.[8] Solving this problem will require corporate rethinking, a subject that will be addressed in later chapters. *Innovate or Evaporate 2.1* portrays a situation that is, unfor-

Innovation: The Turning Point

Chapter 2

tunately, typical of the conditions prevailing in many U.S. organizations. It provides insight into the problems that can result from the pursuit of knowledge for its own sake.

Some Startling Facts

The trends just described are merely the tip of the iceberg. Until you examine some critical information, it is difficult to grasp just how serious the problem is. Let me share some startling facts with you:

1. **Patents:** Patents filed in Japan outnumber those filed in the United States five to one on a per capita basis.[9] Almost half of the patents filed in the United States are filed by foreigners. In fact, six of the largest ten corporate filers of U.S. patents in 1993 were foreign companies. The good news was that for the first time since 1985, a U.S. firm—IBM—led the list. It was followed in order by Toshiba, Canon, Eastman Kodak, Hitachi, Mitsubishi, General Electric, Motorola, Matsushita Electric, and Fuji Photo Film Company.[10]

   In Japan, in contrast, certain safeguards, especially bureaucratic measures, have been installed to prevent most foreign firms from ever filing a timely patent in Japan.[11] It takes up to thirty months to receive a patent, and while under application the file is published, giving the public (for example, Japanese firms) access to the concepts contained therein.[12] And the Japanese file patents for every potential variation in a product, known as patent flooding, helping to lock out foreign competitors as well as domestic ones. This practice, plus Japanese firms' applications orientation, leads to the fact that more patents are filed in Japan than in the United States, Germany, and Great Britain combined.[13] The Japanese view patents as a way of disseminating information while the U.S. patent system is designed to protect innovators.[14] By design, the Japanese patent system favors the larger firm against the smaller one, the domestic firm against the foreign firm.

2. **R&D Expenditures:** On average, U.S. firms spend significantly less on R&D as a percentage of GNP/GDP (1.9 percent from 1986 to 1992) than their Japanese counter-

WHERE ARE THE PRODUCTS?

At MIT's Media Labs, products have been slow in coming. Founded in 1985 as a way to help corporations to work with the latest in computer technology, Media Labs has had outstanding success in creating new ideas. The Lab's 48-year-old founder, Nicholas Negroponte, has raised $42 million in research funds. Researchers at the lab have won nine patents, filed for seventeen more, and signed three licensing deals, but only two of their inventions have been transformed into innovationsæactual products that could be taken to market. And twelve corporate sponsors have dropped out in the past thirty months.

The lab's founder feels that the companies want too much too fast and that research takes a long time to bear fruit. But others believe that not enough is done to create productsæin other words, the lab is not product oriented. For some, who pay $1 million a year just for access to results, the product *is* the process. NEC officials, for example, say that they have learned a lot about research by just being associated with the lab. However, this approach does not produce a steady stream of new products.

In many ways the lab resembles many others in the United States: It is strong on basic research but lacks a product orientation. For example, in 1987, Stephen Benton drew raves for his unique hologram of a Chevy Camaro. Projected off a clear film, it seemed to hing in mid-air. GM was very interested in the possibilities for designing new cars using his projections, rather than building car models from clay. But after three years, and at least as many more to go before something useable would emerge, GM withdrew its $1 million a year in support.

Source: Gary McWilliams, "Ideas Galore, but Where Are the Goods?" *Business Week* (February 10, 1992), pp. 122-123; Alan Murray and Urban C. Lehner, "Strained Alliance: What U.S. Scientists Discover, the Japanese Convertæinto Profits," *Wall Street Journal* (June 25, 1990), pp. A1, A16.

INNOVATE OR EVAPORATE 2.1

parts (2.7 percent to 3 percent in the same period), and studies indicate that U.S. firms receive a lower return on their R&D investment than Japanese firms.[15] (See Figure 2.1.) However, both spend more, on average, than European firms.[16] *Business Week's* survey of R&D expenditures by the top 900 U.S. firms, reveals they spent an average of 3.7 percent of sales on R&D in 1992, compared to the 4.5 percent of sales spent by a composite of 200 foreign firms. The Japanese firms in the sample spent 5.5 percent of sales on R&D; the German firms, 5.7 percent.[17]

FIGURE 2.1 CLOSING THE INNOVATION GAP

Nondefense R&D Expenditures as a Percent of GNP/GDP

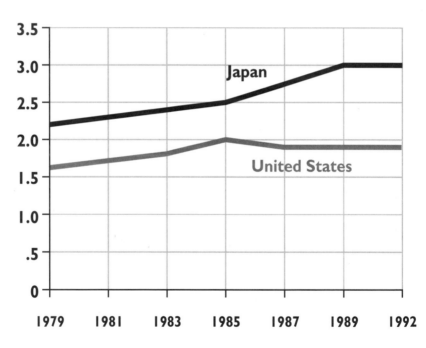

Sources: "U.S. Patents: Big Blue Tops Japanese Firms," *U.S. News & World Report* (March 28, 1994), p. 16; Brian Dumaine, "Closing the Innovation Gap," *Fortune* (December 2, 1991), p. 58.

3. **Composition of R&D:** Despite the apparent all-time highs in R&D budgets for U.S. business, there is concern that these allocations are not sufficient when adjusted for inflation. Moreover, R&D expenditures are expected to decline in the rest of the 1990s, at least relative to past growth.[18] For example, a survey of 253 firms that spend large amounts in R&D found that 41 percent planned reductions in R&D spending in 1994, compared to only 20 percent that planned increases.[19] Moreover, IBM, the patent filing leader in 1993, plans a 15 percent reduction in R&D expenditures from $6 billion to $5 billion in 1994.[20]

4. **Federal R&D Expenditures:** The U.S. government pumped about $80 billion a year into scientific R&D in the mid and late 1980s. In 1993 the government accounted for slightly over 42.3 percent of all R&D expenditures in the United States (private industry 52 percent, colleges and universities 3.7 percent, other nonprofit institutions 2 percent). Government R&D funds were spent mostly for defense. Major weapon systems received the lion's share.[21] Although the U.S. government pumps $30 billion a year into nondefense research, spending decisions are made largely without consulting industry leaders.[22] Budget cuts mandate continued reductions in federal R&D funds in the future.

5. **Japanese Commitment to Product Innovation:** In 1986 Japan made a national commitment to stop being imitators and instead become innovators in product development. This commitment has been renewed each year since then, with massive corporate investment and changes in government policy as well as attempts to change corporate cultures.[23] This is extremely significant. If the Japanese can be as successful at basic research aimed at creating new products as they have been at applications research, they will undermine the last major established competitive edge of U.S. firms.[24] Japanese companies, for example, are making progress in the development of artificial intelligence and the space plane.

    It is also important to note that Japanese firms have always been innovators in operations and human resource management, focusing on process innovation.[25] Such innovation has been a key factor in their economic success. If they are successful in both product and process innovation, the competitive position of American and European firms will suffer. As of 1991 the United States had 257 Nobel Prize winners in physics and chemistry compared to Japan's 3, but that ratio could change drastically in the future.[26] The Japanese now have their own versions of Silicon Valley and the Research Triangle: Kumamoto and Tsukuba Science City.[27] Similarily, Korea has established a goal of increasing its global technological competitiveness in the five year period 1993-1997. It has targeted 11 technologies for development. It has invested significant sums in R&D and is encouraging its firms to form alliances with high-tech firms from advanced countries.[28]

One of Japan's best product innovators is Sony, described in *Innovate or Evaporate 2.2.*

6. **European R&D Expenditures:** Many European businesses are becoming far more competitive. Through mergers and acquisitions and through increased funding for R&D, increasing numbers of firms are becoming globally competitive with respect to technology.[29] However, there remains much concern in Europe that European firms are still falling behind.[30]

7. **U.S. Ph.D.s:** Fifty-nine percent of the Ph.D. candidates in engineering in the United States are foreign nationals.[31] Even though Japan's population is less than half of that of the United States, Japanese universities produce more engineers.[32]

8. **The Faculty Crisis in the United States:** Faculty members in math, science, and engineering in American colleges and universities are retiring and not being replaced. What replacements there are, are foreign nationals.[33]

9. **Technochauvinism:** U.S. firms are guilty of "technochauvinism"—assuming that all good ideas blossom in America and ignoring the substantial volume of research done elsewhere, principally in Japan, Europe, and Russia.[34] A few U.S. firms have begun searching elsewhere, especially Japan, for new technological ideas.[35]

HOW SONY KEEPS THE MAGIC GOING

In a land of copy-cat companies, Japan's Sony ranks as the world's most innovative consumer electronics firm. Throughout its nearly 50 years of doing business, Sony has consistently cranked out one product hit after another. Often, it has created new markets from thin air. Sony popularized the pocket transistor radio, the battery-powered TV set, the VCR, the camcorder, the compact disc player. Sony gave us the Walkman, TVman, Data Discman, and Mini Disc. The company generates 1000 products a year, almost four per work day. 800 of these are enhanced products with new features and better performance, but 200 are totally new products aimed at creating new markets. The firm spends about 5.7 percent of its sales on R&D. It employs 9000 engineers and scientists in the Tokyo area, working to develop new products, most of them working ten to twelve hour days. One of its primary goals for the 1990s is to do for the computer what it did for the stereo hi-fi—create lots of useful, inexpensive gadgets that anyone can use just about anywhere.

So how does Sony keep the magic going? Sony founder and honorary chairman Masaru Ibuka reveals his secret, "The key to success for Sony, and to everything in business, science, and technology for that matter, is never to follow the others." The former chairman, and co-founder Akio Morita, put it another way, "Our basic concept has always been this—to give convenience, or new methods, or new benefits, to the general public with our technology."

What makes Sony's magic work on the practical level is what is called "Sony's way." Sony's way begins with the recruitment of

continued next page

SONY

Neyaka, which translates roughly as people who are optimistic, open-minded, and have wide ranging interests. The firm hires engineers and scientists like other firms, but tries to avoid the overspecialized. Sometimes the firm will take a flyer and hire a really unconventional employee.

Next, the firm has several human resource management practices which guide researchers. For example, the process of self-promotion allows an engineer or scientist to seek out a project in another part of the firm. If he or she (the firm employs 400 female engineers in Tokyo) finds a job, the individual's supervisor is expected to release that employee. The firm almost never pays for breakthrough performances. Rather, Sony tries to match the employee to the right project so that intrinsic motivation occurs. Furthermore, Sony likes to match enhancement type product projects to the experienced researcher, and the breakthough projects to "the rookies."

Many of the firm's big ideas have stemmed from Ibuka himself, for example, the VCR, the camcorder, and the Walkman. But breakthroughs also trickle up from individual engineers or teams of engineers as occured with the Palmtop and the Data Discman. And, while the engineers and scientists come up with the products, the Design Center gives each product that distinctive Sony look. To help cut redundancy, the Sony Corporate Research division coordinates the R&D of 23 business groups and hundreds of research teams. Corporate Research also organizes a huge annual exposition of projects that employees are working on. The top people at Sony, including Ibuka and Morita have always made a point of visiting each and every project exhibited.

Source: Brenton R. Schlender, "How Sony Keeps the Magic Going," *Fortune* (February 24, 1992), pp. 76-84.

10. **The Lab Crisis:** Less than one-fifth of the equipment in research labs in U.S. universities is state of the art, and funding for replacements is dwindling.[36]

11. **Japanese Intelligence Systems:** Japanese firms have a sophisticated intelligence network that gathers information about other countries' technologies. They (and others from the Pacific Rim) often appropriate the information and use it to duplicate products in their own laboratories.

12. **Japanese Acquisitions and Research Sponsorship:** Japanese firms are quick to buy out U.S. technology firms.[37] They also sponsor significant levels of research in U.S. universities and laboratories.[38]

13. **Differential Emphasis on Innovation:** Historically there has been much less emphasis on innovation in the United States than in Europe and Japan. A 1985 study by Arthur D. Little, examining innovation management practices among major North American, European, and Japanese firms, revealed quite clearly that chief executives in North American firms were much less concerned about innovation than their European and Japanese counterparts and that they had installed fewer mechanisms for making creativity and innovation prominent forces in their organizations. Only 51 percent of North American managers, for example, reported that their organizations expected specific profit contributions resulting from innovation for the next five years, compared to 71 percent of European executives and 82 percent of Japanese executives.[39]

    A 1991 study of innovation practices in fourteen major U.S. and Japanese firms, conducted by James Swallow of the consulting firm of A. T. Kearney, suggests that the Japanese spend more time planning their innovations, suffer development setbacks in a smaller proportion of products, and spend less time debugging finished products than do their U. S. counterparts. They also invest more of their management time in new products and receive more revenues from them.[40] (See Figure 2.2.)

A 1991 study of European, Japanese and U.S. firms by consulting firm Arthur D. Little reveals that U.S. and European firms trail Japanese firms in the amount of effort put forth in product innovation.[41] Another 1992 study, commissioned by Grant Thornton, a Chicago-based consulting firm, surveyed 250 executives from midsized U.S. manufacturing firms and found that 90 percent of these executives believed the United States had lost or was losing its lead in global product innovation. 50 percent said that the United States was clearly behind; of these 50 percent, 75 percent said that the new leader was Japan.[42] Ironically, although European firms have been strong proponents of innovation, they still lag behind the United States and Japanese firms.

FIGURE 2.2 U.S. AND JAPAN FIRMS COMPARED IN INNOVATION PRACTICES

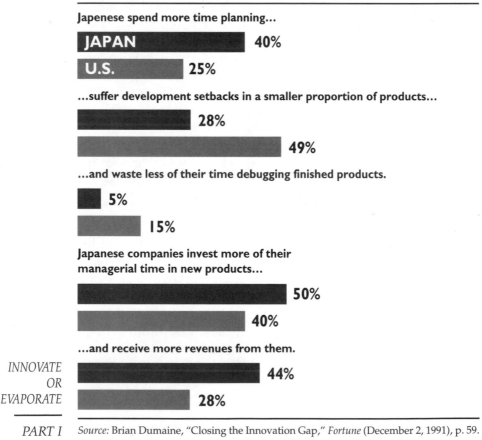

Japenese spend more time planning...

JAPAN 40%

U.S. 25%

...suffer development setbacks in a smaller proportion of products...

28%

49%

...and waste less of their time debugging finished products.

5%

15%

Japanese companies invest more of their managerial time in new products...

50%

40%

...and receive more revenues from them.

44%

28%

Source: Brian Dumaine, "Closing the Innovation Gap," *Fortune* (December 2, 1991), p. 59.

14. **The Impact of Mergers and Acquisitions:** Mergers and acquisitions, both of which are commonplace in the United States, tend to reduce both investment in R&D and the number of patents registered.[43]

15. **Insufficient Process R&D:** Historically, U.S. firms have spent far too much time and money on product R&D relative to process R&D. Most of the major setbacks that U.S. industry has suffered in industries such as electronics, autos, steel, and textiles have been due not to lack of product innovation, but rather to lack of process innovation.[44] Historically, about 80 percent of U.S. nondefense R&D has gone to product innovation and only 20 percent to process innovation.[45] One U.S. firm which has engaged in significant process research in recent years is Norfolk Southern. Its innovation activities are described in *Innovate or Evaporate 2.3*.

The Competitive Environment

The United States has experienced sharp setbacks in numerous industries in recent years. We have seen the competitive position of U.S. firms decline in steel, autos, textiles, cameras, appliances, computer chips, and more recently personal computers.[46] We reviewed earlier the pronouncements of Hayes and Abernathy, and those of Hill, Hitt, and Hoskisson, regarding U.S. firms' declining competitiveness due to a decline in innovativeness.[47] More recently, *Fortune* writer Brian Dumaine, after examining the trends in numerous industries, observed that American firms are not creating products fast enough for global competition.[48] One must wonder why so many U.S. firms are not getting the message: They are facing a more competitive international environment and need to take action to halt current trends.

Even within the United States, business is becoming more competitive. The consequences of deregulation and a freer economy, plus the accelerated rate of change which shortens product life cycles, have caused firms in virtually all segments of the economy to experience greatly increased competition. Banks, airlines, computer chip manufacturers, hospitals, hotels, auto manufacturers, and a host of other industries are facing increased domestic competition.

Competitiveness depends on two primary strategies: being relatively differentiated from the competition and/or having a relatively low cost structure compared to the competition. If a firm is not doing something different or doing it more cheaply, it is not going to survive very long in a competitive environment.[49] *The bottom line is that creativity leading to innovation is needed to combat competition.* To do something different or more cheaply, a firm has to be creative. And to make it count on the bottom line, it has to turn that creativity into an innovation.

Thomas J. Peters and Robert H. Waterman, Jr. expounded on the importance of innovation to successful business operations in *In Search of Excellence*. Like Hayes and Abernathy and Hill, Hitt, and Hoskinson, Peters and Waterman believed that U.S. firms have become too concerned with short-term analytical thinking and too concerned with short-term objectives, such as return on investment. They feel that U.S. executives have become less willing to take risks, which means that they are less likely to invest in ideas.[50] More recently in *Passion for Excellence*, (coauthored with Nancy K. Austin) and *Thriving on Chaos: Handbook for a Management Revolution*, Peters cites innovation as one, if not the *key*, solution to the problem of reduced competitiveness.[51]

American, Japanese, and European managers are all reading the same books. We all sit at the feet of the same management gurus. We all learn the same ways to compete and solve problems. If you consider that the ability to compete is at the heart of any business, you will recognize that *the only long-term sustainable competitive advantage is innovation*. Without innovation, we become predictable to our competitors because they are reading from the same page. They know the same techniques we do. They use the same software. They come up with the same solutions. We need to be more creative, more innovative. Otherwise we will lose the ability to compete. *Innovate or evaporate!*

NORFOLK SOUTHERN: ON THE RIGHT TRACK

The railroad industry was mired in a depressed condition just fifteen years ago. But with productivity increases that averaged 157 percent over that time frame, increased use of technology, significant captial investment, quality management programs, and a stronger customer focus, the railroads have made a comeback. At the head of the herd is Norfolk Southern, whose lone black stallion advertising symbol epitomizes its leadership role in the industry. Norfolk Southern, the nation's fourth largest railroad, was one of only two of the nation's major railroads to make enough money to cover its cost of capital in 1992. In 1993, it made $772 million on sales of $4.5 billion.

Chairman David Goode is steering the company toward a strategy of marrying the traditional efficiencies of railroad freight hauling with the needs of today's just-in-time economy, requiring rapid, flexible, and dependable service. To make that strategy work requires a significant amount of innovation. Fortunately, Norfolk Southern is a firm with a recent history of innovation, and a firm still concerned with innovation. Innovation in managing boxcar loading, sorting cars in various hubs, and eliminating the need for certain hubs on some routes, for example, has enabled Norfolk Southern to garner a significant share of both the automobile delivery business and the truck trailer hauling business. The firm can, for example, guarantee that a delivery will be made at a precise minute to the Atlanta Ford Motor Company assembly plant. This enables Ford to use boxcars as inventory bins, cutting their own inventories and making just-in-time inventorying possible. There is some room for leeway, but being late more than a few minutes would idle some 2400 workers at the plant.

continued next page

NORFOLK SOUTHERN

Significant technology investment has gone into communications technology enabling better tracking of the various types of railroad cars, their loads, and where they are in the system relative to where they need to be. Another focus of information technology has been to improve customer satisfaction with railroad operations, for example, in bringing new service ideas to customers. Innovative quality and safety management programs have helped improve efficiency while cutting accidents by two-thirds.

Norfolk Southern's focus on innovation springs from a series of three- and four-day seminars on creative problem solving attended by virtually all upper and middle managers and many professional staff members from 1981 to 1988. The basic creative problem solving model was used as the focal point for the course. Traditional creativity processes such as brainstorming were taught, along with less traditional but very useful processes such as excursion. In 1982, Southern Railway merged with Norfolk and Western Railway. The creative problem-solving course provided an extra benefit to the new firm by offering a way for the two merged firms' managers to learn to solve problems together. That focus on innovation and collaboration has remained with the firm.

In 1990, the firm began to think in terms of developing an innovation research program. "Thoroughbred Innovation" was formalized in early 1993 with the creation of the Innovation Research Group. The Group's specific mission is to locate new technology that can be applied to railroad operations. Therefore, most of its efforts are aimed at process innovation. The 1993 objective for the Group was very modest—obtain $1 million in savings. But within five years, the firm expects to save a minimum of $40 million a year from the Group's efforts. Some of the innovations produced include: a new type of trainman's lantern, a strong yet lightweight coupler knuckle (which couples cars together), Timbrex crossties made of recycled materials, and high-hardness wheels. The firm is also examining the possibilities of fuel injection for locomotives and alternative fuels such as liquefied natural gas.

NORFOLK SOUTHERN

Sources: David Hage, "On the Right Track," *U.S. News & World Report* (March 21, 1994), pp. 46-53; William G. Vantuono, "Productivity Propels Rolling Stock Buying Decisions," *Railway Age* (January 1994), p. 15; William G. Vantuono, "C&S: State-of-the-Art Improves State-of-the-Art Railroad," *Railway Age* (January 1994), p. 40; Michael A. Verespej, "Better Safety Through Empowerment," *Industry Week* (November 15, 1993), pp. 56-68; Gus Welty, "NS's 'Thoroughbred' Innovators," *Railway Age* (August 1993), pp. 95-96; Robert J. Bowman, "Quality Management Comes to Global Transportation: Riding the Rails," *World Trade* (February 1993), pp. 40-42; interview with Norfolk Southern management development personnel, fall 1989.

THE BUSINESS ORGANIZATION: CREATIVITY AND INNOVATION

The business organization is composed not only of individuals and groups but also of the organizational context itself, which includes its purposes, strategies, structure, systems, management style, its employees, and culture. Every person is creative to some degree. So is every group and organization. There are differences in the quality and quantity of demonstrated creativity, but the potential creativity of individuals, groups, and organizations is virtually unlimited. It is also virtually untapped by most individuals and firms. Fortunately, however, any person, group, or organization can be more creative and innovative—but only if they take the necessary actions. This book describes these actions and shows how they enable a firm to obtain an innovative edge (that is, a sustainable competitive edge) over other firms.

For the organization, becoming more innovative is a matter of changing the seven S's of organizational success—strategy, structure, systems, style, staff, skills, and shared values—to require and support innovation.[52] For the organization, becoming more creative involves total commitment to the concept and decisive action in each of these seven critical areas. The organization must also manage individual and group creativity if it is to become highly innovative.

Innovation: The Turning Point

Chapter 2

For the individual, becoming more creative can be seen as having three components: accepting one's own creative potential (20 percent), learning the processes that can produce ideas (60 percent), and developing intuition (20 Percent). Organizations need to provide training, in examining one's potential, in these creative processes, and in intuition development to their members in order to raise the level of innovation in the organization as a whole.

For the group, becoming more creative means using group dynamics to enhance the creative process. It also means learning the processes, such as brainstorming, that groups may use to unleash creative ideas. For the group, becoming more creative has two basic components: learning appropriate group dynamics (30 percent), and learning group processes that produce ideas (70 percent). Again, organizations need to provide training and development in these processes in order to raise the level of innovation in the organization as a whole.

INNOVATION:
THE TURNING POINT

U.S. firms are at a turning point. There is a sizable gap between where they are and where they ought to be in terms of individual, group and organizational innovation. Many U.S. firms, their managers, and their employees are in danger of falling further behind their global competitors, especially Japanese and other Pacific Rim firms, and of not being able to cope with the major challenges they face in the coming years. Without significant changes, they simply won't be able to conduct business as effectively and efficiently as they should.

Far too few U.S. firms actively pursue innovation, but that is changing. Because of the need to cope with the strategic challenges confronting corporations and their managers, more organizations are beginning to recognize the need to innovate. For example, many organizations are trying to improve their ratio of R&D expenditures to new products and processes resulting from R&D. They are trying to spend less on R&D, while getting more results from their R&D investments.[53] This book is designed to assist companies in achieving innovation by providing a model for successful implementation of a program to increase creativity and innovation in the organization as a whole.

Innovation:
The Turning
Point

Chapter 2

43

REFERENCES

1. Robert H. Hayes and William J. Abernathy, "Managing Our Way to Economic Decline," *Harvard Business Review* (July/August 1980), pp. 67-77.

2. Neil Gross, "Japan: Hustling to Catch Up in Science," *Business Week* (June 15, 1990), pp. 72-82, 114-115; Thane Peterson, "Europe: Suddenly High Tech is a Three-Way Race," *Business Week* (June 15, 1990), pp. 116-123,148-149.

3. Charles W. L. Hill, Michael A. Hitt, and Robert E. Hoskisson, "Declining U.S. Competitiveness: Reflections on a Crisis," *Academy of Management Executive* (January 1988), pp. 51-60.

4. Stephen Kreider Yoder, "Shoving Back: How H-P Used Tactics of the Japanese to Beat Them at Their Own Game," *Wall Street Journal* (September 8, 1994), pp. A1, A9; Bill Powell, "Losing Their Lead," *Newsweek* (December 13, 1993), pp. 51-53.

5. John Carey, "Could America Afford the Transistor Today?" *Business Week* (March 7, 1994), p. 81; Gene Koretz, "Business Talks a Better R&D Game than It Plays," *Business Week* (August 21, 1989), p. 20.

6. J. Madeline Nash, "Tigers in the Lab," *Time* (November 21, 1994), pp. 86-87.

7. Neil Gross, "Who Says Science Has to Pay Off Fast?" *Business Week* (March 21, 1994), pp. 110-111; John Carey, "Could America Afford the Transistor Today?" *Business Week* (March 7, 1994) pp. 80-84.

8. Most authorities agree. For example, see Robert M. White, "Inventors, Invention and Innovation: The Sources of Corporate Competitiveness," *Vital Speeches* (July 15, 1990), pp. 593-596; and a lengthy discussion in Otis Port, "Back to Basics," *Business Week* (June 15, 1989), pp. 14-19.

9. Susan G. Strother, "Government Hopes to Light Fire of Genius," *Orlando Sentinel* (January 31, 1988), pp. D1, D3.

10. Associated Press, "Most Inventive Company is American Again," *Orlando Sentinel* (January 13, 1994), pp. C1, C4; Peter Coy, "The Global Patent Race Heats Up," *Business Week* (August 9, 1993), pp. 57-58.

11. Joseph F. Dunphy, "Japan's Patent System Comes Under Fire," *Chemical Week* (July 27, 1988), pp. 26-28.

12. Peter Langan, "Less Patience for Patents," *Asian Business* (May 1993), pp. 63-64.

13. Masaaki Kotabe and Eli P. Cox III, "Assessment of Shifting Global Competitiveness: Patent Applications and Grants in Four Major Countries," *Business Week* (January/February 1993), pp. 57-64.

14. Donald M. Spero, "Patent Protection or Piracy—A CEO Views Japan," *Harvard Business Review* (September-October 1990), pp. 58-67.

15. Brian Dumaine, "Closing the Innovation Gap" *Fortune* (December 2, 1991), pp. 57-59.

16. Frederick Shaw Myers, "Japan Pushes the "R" in R&D," *Chemical Engineering* (February 1990), pp. 30-33, 48; Bruce C. P. Rayner, "The Rising Price of Technological Leadership," *Electronic Business* (March 18, 1991), pp. 52-56; Fumiaki Kitamura, "Japan's R&D Budget Second Largest in World," *Business Japan* (November 1990), pp. 35-47; "Cash Rich Japan and a Unifying Europe Are Closing the Gap in Science," *Business Week* (June 15, 1990), pp. 35-36.

17. Peter Coy, "In The Labs, the Fight to Spend Less, Get More," *Business Week* (June 28, 1993), p. 104.

18. John Carey, op. cit., pp. 80-84; Ralph E. Winter, "R&D Outlays Slowing After Sharp Rise," *Wall Street Journal* (December 27, 1990), p. A2; Emily Smith, "Statistics: Ranking the World's Big Spenders on R&D; R&D Scoreboard," *Business Week* (June 15, 1990), pp. 192-223; Otis Port, "The Global Race: Why the U.S. is Losing its Lead," *Business Week* (June 15, 1990), pp. 32-39; Lindley H. Clark, Jr., and Alfred L. Malabre, Jr., "Evolving R&D: Slow Rise in Outlays for Research Imperils U.S. Competitive Edge, " *Wall Street Journal* (November 16, 1989), pp. A1, A10.

19. John Carey, op. cit., p. 82.

20. "U.S. Patents: Big Blue Tops Japanese Firms," *U.S. News & World Report* (March 28, 1994), p. 16.

21. John Carey, op. cit., calculated from table on p. 82; Susan Dentzer, "Sharpening Our High-Tech Edge," *U.S. News & World Report* (December 16, 1991), pp. 71-77; Ralph E. Winter, loc. cit.

22. John Carey, "A Think Tank for, Er, 'Competitiveness'," *Business Week* (April 20, 1992), p. 90.

23. Neil Gross, "Who Says Science Has to Pay Off Fast?" *Business Week* (March 21, 1994), pp. 110-111; Neil Gross, "Japan Hustling to Catch Up in Science," op. cit., pp. 72-82, 114-115.

24. Neil Gross, Ibid.; Bernard Wysocki, Jr., "Japan Assaults the Last Bastion: America's Lead in Innovation—The Final Frontier," *Wall Street Journal* (November 14, 1989), special edition on "Technology."

25. Gene Bylinsky, "Trying to Transcend Copycat Science," *Fortune* (March 30, 1987), pp. 42-46.

26. "Figure 994: Nobel Prize Laureates in Physics, Chemistry, and Physiology/Medicine—Selected Countries 1901-1991," *Science and Technology*, Statistical Abstracts of the U.S. (Washington D.C.: U.S. Department of Commerce, Economics and Statistical Administration, Bureau of the Census, 1993), p. 604.

27. Frederick Shaw Myers, op. cit.; Michael Rogers, "Breeding New Ideas," *Newsweek* (August 8, 1988), pp. 54-55.

28. "Korea Continues to Emphasize Science and Technology," *East Asian Executive Reports* (October 15, 1993), pp. 20-22.

29. Francine S. Kiefer, "Europe Lags Behind U.S., Japan in Research and Development: But EC Proposes More Then Doubling Funding for 'Big Science' Research From 1994-1998," *Christian Science Monitor* (February 10, 1993), pp. 10-11; Thane Peterson, op. cit.

30. Daniel Benjamin, "The Trailing Edge: Some Germans Fear They're Falling Behind in High-Tech Fields," *Wall Street Journal* (April 27, 1994), pp. A1, A6; Jonathan B. Levine, "How Europe Swings the Big Science Tab," *Business Week* (March 22, 1993), pp. 62-64.

31. "Figure 993: Doctorates Conferred by Recipients' Characteristics, 1980-1991 and by Selected Science and Engineering Fields, 1991," *Science and Technology*, Statistical Abstracts of the U.S. (Washington D.C.: U.S. Department of Commerce, Economics and Statistical Administration, Bureau of the Census, 1993), p. 604.

32. Lewis J. Lord and Miriam Horn, "The Brain Battle," *U. S. News & World Report* (January 19, 1987), pp. 58-65.

33. Ezra Bowen, "Wanted: Fresh, Homegrown Talent." *Time* (January 11, 1988), p. 65; "The Foreign Accent Gets Stronger in U.S. Science," *Business Week* (September 21, 1987), p. 64.

34. John A. Young, "Myths of Technology Leadership Lull US into Risky Comfort Zone," *Financier* (February, 1990), pp. 32-36; Daniel Greenberg, "High-Tech America's Myopic Mind Set," *U.S. News & World Report* (September 22, 1986), pp. 64-65.

35. Susan Moffat, "Picking Japan's Research Brains," *Fortune* (March 25, 1991), pp. 84-96.

36. Steven Soloman, "Machines Kill New Ideas?" *New York Times* (May 24, 1987), p. 48.

37. Stephen Budiansky, "Japan's Research Raid," *U.S. News and World Report* (March 22, 1993), pp. 46-47; Barbara Buell, "Japan: A Shopping Spree in the U.S.," *Business Week* (June 15, 1990), pp. 86-87; Otis Port, "The Global Race: Why the U.S. is Losing Its Lead," *Business Week* (June 15, 1990), pp. 32-39.

38. Stephen Budiansky, loc. cit.; Otis Port, "The Global Race: Why the U.S. is Losing Its Lead," *Business Week* (June 15, 1990), pp. 32-39; Evan Herbert, "Japanese R&D in the United States," *Research-Technology Management* (November/December 1989), pp. 11-20.

39. Arthur D. Little, Inc., "Management Perspectives on Innovation: Innovation Management Practices in North America, Europe, and Japan," (Cambridge, Mass.: Arthur D. Little, Inc. 1985), p. 4.

40. Brian Dumaine, loc. cit.

41. Arthur D. Little, Inc., "The Arthur D. Little Survey on the Product Innovation Process," (Cambridge, Mass: Arthur D. Little, 1991), p.1.

42. "Product Development," *Wall Street Journal* (March 17, 1992), p. A1.

43. Michael A. Hitt, Robert E. Hoskisson, R. Duane Ireland, and Jeffrey S. Harrison, "Effects of Acquisitions on R&D Inputs and Outputs," *Academy of Management Journal* (September 1991), pp. 693-706.

44. Ralph E. Gomory, "From the Ladder of Science to the Product Development Cycle," *Harvard Business Review* (November/December 1989), pp. 99-105.

45. Marie-Louise Caravatti," Why the United States Must Do More Process R&D," *Research-Technology Management* (September/October 1992), pp. 8-9.

46. Andrew Kupfer, "How American Industry Stacks Up," *Fortune* (March 9, 1992), pp. 30-46.

47. Charles W. L. Hill, Michael A. Hitt, Robert E. Hoskisson, "Declining U.S. Competitiveness: Reflections On a Crisis," *The Academy of Management Executive* (January 1988), pp. 51-60.

48. Brian Dumaine, op. cit., p. 56.

49. William K. Hall, "Survival Strategies in a Hostile Environment," *Harvard Business Review* (September/October, 1980), pp. 73-86; Michael E. Porter, *Competitive Strategy* (New York: Free Press, 1980), p. 178.

50. Thomas J. Peters and Robert H. Waterman Jr., loc. cit.

51. Thomas J. Peters and Nancy K. Austin, *Passion for Excellence* (New York: Random House, 1985); Thomas J. Peters, *Thriving on Chaos: Handbook for a Management Revolution* (New York: Knopf, 1987), pp. 27, 191-280.

52. Ibid.

53. Peter Coy, op. cit., pp.102-104.

THE FOUR TYPES OF INNOVATION
CHAPTER 3

Ultimately, speed (of innovation) is the only weapon we have.
Andrew Grove, CEO
Chairman, Intel

In business the desired result or product of the innovative process is *an innovation*. To be **an innovation**, the result of the creative process must have a useful application and have a significant impact on an individual, a group, an organization, an industry, or a society. As noted in Chapter 1, there are four principal types of innovation that result from the creative process. These are the "product" of innovation, and they are defined as follows:

1. **A product innovation** — a physical product or service, or an enhancement to either.
2. **A process innovation** — a process for improving efficiency or effectiveness.
3. **A marketing innovation** — a new marketing concept or action.
4. **A management innovation** — a new way of managing.

STRATEGY AND INNOVATION

There are three primary types of organizational strategies: corporate, business, and functional. The focus of **corporate strategy** is on determining what business (or businesses) the company is or should be in and how that business is to be operated in a very fundamental sense. For example, should the company grow, stabilize, or reduce its asset base? The focus of **business strategy** is on determining how a particular business will compete—how it will obtain a strategic advantage, and use it. Marketing issues are the primary concern here. The focus of **functional strategy** is on determining how best to use the company's resources to support the competitive efforts defined in the business strategy. Marketing, operations, finance, human resources, information management, and R&D are critical functional strategies. Our concern in this book is primarily with strategies at the business level, but much of the innovation necessary to make those strategies successful occurs at the functional level.

According to the widely accepted strategy research of Professors William K. Hall and Michael E. Porter, firms compete strategically at the business level on the basis of two primary factors: the relative differentiation of the firm's products or services from those of competitors, and/or the relatively low cost of its products or services compared to those of the competition. Functional strategies should be designed to support these two business strategies. Thus, for example, a firm's promotion strategy could be designed to create a perception of differentiation, either real or imagined. When Wendy's CEO, Dave, tells you about how he dreams of his firm's bacon-mushroom-cheeseburger melt, he is telling you that it is different from anything McDonald's, Burger King, Hardees, or Checkers has. Similarly, a firm's operations strategy could be designed to create a relatively low-cost product. Wendy's side salad is only 99¢ compared to higher-priced side salads at other chains. After researching a number of firms, Hall concluded that there are varying degrees of ability to compete, according to combinations of these two strategies.[1] Hall's Competitiveness Model is shown in Figure 3.1.

FIGURE 3.1 HALL'S COMPETITIVENESS MODEL

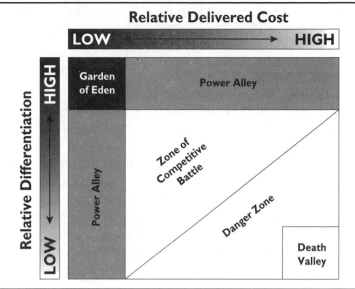

Source: Adapted and reprinted by permission of the *Harvard Business Review.* An exhibit from "Survival Strategies in a Hostile Environment" by William K. Hall (September/October 1990), pp. 73-86. Copyright 1980 by the President and Fellows of Harvard College; all rights reserved.

Hall's research indicates that firms that have a very high degree of differentiation relative to competitors, or a low-cost position relative to competitors, operate within competitive power alleys. (See Figure 3.1.) The Mercedes Benz line of automobiles has been successfully differentiated from competitors by its quality and emphasis on engineering. Thus, Mercedes has competed from the differentiation power alley. Recently, of course, Lexus and Infiniti have equaled that differentation, but at substantially lower costs, significantly eroding Mercedes' market share in the United States. The Korean car Hyundai competed from the low-cost power alley during its first two years in the market, after which rising wages for Korean workers made this advantage less significant. (Incidentally, Hyundai then had low quality and, therefore, a very poor degree of relative differentiation. The company has taken steps to improve its quality substantially.)[2]

The Toyota Lexus, the Nissan Infiniti, the Mazda Miata, the Cadillac SST, and the Dodge Stealth are examples of those rare products that have both a high degree of relative differentiation and a relative low cost position. They compete from the "Garden of Eden." General Motors' Buick Reatta, by contrast, had no

The Four Types of Innovation

Chapter 3

apparent positive differentiation factors and was a high-cost item. (The company actually lost $27,000 on every unit it sold.) This product was in "Death Valley" and was therefore dropped from the company's product line in 1990. *It is in order to achieve relative differentiation and/or relative low cost, as described in Hall's model, that organizations must innovate.*

Product innovation leads principally to competitive advantage through differentiation, while *process innovation* leads principally to a low-cost advantage. *Marketing innovation* helps achieve relative differentiation and/or relative low-cost objectives by improving strategies and tactics concerned with the marketing mix—product, price, promotion, distribution, and target market.[3] *Management innovation* can help achieve both differentiation and low-cost competitive advantages by improving the effectiveness and efficiency of efforts to achieve these goals. In the following pages we examine each of the four types of innovation in more detail.

PRODUCT INNOVATION

Product innovations are new physical products or services or enhancements to existing products or services. In modern firms they are normally developed by a cross-functional team representing marketing, operations, R&D, customers, and often suppliers. They may also be developed by corporate units either singly or in other combinations, or by a single inventor or creator. The easiest way to understand what product innovations are is to look at some. Exhibit 3.1 examines some recent and anticipated new-product developments and enhancements.

Product Innovation at Three Levels

Leading U.S. and Japanese firms have developed a three-tiered model of product development.

 改 The first level is **Kaizen,** or continuous improvement.

善 再 利 用 The second is **leaping,** developing new products out of old ones. For example, the Sony Walkman was developed from the newly created portable tape recorder.

発 想 Finally, there is genuine **big bang innovation.** All three types are increasingly being pursued simultaneously.[4]

Perhaps no one manages new-product cycles as well as Intel. When the company found itself face-to-face with new competitors using new technologies, CEO Andrew Grove launched a new-product development program that left the competitors eating Intel's dust. *Innovate or Evaporate 3.1* describes Intel's product development process.

EXHIBIT 3.1 EXAMPLES OF PRODUCT INNOVATION

Recent New Products and Services

Books on audio cassettes
Career ladder plans for teachers
Casio's Data Bank Watch
Cellular phones
Color copiers
Color laser printers
Compact discs
Computerized cars
Electronic maps for cars
Empathy belly pregnancy simulators
Eye controlled computing
Flat screen TV
Foam homes
Genetic engineering
Gillettes' Sensor razor
High-tech special effects for movies
Home Shopping Network

Leasing maternity clothes
Notebook PC's
Overnight fresh fish deliveries
Personal digital assistant
Pentium computer chip (586)
Promethics—air traffic control for cars
Propeller driven planes that are faster
    than jet planes
Rollerblades
Save now, pay later tuition for colleges
Shoes that log mileage
Talking Teddy Bear
Video rental company that delivers
    pizza too
Video yearbooks
Walker Pocket Phone

Recent Product and Service Enhancements

Color based trade books
Diet Cherry Coke
Drink holders in automobiles
Lemon, Peach, Meadow Grass flavored
    vodka
Miniature CD's

Overnight parcel delivery
PCs with ever expanding memory
600 dpi laser printers
Sneakers that pump-up
WordPerfect 6.2

Anticipated New Products and Services

Auto engines that achieve 100 mpg
Computers that think like humans
A cure for AIDS
A practical electric car
Fusion reactors
Holography for home use
Human-produced artificial organs
Inexpensive color laser printers
Lifelike computer simualtions/games

New energy sources
New financing instruments
Neural network computers
Robot surgeons
Robots as home servants
686 and 786 computer chips
Spaceship for interplanetary travel
Space plane
Superpowered home computers

PROCESS INNOVATION

A **process innovation** is a significant improvement in an organizational process. Process innovations occur throughout the organization. They help increase both effectiveness and efficiency; however, most are aimed at increasing efficiency. Although this book deals separately with marketing and management process innovations because of their significance, it is important to note that there are as many types of process innovations as there are processes. For example, each of the major functions of the organization—marketing, operations, finance, human resources, information systems and R&D—can benefit from process innovations.[5] Exhibit 3.2 presents some examples of process innovations that are common to most firms.

EXHIBIT 3.2 RECENT PROCESS INNOVATIONS

Marketing
800 numbers for customer querries, electronic data enterchange, relationship marketing.

Operations
Computer integrated manufacturing, group software programming (as opposed to individual programming).

Finance
"Rescue financing" to save ailing banks, strategic cost accounting, swap financing, derivative securities.

Human Resource Management
Corporate culture management, collaboration between management and labor, change management.

Information Systems Management
Distributed data processing, decision support systems, management information systems, expert systems, networked PCs.

Research and Development (R&D)
Product oriented R&D, three teirs of R&D

Management
Reengineering, empowerment, process redesign, creativity circles, strategic scenarios.

INSIDE INTEL

Today, everyone who uses computers knows to look for "Intel inside." This advertising theme has made everyone aware of Intel computer chips. This might not have happened were it not for CEO Andrew Grove's belief in innovation as the key to sustainable competitive advantage. In the late 1980s and early 1990s Intel was confronted with new and especially capable competitors armed with new technologies. Grove's solution was to create so many new and superior products so quickly that competitors could not keep pace. "Ultimately, speed [of innovation] is the only weapon we have," he claims. In the 1990s, Intel will give birth to a new family of chips every two years, instead of one every three or four years as it has in the past. And the firm won't produce just one or two models. In 1992, for example, it introduced thirty variants of its successful 486 chip.

Virtually every PC and cash register has a computer chip, and most of these chips are made by Intel. Every time Intel has introduced a new chip, increased productivity has resulted and new products and services based on the chip have been developed. However, as the market for its products grows even larger, Intel's competitors grow more numerous, hoping to stake a claim to part of Intel's market share.

Intel teams work on alternating series of chips. The 486 team is now working on the 686 chip, and the 586 (Pentium) team is working on the 786 chip. The advances incorporated into Intel's chips are staggering. The 386 had 500,000 transistors and 5 mips (millions of instructions per second). The 486 had 1.2 million transistors and 20 mips; the 586, 3 million transistors and 100 mips. The 686 will have 7 million transistors and 175 mips, and the 786 will have 20 million transistors and 250 mips.

This rapid pace of technological progress is impressive, but customers have difficulty assimilating it quickly. Therefore, Intel

continued next page

INNOVATE OR EVAPORATE 3.1

INTEL

has begun to include key customers in its chip design process. The goal is to build in features that customers like. Intel is also trying to stimulate computer advances, for example, moving to make it easier for PC's to do the complex graphics that workstations can do.

Using concurrent engineering and "enablers" (software and hardware that make the design process easier and faster), Intel has forged ahead with its new chip designs without major manufacturing glitches. And by becoming more customer oriented, the company can open markets for its products that probably wouldn't exist otherwise. For example, by helping software writers understand its chips and their power, Intel encourages them to create programs that will increase demand for these chips. Intel's 1992 R&D budget of $800 million was the highest of any chipmaker in the world.

But Intel isn't stopping with chips. It intends to transform the computer and communications industries. CEO Grove's vision of the future includes jazzing up the PC with new application programs, adding new hardware features to make it as useful for communications as it is for number crunching. As he puts it, "We have to make the PC the ubiquitous interactive access device." Grove's strategy has two objectives: First, by pushing PC's to their limits, Intel will oblige owners to buy models using new Intel chips that clonemakers don't sell. Second, by giving the PC new life, Intel will enable users to rely less on workstations based on the RISC (reduced instruction set computing) chips sold by competitors. Personal conferencing, video conferencing, cable TV access, and VCR-like playback capabilities are all product features that Intel has in mind for PC's in the near future.

Source: Michael Meyer, "Chipping at Intel," *Newsweek* (February 21, 1994), pp. 70-72; Robert D. Hof, "Intel Steers the PC onto the Info Highway," *Business Week* (January 31, 1994), pp. 68, 69; Alan Deutschman, "If They're Gaining on You, Innovate," *Fortune* (November 2, 1992), p. 86; Robert D. Hof, "Inside Intel," *Business Week* (June 1, 1992), pp. 86-94. "Inside Intel," *Business Week*, June 1, 1992, pp. 86-94.

INNOVATE
OR
EVAPORATE

PART I

54

Individual companies may have hundreds, and large companies even thousands of innovative processes that are appropriate to their specific situations. *Innovate or Evaporate 3.2* examines a unique situation in process innovation: reducing the use of robotics and reintroducing human workers into a manufacturing environment.

THE INTERACTION OF PRODUCT AND PROCESS INNOVATIONS

In the best-managed firms product and process innovations are coordinated. One study of seventy-four highly successful firms over a fifteen-year period, as rated by *Business Month*, found commitment to *both* product and process innovation to be one of the six common characteristics of those firms.[6] Other research suggests that product and process innovations are so intertwined that product innovations can lead to process innovations and that the reverse is also true, though less likely.[7] Most of the major sucessful firms in the U.S. and Japan, and many of those in Europe, integrate product and process innovation.[8]

There is evidence that product innovations alone are not likely to lead to sustained competitive advantages.[9] Rather, both product and process innovations are necessary, or, as another study shows, product innovation must be substantial if it is to lead to high levels of profitibility in manufacturing.[10] Many North American firms are taking steps to adopt continuous-improvement programs that require both product and process innovation and coordination of the two.[11] *Such efforts help the firm move toward both differentation and relative low-cost-competitive positions.* The use of cross-functional design teams is an effective way of coordinating product and process innovations in manufacturing firms.

Innovation researchers Michael Tushman and David Nadler have suggested that the relationship between product and process innovation in terms of corporate focus is a function of the product life cycle, as shown in Figure 3.2. As you can see, they suggest that product and process innovation should receive varying amounts of corporate focus at different stages of the product life cycle.

The Four Types of Innovation

Chapter 3

FIGURE 3.2 DOMINANT INNOVATION TYPES OVER THE PRODUCT LIFE CYCLES

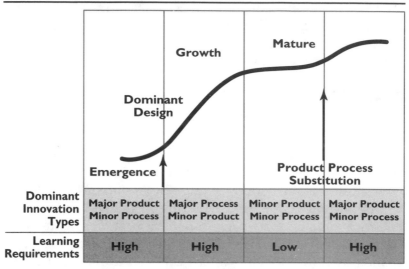

Dominant Innovation Types	Major Product Minor Process	Major Process Minor Product	Minor Product Minor Process	Major Product Minor Process
Learning Requirements	High	High	Low	High

Source: Michael Tushman and David Nadler, "Organizing for Innovation," *California Management Review* (Spring 1986), p. 78. Copyright © 1986 by the Regents of the University of California. Reprinted from the *California Management Review,* Vol. 28, No. 3. By permission of the Regents.

Innovation and TQM

Commitment to total quality management (TQM) includes a commitment to process innovation—including reengineering, which is process redesign on a grand scale. TQM is often intertwined with product and process. When a manufacturer develops a simplified product with fewer parts to improve quality, a new product results, and the simplified manufacturing process itself also becomes an innovation.

MARKETING INNOVATION

A **marketing innovation** is a significant improvement in any element of the marketing mix—product, promotion, price, distribution, or target market. In an age in which the consumer is bombarded by advertisements, innovative marketing techniques are critical to successful sales.[12] Sometimes real differentiation and relative low cost don't matter. What may matter is how customers perceive these. Innovative marketing helps create the desired perceptions.

Marketing innovation can support both differentiation (product, promotion, distribution, and target market strategies) and

TOYOTA'S PRODUCTION GURU

We usually think of process innovation in production as involving increased usage of robotics, computers, and other automation related equipment. And for most of its history, that has been true at Toyota. Mikio Kitano, Toyota's director of production engineering since 1990, has long been a proponent of automation. During his career he has led several inititatives which have resulted in increased automation throughout Toyota's plants. Often viewed as a renegade, at least partly for his demanding style when others wanted to go slow, in 1990, Kitano turned renegade again arguing for paring automation in Toyota plants because it wasn't paying for itself to a sufficient degree. He believed that it was because robots were being used in too many places that human beings could do the job just as well and for less cost.

He rejects machines that merely overcomplicate. "The key to productivity is simplicity. Men control machines, not the other way around." Kitano continually visits Toyota plants, finetuning their processes. For example, at the Tahara plant, he replaced a palletized system for inserting the engine and drivetrain into the body of a car with a more traditional chain pulley system. He did so because he felt that litte productivity was gained by the pallets, but that maintenance costs were greatly increased. His actions knocked 75 percent off the price of maintaining the sytem.

Source: Karen Lowry Miller, "The Factory Guru Tinkering with Toyota," *Business Week* (May 17, 1993), pp. 95-97.

INNOVATE OR EVAPORATE 3.2

low cost (and related price strategies). When Dell Computer Corporation became the first firm to market PC's by telephone, it was using a marketing innovation. Dell generated databases derived from its sales efforts and used these to further enhance customer satisfaction through related product development; this too was a marketing innovation.[13]

Examples of innovations in each of the five areas of the marketing mix are presented in Exhibit 3.3.

Innovate or Evaporate 3.3 examines a marketing innovation in more detail. Some innovations cut across all five marketing mix variables. Relationship marketing, for example, is an attempt

EXHIBIT 3.3 EXAMPLES OF MARKETING MIX INNOVATION

Product
L. A. Gear's sneakers that flash a light off and on as you step. Timex's glow watch.

Promotion
A classic example of a promotion innovation was the use of black and white television advertisements by L'Oreal cosmetics to market its products when everyone else was using color advertisements. It isn't clear that its products were actually any different from the competition's, but it is clear that people remembered these products and bought them.

Price
In order to lure customers from its competitors, Boeing Aircraft Company has upon occasion included the cost of financing in the price of its planes, giving it a competitive edge over its less financially sound competitors who couldn't afford to offer low rates on purchase financing.

Distribution
Milliken Company, the $2 billion textile firm, supplies Levi Strauss & Company, one of its major customers, with truckloads of raw materials, delivered the day before they are needed, and loaded in the reverse order they are needed so that the first item needed is at the open end of the truck and Levi's people can then unload the truck as they use the material.

Target Market
A classic example of innovative marketing in more effectively reaching the target market is the "infomercial." The recent success of infomercials, television segments (typically a half-hour long) that seem like they are providing information but are actually sales pitches, has demonstrated that there are new ways of reaching the target market, and that new ways are necessary. Most of the products sold in these infomercials are rather generic, with few demonstrable advantages and often higher costs than competing products, but people buy them because of the target market focus of the presentation.

Sources: Tom Peters, "The Home Team Advantage," *U. S. News & World Report* (March 31, 1986), p. 49; Sharon Edelson, "Switching Channels," *Women's Wear Daily* (November 1, 1991), pp. 14,15. Author's personal knowledge of certain strategies.

IKEA: MARKETING INNOVATION DRIVES TOTAL BUSINESS REDEFINITION

IKEA was transformed from a small Swedish mail-order furntiture operation into the world's largest retailer of home furnishings after top management totally redefined the furniture retail business. In an industry where few companies move outside their own countries, IKEA has created a global network of over 100 stores. In 1992, 96 million people visited these stores and purchased $4.3 billion in goods. The key elements of IKEA's successful strategy are well known: simple, high-quality, Scandinavian design; global sourcing of components; knock-down furniture kits that customers transport and assemble themselves; huge suburban stores with plenty of parking and amenities like coffee shops, restaurants, even day-care facilities. Low prices, ranging from 25 percent to 50 perceent below competitors are also an essential ingredient, created by a combination of low cost components, efficient warehousing, and customer self-service.

But if one looks beyond the obvious strategy one finds the real innovation. IKEA attains low costs and translates them into low prices because it fundamentally redefined the business. First, it redefined the relationship with the customer. The new relationship promises the customer low prices and high quality if the customer will perform two tasks that are normally performed by the manufacturer and the retailer: assembly and

continued next page

INNOVATE OR EVAPORATE 3.3

IKEA

delivery. Because IKEA wanted to make it easy for the customer to take on this new role, every aspect of the company was defined accordingly.

For example, each year IKEA prints 45 million catalogs in ten different languages. Each catalog lists between 30 percent and 40 percent of the firm's 10,000 products. Most important, each provides a script describing the role of each participant in the company's business system. When customers enter a store they are given a catalog, tape measures, pens, and notepaper to help them make choices without the aid of a salesperson. Furniture items come complete with simple, readable labels with descriptions of the dimensions, colors, and materials in which they are available, instructions for care, and the location in the store where they may be picked up. After payment, customers cart off the unassembled items. Car roof racks are available. In these ways IKEA has redefined the way value is created. "IKEA wants its customers to understand that their role is not to *consume* value but to *create* it."

In similar ways, IKEA has redefined its relationships with suppliers. For example, it seeks long-term commitment from highly qualified, globally based suppliers, which must meet rigorous tests before becoming members of the IKEA team. And it has created a special unit, IKEA Engineering, to provide technical assistance to suppliers. Finally, IKEA also reinvented its internal processes, which mirror its relationship with its customers and suppliers. For example, its logistics process deals with glo-

IKEA

bal sources to assemble widely dispersed components. The back of a chair may come from Poland, the legs from France, and the screws that hold it together from Spain. For this to be a financially sound strategy high-volume sales are required. At the center of this strategy are fourteen warehouseslinked to retail stores in computer-integrated networks. These warehouses are in fact system integrators, relating supply to demand, holding down warehouse inventories, and keeping stores supplied only as needed.

IKEA's success has occurred because it invented a new way for value to be created rather than trying to systematically create value along a given value chain.

Source: Richard Normann and Rafael Ramíerez, "From Value Chain to Value Constellation: Designing Interactive Strategy," *Harvard Business Review* (July-August 1993), pp. 65-77.

to build strong relationships with customers so that all five marketing mix variables may be strengthened in ways that will benefit the firm.[14]

MANAGEMENT INNOVATION

A **management innovation** is a significant improvement in the management of the organization. Management innovation is necessary if a firm is to cope successfully with the ten strategic challenges identified in Chapter 1. U.S., Canadian, and European firms must improve their management practices to compete successfully with the Japanese and other Pacific Rim firms.[15] The manager's primary function is creative problem solving in the areas of planning, organizing,[1] leading,[2] and controlling. As organizations continue to move toward greater self-management by employees, individuals at all levels will have increased responsibility for creative problem solving.

[1] Includes staffing and human resource management as it pertains to a single manager.

[2] Includes motivating and communicating.

Ray Stata, CEO of Boston-based Analog Devices, Inc., observes that Japan was the first nation to achieve economic success based on management innovation. Virtually all previous national economic successes had been based on technology. But Japanese firms brought new ways of managing to the same essential product and process areas as their North American and European competitors and used those improved management techniques, most of which resulted in product and process innovations, to transform Japan into a major force in the world economy.[16] Japanese management practices are different from those of firms elsewhere in the world, and they are clearly very effective.[17]

Exhibit 3.4 presents examples of some recent management innovations. *Innovate or Evaporate 3.4* describes a management innovation that has helped Cypress Semiconductors achieve its unique brand of success.

EXHIBIT 3.4 EXAMPLES OF MANAGEMENT INNOVATION

Creative Problem Solving
Expert systems, creativity techniques, lateral thinking, knowledge management.

Planning
Strategic alliances, joint ventures, scenerio forecasting, business plan software, speed strategies.

Organizing
Reengineering, process redesign, creativity circles, restructuring to the lean and mean look, intrapreneurship, networked organizations.

Leading
Transformational leadership, empowerment, management by wandering around (MBWA).

Controlling
Comshare's "Commander" Executive Information System, self-management, activity-based costing.

CYPRESS SEMI-CONDUCTOR SUCCEEDS THROUGH MANAGEMENT INNOVATION

Cypress Semiconductor is the only U.S. semiconductor firm that has made a profit every year since 1983. Cypress is a niche manufacturer headquartered in the Silicon Valley that makes specialty chips. At the heart of Cypress's success is "Turbo MBO," its innovative management planning and control system established by CEO T. J. Rogers. The system is computerized and allows for the establishment and review of objectives for all 1400 employees on a weekly basis. Objectives are set on Monday, reviewed on Wednesday for progress, and reviewed again on Friday for completion. Some objectives are for longer periods, but seldom for more than six weeks. Rogers attributes much of the firm's success to this system. It is important to note that the firm seeks innovation in <u>both</u> product and process areas. It spends 24 percent of sales on R&D, far above the industry average of 8 percent.

Source: Stephen J. Govoni, "The Systems Are the Solution at Cypress," *Electronic Business* (October 7, 1991), pp. 154-156; Charles Procter, "Top 100 R&D Spenders: Dog Days for R&D," *Electronic Business* (August 5, 1991), pp. 44-47; T. J. Rogers, "No Excuses Management," *Harvard Business Review* (July-August 1990), pp. 84-98; Kathleen Melymuka, "Controlled Fusion," *CIO* (August, 1990), pp. 57-59.

INNOVATE OR EVAPORATE 3.4

HOW MANAGEMENT MUST CHANGE TO MEET THE STRATEGIC CHALLENGES OF THE 1990s

The ten strategic challenges identified in Chapter 1 will force management to change in the next decade, sometimes dramatically, sometimes incrementally.[18] Many of the changes have already begun, but many more will be needed. Some of the innovations needed include: ways of empowering employees, ways of coping with strategic discontinuity, new techniques for generating ideas, computerized idea generators, resource-based strategies, speed strategies for specific situations and firms, redesigning jobs in new ways, self-management techniques, knowledge management, and self-control processes. Among the most important changes in the management process according to what has been described as **the new management,**[19] is an increased emphasis on innovation.

The following list examines how each management challenge might lead to innovation:

1. Accelerating change—new approaches to managing change, new ways of managing stress, improved information systems.

2. Increasing competition—improvements in competitor intelligence systems, new strategies, new customer linkages.

3. Globalization of business—global strategies, global structures, global systems, global cultures, creative management styles.

4. Changing technology—a new way of accelerating product life cycles, new competitive advantages, new product concepts.

5. Diverse work force—new leadership and management styles, new management processes, new benefits, new motivation systems.

6. Resource shortages—substitutes, scarcity management strategies, more efficient processes.

7. Transition to knowledge-based society—new management paradigms, knowledge management techniques.

8. Unstable economic and marketing conditions—adaptive management, scenario management, stability enhancers.

9. Constituent demands—new relationships with constituents, new processes for transforming inputs into outputs.

10. Increasing complexity—more expert systems, more computer simulations, new ways of managing.

Innovation is a misunderstood phenomenon. As you have seen from the discussion of the four types of innovation, innovation and creativity are not restricted to marketing nor to new product development as so many people seem to believe. Innovation is not only the realm of scientists, engineers, and advertisers. Quite to the contrary. There are thousands of men and women everyday who are innovative in all sorts of jobs. For example, they may develop a more efficient compensation program, or they may find a new way of manufacturing a product for half a cent less per unit. Their work group, quality group, or creativity team may develop a new way of cutting customer complaints by 10 percent. They may determine new ways of achieving a tax break. Yes, they may even invent new products and develop new ways to advertise them. Creativity and innovation are common occurrences, but they are still not as common as they need to be. Everyone in an organization must be creative in order to achieve product, process, marketing, and management innovations.

There are three major ways to develop and stimulate creativity and turn it into innovation—the **product:**

1. Increase **personal and group creativity.**

2. Use creative **processes** that improve creative thinking.

At the same time:

3. Improve the **possibilities** through organizational culture and management style. The rest of this book describes ways of improving organizational possibilities for innovation.

REFERENCES

1. William K. Hall, "Survival Strategies in a Hostile Environment," *Harvard Business Review* (September/October 1980), pp. 73-86; Michael E. Porter, *Competitive Strategy* (New York: Free Press, 1980). Porter also identifies a third strategy, focus, meaning that the firm focuses primarily on a particular target market or product. But since a firm's strategy ends up being either a focus differentiation or a focus low cost strategy, Hall's two options are used here rather than Porter's three.

2. James R. Healey, "Hyundai Revs Up for Change as Sales Soar," *USA Today* (May 11, 1993), pp. 1B, 2B.

3. Michael E. Porter, *Competitive Strategy* (New York: Free Press, 1980), pp. 177-178.

4. Peter F. Drucker, "Japan: New Strategies for a New Reality," *Wall Street Journal* (October 2, 1991), p. A12.

5. For a discussion of 10 types of innovation see: Mathew J. Manimala, "Rules of Thumb That Help Innovators: A Tale of Two Entrepreneurs," *Creativity and Innovation Management* (September 1993), pp. 197-206.

6. P. Rajan Varadarajan and Vasudevan Ramanujam, "The Corporate Performance Condundrum: A Synthesis of Contemporary Views and an Extension," *Journal of Management Studies* (September 1990), pp. 463-483.

7. Masaaki Kotabe and Janet Y. Murray, "Linking Product and Process Innovations and Modes of International Sourcing in Global Competition: A Case of Foreign Multinational Firms," *Journal of International Business Studies* (Third Quarter 1990), pp. 383-408; Kornelius Kraft, "Are Product- and Process-Innovations Independent of Each Other:" *Applied Economics* (August 1990), pp. 1029-1038.

8. Masaaki Kotabe, "Corporate Product Policy and Innovative Behavior of European and Japanese Multinationals: An Empirical Investigation," *Journal of Marketing* (April 1990), pp. 19-33. U.S. firms are included as a result of my observation.

9. Noel Capon, John U. Farley, Donald R. Lehman, and James M. Hulbert, "Profiles of Product Innovators Among Large U.S. Manufacturers," *Management Science* (February 1992), pp. 157-169; Masaaki Kotabe and Janet Y. Murray, loc. cit.; Kornelius Kraft, loc. cit.; Noel Capon, et.al., loc. cit.

10. Noel Capon, et.al., loc. cit.; Masaaki Kotabe and Janet Y. Murray, loc. cit.; Kornelius Kraft, loc. cit.

11. For a discussion of the relationship between continuous improvement and product and process innovation see: J. Stephen Sarazen, "Continuous Improvement and Innovation," *Journal for Quality & Participation* (September 1991), pp. 34-39.

12. Regis McKenna, "Marketing is Everything," *Harvard Business Review* (January/February 1991), pp. 65-79.

13. Joel Kotkin, "The Innovation Upstarts", *Inc.*, (January, 1989), pp. 70-73.

14. Robert Stacey, "Canada: The Many Benefits of Relationship Marketing," *Direct Marketing* (September 1993), pp. 65-69; Philip Kotler, "Marketing's New Paradigm: What's Really Happening Our There," *Planning Review* (September/October 1992), pp. 50-52.

15. James M. Higgins, *The Management Challenge*, 2nd ed (New York: Macmillan, 1994), Chapter 1.

16. Ray Stata, "Organizational Learning: The Sustainable Competitive Advantage," *Sloan Management Review* (Spring 1989), pp. 63-74.

17. For example, see, William G. Ouchi, *Theory Z: How America Can Meet the Japanese Challenge* (Reading, Mass.: Addison-Wesley, 1981)

18. Higgins, loc. cit.

19. Higgins, op. cit., p. 70.

The Four
Types of
Innovation

Chapter 3

67

MEASURING YOUR ORGANIZATION'S IQ

CHAPTER 4

We have to be willing to cannibalize what we're doing today in order to ensure our leadership in the future. It's counter to human nature, but you have to kill your business while it is still working.

Lewis Platt, CEO
Hewlett-Packard

On the basis of an extensive examination of research and case studies, it is evident that what separates extremely creative/innovative organizations from less creative/innovative ones is a set of readily identifiable characteristics. To make these characteristics more meaningful and more understandable, they have been grouped according to the seven categories of the familiar Seven S's framework: Strategy, Structure, Systems, Style, Staff, Shared Values, and Skills.[1] *(See "A Brief Summary of the Seven Ss" which follows for brief definitions of these terms.)*

THE SEVEN S's AND INNOVATION

After examining successful companies such as Hewlett-Packard, The Walt Disney Companies, 3M, Xerox, IBM, Delta Airlines, and others, Thomas J. Peters and Robert H. Waterman, Jr., conceived of the Seven S's model as a way of describing the key characteristics of successful organizations.[2] This framework, shown in Figure 4.1, can be used to examine an organization's capacity to survive and prosper, through the use of innovation, in an environment characterized by major challenges like those identified in Chapter 1. The evidence cited throughout this book suggests that organizations that possess these seven groups of characteristics (as applied here to innovation) are consistently more innovative than those that do not.[3] As shown in Figure 4.1, shared values, or culture, form a hub around which the other six S's are clustered.

A BRIEF SUMMARY OF THE SEVEN S'S

1. *Strategy:* There are three types of strategy: corporate, business, and functional. The corporate strategy defines what business or businesses the firm is in or should be in and how the firm will conduct that business or those businesses in a fundamental way. The business strategy describes how a firm will compete in a particular business. A firm's business strategy is the major plan of action aimed at gaining a sustainable advantage over the competition. Relative differentation and relative low cost are the two most generic business strategies. Functional strategies such as marketing, finance, operations, human resources management, information systems management, and R&D, should be aligned with the business strategy.

2. *Structure:* The organization's structure consists of five parts: jobs, the authority to do those jobs, departmentalization of jobs, the managers' span of control, and mechanisms of coordination. The first four of these are normally shown in an organization chart. The last of these is usually described in the firm's operating policies and procedures.

3. *Systems:* "The processes and flows that show how an organization gets things done from day to day (information systems, capital budgeting systems, manufacturing processes, quality-control systems, performance measurement systems)."

4. *Style (Leadership/Management Style):* The consistent pattern of behavior exhibited when relating to subordinates and other employees.

5. *Staff*: This is corporate demographics. It is the number and type of employees the firm needs to do what, when, and where. It is not about personalities.

6. *Shared values (or organizational culture)*: The values that are shared in the organization that make it different from all other organizations.

7. *Skills*: "A derivative of the rest. Skills are those capabilities that are possessed by an organization as a whole, as opposed to the people in it. (The concept of corporate skill as something different from the skills of the people in it seems difficult for many people to grasp; yet some organizations that hire only the best and the brightest cannot get seemingly simple things done, while others perform extraordinary feats with ordinary people.)"

Source: Based loosely on Robert H. Waterman, Jr., "The Seven Elements of Strategic Fit." *Journal of Business Strategy* (Winter 1982), p. 71. I have modified his definitions of five of the seven S's to make them more consistent with general management terminology.

The behavior required by the characteristics of each of the Seven S's should be coordinated and consistent. These characteristics should not be designed or operated independently; but rather, they should be designed and used in a way that recognizes their interdependence. When an organization is undergoing strategic change, strategy would be the first of the S's to be reformulated. Structure, systems, style, staff, and shared values would then be aligned with the new strategy. When strategy, structure, systems, style, staff, and shared values are in place and properly aligned with one another, organizations will possess the seventh of the Seven S's, the set of *skills* required to succeed strategically—in this case, the innovation skills necessary to compete in today's highly competitive and changeful environment.

Figure 4.2 portrays a company's Seven S's, which are aligned in an appropriate way. All of the directional arrows are pointing the same way. Strategy will be achieved and skills obtained because the other five S's support the company's strategy. Conversely, Figure 4.3 represents an organization in which structure, systems, style, staff and shared values are not aligned with strategy. Hence, strategy and skills will not be achieved. The Seven S's framework is designed to help a firm implement its strategy successfully and obtain synergistic skills by designing the other five S's in such a way that they support strategy.

If the firm adopts goals and objectives for innovation and formulates a strategy to achieve them, it must also have the proper structure, systems, style, staff, and shared values. It won't do any good to set innovation goals and objectives for managers, professional staff, and other employees if, for example:

- structure is too centralized—for example, if individuals are not given enough authority to achieve their goals and objectives.

- systems are not designed to encourage, track, and reward innovation.

- management styles do not encourage and reward innovation.

- the staff (all employees) is not capable of innovation, perhaps because of lack of training.

- the firm's shared values do not require and support innovative behavior.

Only if strategy, structure, systems, style, staff, and shared values work together will the organization and its members develop the skills necessary for innovation. If you examine Figures 4.1, 4.2, and 4.3, you will note the interdependency indicated by the lines connecting the S's to one another. Everything affects everything else. A change in one "S" affects all the others. *Innovate or Evaporate 4.1* describes Hewlett-Packard, a firm that has all its Seven S's aimed in the same direction—that is, toward achieving innovation. But even Hewlett-Packard has sometimes experienced difficulty keeping its Seven S's coordinated, as this vignette explains.

The remainder of this chapter examines the forty-nine characteristics of innovative organizations through two questionnaires, each with two parts. The questionnaires can help you evaluate your firm with respect to the four types of innovation. The first questionnaire deals with product and process innovation, the second with marketing and management innovation.

FIGURE 4.1 THE SEVEN S'S FRAMEWORK

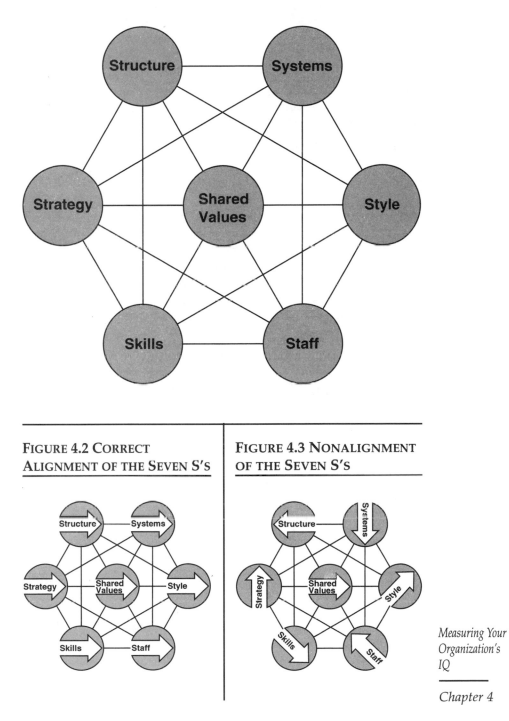

FIGURE 4.2 CORRECT
ALIGNMENT OF THE SEVEN S'S

FIGURE 4.3 NONALIGNMENT
OF THE SEVEN S'S

*Measuring Your
Organization's
IQ*

Chapter 4

THE INNOVATION QUOTIENT INVENTORY:

Determining Your Organization's IQ

The forty-nine characteristics that are shared by innovative organizations serve as the foundation for the organizational self-examination questionnaires presented in Exhibits 4.1, 4.2, 4.3, and 4.4. Exhibit 4.1 deals with characteristics related to product innovation; 4.2 deals with characteristics related to process innovation; 4.3 with characteristics related to marketing innovation; and 4.4 deals with characteristics related to management innovation. You may complete these questionnaires from the perspective of the organization as a whole or from that of the division or department in which you work. However, answering from the perspective of the unit for which you work is probably best since an overall organization perspective tends to gloss over specific weaknesses. Organizational summaries of responses will provide a fatal corporate overview. If you are unaware of your organization's programs relative to the subjects of these questionnaires—for example, its marketing programs—you should not complete that questionnaire.

Instructions for Completing the Questionnaires

To determine your organization's *Innovation Quotient (IQ)*, complete all four questionnaires.[4] Respond in an open and honest way. If you do, your responses will be more likely to help you gain a better understanding of your organization's capacity for innovation. After you have finished, follow the scoring instructions provided. Note that in all four questionnaires the term *product* refers to products, services, and enhancements to both.

Making Copies of the Questionnaires

Persons and companies who have purchased a copy of this book may make up to ten copies of each questionnaire for use in their organization at no charge. Site licenses are available for companies, managers, professionals, team leaders, and other employees who wish to make more than ten copies.

Please contact:

James M. Higgins & Associates, Inc., 400 North New York Avneue, #215, Winter Park, FL, USA 32789. (407) 647-5344, fax (407) 647-5575.

EXHIBIT 4.1 PRODUCT INNOVATION

Read the questions on the left and mark a score in the appropriate column to the right. Please circle the number on the scale of 1 (low) to 10 (high) to indicate the degree to which your company possesses the characteristic in question.

PRODUCT INNOVATION CHARACTERISTICS	PRODUCT INNOVATION RATING LOW HIGH 1 2 3 4 5 6 7 8 9 10
TO WHAT EXTENT DOES YOUR ORGANIZATION	
1a. Have a stated and working strategy of product innovation	1 2 3 4 5 6 7 8 9 10
2a. Develop structural mechanisms for intrapreneurship	1 2 3 4 5 6 7 8 9 10
3a. Reward product creativity and innovation	1 2 3 4 5 6 7 8 9 10
4a. Create a vision/strategic intent for product innovation	1 2 3 4 5 6 7 8 9 10
5a. Treat employees as a vital resource for building competitive advantage in products	1 2 3 4 5 6 7 8 9 10
6a. Hold creative product employees and their contributions in high esteem	1 2 3 4 5 6 7 8 9 10
7a. Proactively create new opportunities, and respond to change relative to new products	1 2 3 4 5 6 7 8 9 10
8a. Possess a market orientation for creating products (it is close to its customers)	1 2 3 4 5 6 7 8 9 10
9a. Require cross-functional and customer/supplier new-product teams	1 2 3 4 5 6 7 8 9 10
10a. Celebrate new product successes	1 2 3 4 5 6 7 8 9 10
11a. Allow employees to make mistakes when innovating products	1 2 3 4 5 6 7 8 9 10
12a. Have product idea people	1 2 3 4 5 6 7 8 9 10
13a. Encourage new ideas and risk taking with products	1 2 3 4 5 6 7 8 9 10
14a. Continuously create new products or services and/or enhance old ones	1 2 3 4 5 6 7 8 9 10
15a. Require relevant managers to have objectives for product innovation and evaluate their performance relative to these objectives	1 2 3 4 5 6 7 8 9 10

16a. Have new product/research centers	1 2 3 4 5 6 7 8 9 10
17a. Have management information systems for product innovation to scan the environment, monitor and benchmark competitors,determine best practices, keep abreast of new technologies, monitor market conditions, and exchange information internally	1 2 3 4 5 6 7 8 9 10
18a. Suspend judgment on new product ideas	1 2 3 4 5 6 7 8 9 10
19a. Have product idea/innovation champions	1 2 3 4 5 6 7 8 9 10
20a. Value and practice openness with respect to products	1 2 3 4 5 6 7 8 9 10
21a. Successfully practice continuous as well as "big bang" product innovation	1 2 3 4 5 6 7 8 9 10
22a. Put each and every product on trial for its life every 18 months to two years	1 2 3 4 5 6 7 8 9 10
23a. Have open communication between product innovation centers/teams and the rest of the organization	1 2 3 4 5 6 7 8 9 10
24a. Have formal product idea assessment systems that separate creation from evaluation and look beyond simple financial analysis	1 2 3 4 5 6 7 8 9 10
25a. Empower subordinates: delegate sufficient authority for employees to innovate new products	1 2 3 4 5 6 7 8 9 10
26a. Train employees to be creative for product development	1 2 3 4 5 6 7 8 9 10
27a. Possess a shared value that this is an innovative organization insofar as products are concerned	1 2 3 4 5 6 7 8 9 10
28a. Engage in knowledge management for product development—identifying knowledge assets, sharing information, tapping innate knowledge of individuals	1 2 3 4 5 6 7 8 9 10
29a. Make commercialization of new ideas a priority	1 2 3 4 5 6 7 8 9 10
30a. Structure for flexibility to adapt and seize the opportunity for new products	1 2 3 4 5 6 7 8 9 10
31a. Have a system for getting the products from the lab to the marketplace	1 2 3 4 5 6 7 8 9 10
32a. Use a problem-solving management style for developing new products	1 2 3 4 5 6 7 8 9 10
33a. Use many of the 100 or more creativity processes such as brainstorming, verbal checklists, mind mapping, storyboarding, lotus blossom and so on for product development	1 2 3 4 5 6 7 8 9 10

34a. Manage organizational culture to make it more innovative for product development	1 2 3 4 5 6 7 8 9 10
35a. Practice organizational learning—learn from experience and share knowledge about products	1 2 3 4 5 6 7 8 9 10
36a. Use speed strategies for new-product development	1 2 3 4 5 6 7 8 9 10
37a. Use alliances to obtain product innovation	1 2 3 4 5 6 7 8 9 10
38a. Use both formal and informal product innovation information exchanges within the company	1 2 3 4 5 6 7 8 9 10
39a. Use transformational leadership for product development	1 2 3 4 5 6 7 8 9 10
40a. Provide time for/encourage reflection about products	1 2 3 4 5 6 7 8 9 10
41a. Place a high value on change and make it part of the organization's culture with respect to product development	1 2 3 4 5 6 7 8 9 10
42a. Leverage resources to achieve seemingly unobtainable product objectives	1 2 3 4 5 6 7 8 9 10
43a. Know when and how to lead the customer to new or enhanced products or services	1 2 3 4 5 6 7 8 9 10
44a. Have an effective and efficient structure for creating new products	1 2 3 4 5 6 7 8 9 10
45a. Have effective suggestion programs for products	1 2 3 4 5 6 7 8 9 10
46a. Use special approaches in managing innovative product-development employees	1 2 3 4 5 6 7 8 9 10
47a. Provide physical facilities conducive to idea exchange and creative thinking about products	1 2 3 4 5 6 7 8 9 10
48a. Require relevant nonmanagerial employees to have objectives for product innovation and evaluate their performance in relation to those objectives	1 2 3 4 5 6 7 8 9 10
49a. Invest heavily and appropriately in product R&D	1 2 3 4 5 6 7 8 9 10

EXHIBIT 4.2 - PROCESS INNOVATION

Read the questions on the left and mark a score in the appropriate column to the right. Please circle the number on the scale of 1 (low) to 10 (high) to indicate the degree to which your company possesses the characteristic in question.

PROCESS INNOVATION CHARACTERISTICS	PROCESS INNOVATION RATING
	LOW HIGH
	1 2 3 4 5 6 7 8 9 10

TO WHAT EXTENT DOES YOUR ORGANIZATION

1b. Have a stated and working strategy of process innovation (includes process redesign/reengineering)	1 2 3 4 5 6 7 8 9 10
2b. Develop structural mechanisms for process redesign/reengineering initiatives	1 2 3 4 5 6 7 8 9 10
3b. Reward process creativity and innovation	1 2 3 4 5 6 7 8 9 10
4b. Create a vision/strategic intent for process innovation	1 2 3 4 5 6 7 8 9 10
5b. Treat employees as a vital resource for building competitive advantage in processes	1 2 3 4 5 6 7 8 9 10
6b. Hold creative process employees and their contributions in high esteem	1 2 3 4 5 6 7 8 9 10
7b. Proactively create new opportunities, and respond to change relative to new processes	1 2 3 4 5 6 7 8 9 10
8b. Possess a market orientation for creating processes (it is close to its customers)	1 2 3 4 5 6 7 8 9 10
9b. Require cross-functional and customer/supplier process redesign/reengineering teams	1 2 3 4 5 6 7 8 9 10
10b. Celebrate new process successes	1 2 3 4 5 6 7 8 9 10
11b. Allow employees to make mistakes when innovating processes	1 2 3 4 5 6 7 8 9 10
12b. Have process idea people	1 2 3 4 5 6 7 8 9 10
13b. Encourage new ideas and risk taking with processes	1 2 3 4 5 6 7 8 9 10
14b. Continuously create new processes for manufacturing products or delivering services	1 2 3 4 5 6 7 8 9 10

15b. Require relevant managers to have objectives for process innovation and evaluate their performance relative to these objectives   1 2 3 4 5 6 7 8 9 10

16b. Have process redesign/reengineering programs/centers   1 2 3 4 5 6 7 8 9 10

17b. Have management information systems for process innovation to scan the environment, monitor and benchmark competitors, determine best practices, keep abreast of new technologies, monitor market conditions, and exchange information internally   1 2 3 4 5 6 7 8 9 10

18b. Suspend judgment on new process ideas   1 2 3 4 5 6 7 8 9 10

19b. Have process idea/innovation champions   1 2 3 4 5 6 7 8 9 10

20b. Value and practice openness with respect to processes   1 2 3 4 5 6 7 8 9 10

21b. Successfully practice continuous process innovation and reengineering   1 2 3 4 5 6 7 8 9 10

22b. Put each and every process on trial for its life every 18 months to two years   1 2 3 4 5 6 7 8 9 10

23b. Have open communication between process innovation teams and the rest of the organization   1 2 3 4 5 6 7 8 9 10

24b. Have formal process idea assessment systems that separate creation from evaluation and look beyond simple financial analysis   1 2 3 4 5 6 7 8 9 10

25b. Empower subordinates: delegate sufficient authority for employees to innovate new processes   1 2 3 4 5 6 7 8 9 10

26b. Train employees to be creative for process development   1 2 3 4 5 6 7 8 9 10

27b. Possess a shared value that this is an innovative organization insofar as processes are concerned   1 2 3 4 5 6 7 8 9 10

28b. Engage in knowledge management for process innovation—identifying knowledge assets, sharing information, tapping innate knowledge of individuals   1 2 3 4 5 6 7 8 9 10

29b. Make process effectiveness and efficiency a priority   1 2 3 4 5 6 7 8 9 10

30b. Structure for flexibility to adapt and seize the opportunity for new processes   1 2 3 4 5 6 7 8 9 10

31b. Have a system for implementing process innovations   1 2 3 4 5 6 7 8 9 10

32b. Use a problem-solving management style for developing new processes   1 2 3 4 5 6 7 8 9 10

33b. Use many of the 100 or more creativity processes such as brainstorming, verbal checklists, mind mapping, storyboarding, lotus blossom and so on for process development   1 2 3 4 5 6 7 8 9 10

34b. Manage organizational culture to make it more innovative for process redesign   1 2 3 4 5 6 7 8 9 10

35b. Practice organizational learning—learn from experience and share knowledge about processes   1 2 3 4 5 6 7 8 9 10

36b. Use deadlines and/or objectives that stretch performers' capabilities to speed process innovation   1 2 3 4 5 6 7 8 9 10

37b. Use alliances to obtain process innovation   1 2 3 4 5 6 7 8 9 10

38b. Use both formal and informal process innovation information exchanges within the company   1 2 3 4 5 6 7 8 9 10

39b. Use transformational leadership for process development   1 2 3 4 5 6 7 8 9 10

40b. Provide time for/encourage reflection about processes   1 2 3 4 5 6 7 8 9 10

41b. Place a high value on change and make it part of the organization's culture with respect to process redesign   1 2 3 4 5 6 7 8 9 10

42b. Leverage resources to achieve seemingly unobtainable process objectives   1 2 3 4 5 6 7 8 9 10

43b. Know when and how to lead the customer to lower costs and/or higher quality resulting from improved processes   1 2 3 4 5 6 7 8 9 10

44b. Have an effective and efficient structure for creating process improvement innovation   1 2 3 4 5 6 7 8 9 10

45b. Have effective suggestion programs for processes   1 2 3 4 5 6 7 8 9 10

46b. Use special approaches in managing innovative process-redesign employees   1 2 3 4 5 6 7 8 9 10

47b. Provide physical facilities conducive to idea exchange and creative thinking about processes   1 2 3 4 5 6 7 8 9 10

48b. Require nonmanagerial employees to have objectives for process innovation and evaluate their performance in relation to those objectives   1 2 3 4 5 6 7 8 9 10

49b. Invest heavily and appropriately in process R&D   1 2 3 4 5 6 7 8 9 10

EXHIBIT 4.3 - MARKETING INNOVATION

Read the questions on the left and mark a score in the appropriate column to the right. Please circle the number on the scale of 1 (low) to 10 (high) to indicate the degree to which your company possesses the characteristic in question.

MARKETING INNOVATION CHARACTERISTICS	MARKETING INNOVATION RATING LOW HIGH 1 2 3 4 5 6 7 8 9 10
TO WHAT EXTENT DOES YOUR ORGANIZATION	
1c. Have a stated and working strategy of marketing innovation	1 2 3 4 5 6 7 8 9 10
2c. Develop structural mechanisms for marketing innovation	1 2 3 4 5 6 7 8 9 10
3c. Reward marketing creativity and innovation	1 2 3 4 5 6 7 8 9 10
4c. Create a marketing vision/strategic intent	1 2 3 4 5 6 7 8 9 10
5c. Treat employees as a vital resource for building competitive advantage in marketing	1 2 3 4 5 6 7 8 9 10
6c. Hold creative marketing employees and their contributions in high esteem	1 2 3 4 5 6 7 8 9 10
7c. Proactively create new marketing opportunities and respond to change relative to marketing innovations	1 2 3 4 5 6 7 8 9 10
8c. Possess a market orientation (it is close to its customers)	1 2 3 4 5 6 7 8 9 10
9c. Require cross-functional marketing innovation teams	1 2 3 4 5 6 7 8 9 10
10c. Celebrate creative/innovative marketing successes	1 2 3 4 5 6 7 8 9 10
11c. Allow marketing employees to make mistakes when innovating	1 2 3 4 5 6 7 8 9 10
12c. Have marketing idea people	1 2 3 4 5 6 7 8 9 10
13c. Encourage new marketing ideas and risk taking	1 2 3 4 5 6 7 8 9 10
14c. Market products or services innovatively	1 2 3 4 5 6 7 8 9 10
15c. Require relevant managers to have objectives for marketing innovation and evaluate their performance relative to these objectives	1 2 3 4 5 6 7 8 9 10
16c. Have marketing innovation programs/centers	1 2 3 4 5 6 7 8 9 10

17c. Have management information systems for marketing innovation to scan the environment for new opportunities, monitor and benchmark competitors,determine best practices, keep abreast of new technologies, monitor market conditions, and exchange information internally   1 2 3 4 5 6 7 8 9 10

18c. Suspend judgment on new marketing ideas   1 2 3 4 5 6 7 8 9 10

19c. Have marketing idea/innovation champions   1 2 3 4 5 6 7 8 9 10

20c. Value and practice openness with respect to marketing   1 2 3 4 5 6 7 8 9 10

21c. Successfully practice continuous as well as "big bang" marketing innovation   1 2 3 4 5 6 7 8 9 10

22c. Put each and every marketing practice on trial for its life every 18 months to two years   1 2 3 4 5 6 7 8 9 10

23c. Have open communication between marketing innovation centers/teams and the rest of the organization   1 2 3 4 5 6 7 8 9 10

24c. Have formal marketing idea assessment systems that separate creation from evaluation and look beyond simple financial analysis   1 2 3 4 5 6 7 8 9 10

25c. Empower subordinates: delegate sufficient authority for marketing employees to be innovative   1 2 3 4 5 6 7 8 9 10

26c. Train marketing employees to be creative   1 2 3 4 5 6 7 8 9 10

27c. Possess a shared value that this is an innovative marketing organization   1 2 3 4 5 6 7 8 9 10

28c. Engage in knowledge management in marketing—identifying knowledge assets, sharing information, tapping innate knowledge of individuals   1 2 3 4 5 6 7 8 9 10

29c. Make marketing innovation a priority   1 2 3 4 5 6 7 8 9 10

30c. Structure for flexibility to adapt and seize marketing opportunities   1 2 3 4 5 6 7 8 9 10

31c. Have a system for implementing marketing innovation   1 2 3 4 5 6 7 8 9 10

32c. Use a problem-solving management style for solving marketing problems   1 2 3 4 5 6 7 8 9 10

33c. Use many of the 100 or more creativity processes such as brainstorming, verbal checklists, mind mapping, storyboarding, lotus blossom and so on for marketing innovation   1 2 3 4 5 6 7 8 9 10

34c. Manage organizational culture to make marketing more innovative   1 2 3 4 5 6 7 8 9 10

35c. Practice organizational learning—learn from experience
and share knowledge about marketing 1 2 3 4 5 6 7 8 9 10

36c. Use deadlines and/or objectives that stretch performers'
capabilities to speed marketing innovations 1 2 3 4 5 6 7 8 9 10

37c. Use alliances to obtain marketing innovation 1 2 3 4 5 6 7 8 9 10

38c. Use both formal and informal marketing innovation
information exchanges within the company 1 2 3 4 5 6 7 8 9 10

39c. Use transformational leadership in marketing innovation 1 2 3 4 5 6 7 8 9 10

40c. Provide time for/encourage reflection on marketing 1 2 3 4 5 6 7 8 9 10

41c. Place a high value on change and make it part of the
marketing organization's culture 1 2 3 4 5 6 7 8 9 10

42c. Leverage resources to achieve seemingly unobtainable
marketing innovation objectives 1 2 3 4 5 6 7 8 9 10

43c. Know when and how to lead the customer to new or
enhanced product or service opportunities through
innovative marketing 1 2 3 4 5 6 7 8 9 10

44c. Have an effective and efficient structure for creating
marketing innovation 1 2 3 4 5 6 7 8 9 10

45c. Have effective marketing improvement suggestion programs 1 2 3 4 5 6 7 8 9 10

46c. Use special approaches in managing innovative marketing
employees 1 2 3 4 5 6 7 8 9 10

47c. Provide physical facilities conducive to idea exchange and
creative thinking in marketing 1 2 3 4 5 6 7 8 9 10

48c. Require relevant nonmanagerial employees to have objectives
for marketing innovation and evaluate their performance
in relation to those objectives 1 2 3 4 5 6 7 8 9 10

49c. Invest heavily and appropriately in marketing R&D 1 2 3 4 5 6 7 8 9 10

EXHIBIT 4.4 - MANAGEMENT INNOVATION

Read the questions on the left and mark a score in the appropriate column to the right. Please circle the number on the scale of 1 (low) to 10 (high) to indicate the degree to which your company possesses the characteristic in question.

MANAGEMENT INNOVATION CHARACTERISTICS	MANAGEMENT INNOVATION RATING LOW HIGH 1 2 3 4 5 6 7 8 9 10

TO WHAT EXTENT DOES YOUR ORGANIZATION

1d. Have a stated and working strategy of management innovation	1 2 3 4 5 6 7 8 9 10
2d. Develop structural mechanisms for management innovation	1 2 3 4 5 6 7 8 9 10
3d. Reward management creativity and innovation	1 2 3 4 5 6 7 8 9 10
4d. Create a management vision/strategic intent	1 2 3 4 5 6 7 8 9 10
5d. Treat employees as a vital resource for building competitive advantage in management	1 2 3 4 5 6 7 8 9 10
6d. Hold creative managers and their contributions in high esteem	1 2 3 4 5 6 7 8 9 10
7d. Proactively create new management opportunities and respond to change relative to management innovations	1 2 3 4 5 6 7 8 9 10
8d. Possess a market-based management orientation (it is close to its customers)	1 2 3 4 5 6 7 8 9 10
9d. Require cross-functional management innovation teams	1 2 3 4 5 6 7 8 9 10
10d. Celebrate creative/innovative management successes	1 2 3 4 5 6 7 8 9 10
11d. Allow managers to make mistakes when innovating management	1 2 3 4 5 6 7 8 9 10
12d. Have management idea people	1 2 3 4 5 6 7 8 9 10
13d. Encourage new management ideas and risk taking	1 2 3 4 5 6 7 8 9 10
14d. Practice innovative management	1 2 3 4 5 6 7 8 9 10
15d. Require managers to have objectives for management innovation and evaluate their performance relative to these objectives	1 2 3 4 5 6 7 8 9 10
16d. Have management innovation programs/centers	1 2 3 4 5 6 7 8 9 10

17d. Have management information systems for management innovation to scan the environment for new opportunities, monitor and benchmark competitors,determine best practices, keep abreast of new technologies, monitor market conditions, and exchange information internally   1 2 3 4 5 6 7 8 9 10

18d. Suspend judgment on new management ideas   1 2 3 4 5 6 7 8 9 10

19d. Have management idea/innovation champions   1 2 3 4 5 6 7 8 9 10

20d. Value and practice openness with respect to management   1 2 3 4 5 6 7 8 9 10

21d. Successfully practice continuous as well as "big bang" (reengineering-based) management innovation   1 2 3 4 5 6 7 8 9 10

22d. Put each and every management practice on trial for its life every 18 months to two years   1 2 3 4 5 6 7 8 9 10

23d. Have open communication between management innovation centers/teams and the rest of the organization   1 2 3 4 5 6 7 8 9 10

24d. Have formal management idea assessment systems that separate creation from evaluation and look beyond simple financial analysis   1 2 3 4 5 6 7 8 9 10

25d. Empower subordinates: delegate sufficient authority for managers to be innovative   1 2 3 4 5 6 7 8 9 10

26d. Train management employees to be creative   1 2 3 4 5 6 7 8 9 10

27d. Possess a shared value that this is an innovatively managed organization   1 2 3 4 5 6 7 8 9 10

28d. Engage in knowledge management of the management process itself—identifying knowledge assets, sharing information, tapping innate knowledge of individuals   1 2 3 4 5 6 7 8 9 10

29d. Make management innovation a priority   1 2 3 4 5 6 7 8 9 10

30d. Structure for flexibility to adapt and seize management opportunities   1 2 3 4 5 6 7 8 9 10

31d. Have a system for implementing management innovation   1 2 3 4 5 6 7 8 9 10

32d. Use a problem-solving management style for solving management problems   1 2 3 4 5 6 7 8 9 10

33d. Use many of the 100 or more creativity processes such as brainstorming, verbal checklists, mind mapping, storyboarding, lotus blossom and so on for management innovation   1 2 3 4 5 6 7 8 9 10

34d. Manage organizational culture to make management more innovative   1 2 3 4 5 6 7 8 9 10

35d. Practice organizational learning—learn from experience
and share knowledge about management   1 2 3 4 5 6 7 8 9 10

36d. Use deadlines and/or objectives that stretch performers'
capabilities to speed management innovations   1 2 3 4 5 6 7 8 9 10

37d. Use alliances to obtain management innovation   1 2 3 4 5 6 7 8 9 10

38d. Use both formal and informal management innovation
information exchanges within the company   1 2 3 4 5 6 7 8 9 10

39d. Use transformational leadership in management innovation 1 2 3 4 5 6 7 8 9 10

40d. Provide time for/encourage reflection on management   1 2 3 4 5 6 7 8 9 10

41d. Place a high value on change and make it part of the
organization's management culture   1 2 3 4 5 6 7 8 9 10

42d. Leverage resources to achieve seemingly unobtainable
management innovation objectives   1 2 3 4 5 6 7 8 9 10

43d. Know when and how to lead the customer to lower costs
and/or higher quality resulting from innovative management1 2 3 4 5 6 7 8 9 10

44d. Have an effective and efficient structure for creating
management innovation   1 2 3 4 5 6 7 8 9 10

45d. Have effective management improvement suggestion programs 1 2 3 4 5 6 7 8 9 10

46d. Use special approaches in managing innovative
management employees   1 2 3 4 5 6 7 8 9 10

47d. Provide physical facilities conducive to idea exchange and
creative thinking in management   1 2 3 4 5 6 7 8 9 10

48d. Require relevant nonmanagerial employees to have
objectives for management innovation and evaluate their
performance in relation to those objectives   1 2 3 4 5 6 7 8 9 10

49d. Invest heavily and appropriately in management R&D   1 2 3 4 5 6 7 8 9 10

Instructions for Scoring the Questionnaire

Exhibit 4.1 Product Innovation column

Total your score for all questions: _____

Exhibit 4.2 Process Innovation column

Total your score for all questions: _____

Exhibit 4.3 Marketing Innovation column

Total your score for all questions: _____

Exhibit 4.4 Management Innovation column

Total your score for all questions: _____

THE HP WAY

Examining the Seven S's at Hewlett-Packard is a lesson in the do's, and sometimes the don'ts, of innovation. Hewlett-Packard is dedicated to innovation, but even it has sometimes experienced difficulty keeping its Seven S's pointed in the same direction. This vignette examines HP's Seven S's and describes a recent problem the firm experienced in managing them.

Strategy:

HP has seven stated corporate goals. Included in its growth goal is a statement identifying innovation in products as a means of achieving growth. Included within the management goal is a statement regarding the necessity of providing a creative environment for people to work in. HP's business strategy clearly focuses on innovation as a means of gaining market share and profit. "The HP Way" has always meant innovation. Most recently, HP has positioned itself strategically to take advantage of three key trends in the computer industry: reduced instruction set computing (risc), open systems, and desktop networks of PC's.

Systems:

HP has carefully designed its human resource management systems (winning *Personnel Journal's* 1993 Optima Award for excellence in human resource management). These systems include: its manufacturing systems, which are highly cost efficient; its information systems, which give employees access to the information they need to function properly; its performance/management systems, which allow for large measures of self-control; its idea evaluation systems; and other key systems. In each case the objective has been to provide the kind of culture that leads to innovation and creativity. Entire product lines and related production operations have been totally redesigned to make products more competitive.

INNOVATE OR EVAPORATE 4.1

continued next page

HP

Style:

At HP, management is participatory, major units are autonomous, and employees function with high levels of self-control.

Staff:

Employees are carefully chosen for their creative and innovative potential and are trained in vital creativity skills. Managers are trained in the skills needed to manage creative personnel.

Shared Values:

The belief that HP is an innovative company is evident throughout the firm. The firm instills this culture in its employees.

Skills:

In 1993, HP earned over 70 percent of its revenue from products that didn't exist two years earlier. HP has bombarded the marketplace with new products, most of which have been highly successful financially. It launched a series of PC's that moved it from fourteenth to sixth in market share in just a few months. HP has penetrated the Japanese market and is experiencing growth at a time when other firms are feeling the impact of the recession in Japan. HP's stock more than doubled in response to the increased success of its products from 1991 to 1992.

Structure:

We discuss structure at this point, instead of earlier, for a reason. HP's structure has traditionally facilitated innovation. But in 1990, then CEO John A. Young, normally an even-tempered person, nearly came unglued when he learned that the firm's critical new work station project, code-named "snakes," was a year behind schedule. HP's structure had become extremely bureaucratic in an attempt to make the firm's products more compatible with each other and, hence, more functional for customers' integrated computer networks. Such a structure did not support new-product innovation, the key to HP's future. Rather, it buried it in a plethora of coordinating committees.

HP

Young therefore took decisive action. He moved all new-product development teams out of the traditional hierarchy, assigned autonomous "czars" to run the projects, and made the teams accountable to themselves. Success arrived almost overnight.

Managing the Seven S's

HP learned an important lesson: Firms must manage the Seven S's so as to be sure they are always pointing in the same direction. Even though its problems were caused by efforts to solve legitimate customer concerns, HP failed to monitor those efforts to make sure they were consistent with the company's overall strategy. Once the necessary structural changes were made, HP's strategy was fulfilled through the use of skills that helped it increase its market share and profits.

Sources: Alan Deutschman, "How HP Continues to Grow," *Fortune* (May 2, 1994), pp. 90-100; Tim Clark, "Marketing Key to HP's Battle Plan," *Business Marketing* (July 1993), pp. 15-16; "The Metamorphosis of Hewlett-Packard," *Economist* (June 19, 1993), pp. 67-69; Catherine Arnst, "Now, HP Stands for Hot Products," *Business Week* (June 14, 1993), p. 36; Todd R. Hammel and Laura Rock Kopczak, "Tightening the Supply Chain," *Production & Inventory Management Journal* (Second Quarter 1993), pp. 63-70; Jennifer J. Laabs, "1993 Optimas Award Winners," *Personnel Journal* (January 1993), pp. 49-62; Bob Johnstone, "Revolutionary Servant: Hewlett-Packard Shakes Japan's Comptuer Market," *Far Eastern Economic Review* (December 17, 1992), pp. 55-56; Robert D. Hof, "Suddenly, Hewlett-Packard Is Doing Everything Right," *Business Week* (March 23, 1992), pp. 88, 89; Stephen Kreider Yoder, "A 1990 Reorganization at Hewlett-Packard Already Is Paying Off," *Wall Street Journal* (July 22, 1991), pp. A1, A8; Barbara Buell and Robert D. Hof, "Hewlett-Packard Rethinks Itself," *Business Week* (April 1, 1991), pp. 76-79.

INTERPRETING YOUR ORGANIZATION'S IQ SCORES

IQ scores higher than 400 points for any of the four types of innovation indicate that yours is likely to be an extremely innovative organization in that category. A score of 350-400 is good. A score of 300-350 is acceptable but needs improvement. A score below 300 leaves lots of room for improvement. A score below 200 suggests that there are not many possibilities for innovation in the firm. A company with a score below 100 is in serious trouble. Check its pulse: it may be dead.

Several factors should be noted in interpreting these scores:

- A wide range of scores is possible within the same firm. For example, typically one would expect R&D departments to score higher than finance departments on product innovation. Similarly, a good operations department would probably score higher on process innovation then would the finance department. The daily activities of some functions offer more possibilities for innovation than do those of other functions.

- In organizations with duplicate functions in different locations, scores may vary within the same types of departments. Management style and organizational culture (shared values) have a major impact on the occurrence of such variances. For example, operations departments in better-run organizations typically score higher on process and product innovation than those in less-well-run organizations.

- An organizational or subunit average can be obtained by totaling the scores of the individuals in the unit who have completed the questionnaire and dividing the total by the number of participants. Care must be taken, however, not to overlook the wide variances that are likely to exist. Thus many people may find the firm very innovative and many may not, while "on average" the firm is acceptably innovative.

- There is room for creativity and innovation in all jobs. Sometimes, however, it is necessary to provide opportunities for creativity that will not affect certain specific activities. For example, we don't want a machinist to get creative when drilling holes of a certain size. We need holes of that size and no other. But apart from the drilling operation itself (perhaps in team meetings), we can encourage the machinist to suggest ways of improving the drilling operation. When firms recognize such distinctions, their IQ scores—and their profits—will increase.

Four Companies' IQ Scores

The following paragraphs summarize responses to the questionnaire by a variety of firms in both service and manufacturing industries.

In a major theme park entertainment company, product and process innovation scores among 40 participants ranged from 90 to 401, with a mean of 282. Operations personnel had very low scores; product design personnel had much higher scores. Interestingly, the three personnel managers in the group scored the highest.

In a quality consulting company, results on the product and process innovation questionnaire were low among eleven participants, all of whom were consultants. Scores ranged from 90 to 375, with a mean of 230. This firm followed very rigid procedures in its quality consulting practice, which at the time dealt largely with manufacturing.

In the product development department of a large bank, product and process innovation scores ranged from 125 to 400, with a mean of 220. There were twelve participants in the test group, including both professionals and support staff. They were asked to evaluate either the bank or the product development group. The scores were skewed toward the low end. This is a common scoring profile for banks, where little innovation is allowed. The lowest four scores occurred when the overall bank was being evaluated and not the product development group alone. The highest eight scores occurred when the product development department was being evaluated.

A group of twenty-two managers of a smaller, privately held, equipment manufacturing company with $200 million a year in sales achieved the highest IQ score of the four companies, an average of 375 (on a single questionnaire examining both product and processs innovation). The firm's owner and managers stressed both product and process innovation as a means of competing with several Japanese firms that were fierce competitors in their industry.

EXAMINING EACH OF THE SEVEN S's

To get a better idea of how your firm performed on each of the Seven S's for each of the four types of innovation, complete Tables 4.1, 4.2, 4.3, and 4.4 by recording your scores for each set of questions. Now total your score for each of the Seven S's for each of the four types of innovation. A score of less than 14 points on each of the Seven S's suggests serious problems. Scores higher than 57 are very good.

TABLE 4.1 QUESTIONS REGARDING PRODUCT INNOVATION

Strategy	Structure	Systems	Style	Staff	SV	Skills
1a	2a	3a	4a	5a	6a	7a
8a	9a	10a	11a	12a	13a	14a
15a	16a	17a	18a	19a	20a	21a
22a	23a	24a	25a	26a	27a	28a
29a	30a	31a	32a	33a	34a	35a
36a	37a	38a	39a	40a	41a	42a
43a	44a	45a	46a	47a	48a	49a
Total	Total	Total	Total	Total	Total	Total

TABLE 4.2 QUESTIONS REGARDING PROCESS INNOVATION

Strategy	Structure	Systems	Style	Staff	SV	Skills
1b	2b	3b	4b	5b	6b	7b
8b	9b	10b	11b	12b	13b	14b
15b	16b	17b	18b	19b	20b	21b
22b	23b	24b	25b	26b	27b	28b
29b	30b	31b	32b	33b	34b	35b
36b	37b	38b	39b	40b	41b	42b
43b	44b	45b	46b	47b	48b	49b
Total	Total	Total	Total	Total	Total	Total

TABLE 4.3 QUESTIONS REGARDING MARKETING INNOVATION

Strategy	Structure	Systems	Style	Staff	SV	Skills
1c _____	2c _____	3c _____	4c _____	5c _____	6c _____	7c _____
8c _____	9c _____	10c _____	11c _____	12c _____	13c _____	14c _____
15c _____	16c _____	17c _____	18c _____	19c _____	20c _____	21c _____
22c _____	23c _____	24c _____	25c _____	26c _____	27c _____	28c _____
29c _____	30c _____	31c _____	32c _____	33c _____	34c _____	35c _____
36c _____	37c _____	38c _____	39c _____	40c _____	41c _____	42c _____
43c _____	44c _____	45c _____	46c _____	47c _____	48c _____	49c _____
Total ____	Total ____	Total ____	Total ____	Total ____	Total ____	Total ____

TABLE 4.4 QUESTIONS REGARDING MANAGEMENT INNOVATION

Strategy	Structure	Systems	Style	Staff	SV	Skills
1d _____	2d _____	3d _____	4d _____	5d _____	6d _____	7d _____
8d _____	9d _____	10d ____	11d _____	12d _____	13d ____	14d _____
15d _____	16d _____	17d ____	18d	19d	20d	21d
22d _____	23d _____	24d ____	25d _____	26d _____	27d ____	28d _____
29d _____	30d _____	31d ____	32d _____	33d _____	34d ____	35d _____
36d _____	37d _____	38d ____	39d _____	40d _____	41d ____	42d _____
43d _____	44d _____	45d ____	46d _____	47d _____	48d ____	49d _____
Total ____	Total ____	Total ____	Total ____	Total ____	Total ____	Total ____

THE NEXT COURSE OF ACTION

At the end of Chapters 5, 7, 8, 9, 10, 11, and 12, a form is provided to guide your actions to improve your IQ scores. Before you read those chapters and then complete those forms, you should examine your scores for each of the Seven S's.

THE CHARACTERISTICS OF INNOVATIVE ORGANIZATIONS

The list of characteristics examined in the preceding questionnaires can be considered the distinguishing characteristics of an innovative company. These characteristics were compiled from a number of sources, which are discussed more fully in Chapters 5-12. The examples presented in those chapters provide models that can serve as a basis for an organization's efforts. Relevant research findings are provided as available; in addition, significant references are noted at the end of this chapter.[5] Chapter 5 reviews characteristics related to strategy; Chapter 6, those related to innovation strategy; Chapter 7, those related to structure; Chapter 8, those related to systems; Chapter 9, those related to style; Chapter 10, those related to staff; Chapter 11, those related to shared values; and Chapter 12, those related to skills. Chapter 13 provides a summary overview.

These characteristics apply primarily to U.S. and Canadian firms, although the experiences of Japanese and European firms and related research are also relevant. This is especially important because Japanese firms are currently very successful at providing the right organizational cultures for innovation. Although the list of characteristics of Japanese and European firms would be similar to those of U.S. firms, they would not be identical because of cultural differences. Indeed, they won't be identical for U.S. and Canadian firms, even in the same industries, because of differences in organizational culture. Some characteristics may be more important in some firms and some industries than in others. But taken as a whole, these 49 characteristics provide an excellent guide for increasing innovation in organizations.

REFERENCES

1. Thomas J. Peters and Robert H. Waterman, Jr., *In Search of Excellence*, (New York: Harper & Row, 1982), pp. 8-13; Robert H. Waterman Jr., "The Seven S's of Strategic Fit," *Journal of Business Strategy* (Winter, 1982), pp. 70-75.

2. Thomas J. Peters and Robert H. Waterman Jr., Ibid., pp. 8-12.

3. P. Rajan Varadarajan and Vasudevan Ramanujam, "The Corporate Performance Condundrum: A Synthesis of Contemporary Views and an Extension," *Journal of Management Studies* (September 1990), pp.463-483; Richard N. Foster, *Innovation: The Attacker's Advantage* (New York: Summit Books, 1986), p. 21, where he indicates that in his thirty years at McKinsey & Company, every successful firm he saw was innovative; Michael E. Porter, *Competitive Strategy* (New York: Free Press, 1980), pp. 177-179, where he discusses the criticalness of innovation to competitiveness.

4. Peter J. Neff, "Testing Your Company's IQ," *Industry Week* (October 4, 1993), p. 40. I have used his term to label what is a broad-based investigation of a company's capacity for innovation. Mr. Neff is CEO of Rhône-Poulenc, Inc., Rhône-Poulenc's USA subsidiary.

5. The questionnaire first appeared in a 1986 collection of my management materials on innovation then entitled *Escape From the Maze*. This was part of my classroom materials in an MBA course entitled "The Management of Innovation." The collection appeared under several titles until 1992 when it was broken into the trilogy of which this book is one. Sources for the questionnaire include those several hundred cited in individual sections in Chapters 5-12. In addition, the following helped establish the general perspective:

    Early on, the questionnaire was designed based on these sources. Gary A. Steiner, Ed., *The Creative Organization*, (Chicago: University of Chicago Press, 1965); Jay R. Galbraith, "Designing the Innovative Organization," *Organizational Dynamics* (Winter 1982), pp. 5-15; Michael Tushman and David Nadler, "Organizing for Innovation," *California Management Review* (Spring 1986), pp. 74-92. Shortly thereafter, these resources had an impact: Michael A. McGinnis and Thomas P. Vaney, "Innovation Management and Intrapreneurship," *SAM Advanced Management Journal* (Summer 1987), pp. 19-23; F. Axel Johne and Patricia A. Snelson, "Success Factors in Product Innovation: A Selective Review of the Literature," *Journal of Product Innovation Management* (1988), pp. 114-128; Karl Albrecht with Steven Albrecht, *The Creative Organization* (Homewood, IL: Dow-Jones, Irwin, 1988); Herb Brody, "America's Technology Champions," *High Technology Business* (June 1988), pp. 27-28; Kenneth Labich, "The Innovators," *Fortune* (June 6, 1988), pp. 51-60; T. M. Amabile and S. S. Gryskiewicz, "Creative Human Resources in the R&D Laboratory: How Environment and Personality Affect Innovation," in *Handbook for Creative and Innovative Managers*, R. L. Kuhn (ed.)(New York: McGraw-Hill, 1988).

    More recently, the following have helped substantiate the original and later versions of the questionnaire: Susanne G. Scott, "Determinants of Innovative Behavior: A Path Model of Individual Innovation in the Workplace," *Academy of Management Journal* (September 1994), pp. 580-607; Richard W. Woodman, John E. Sawyer and Ricky W. Griffin, "Toward a Theory of Organizational Creativity," *Academy of Management Review* (May 1993), pp. 293-321; Warren B. Brown and Necmi Karagozoglu, "Leading The Way to Faster New

Product Development," *Academy of Management Executive* (February 1993), pp. 36-47; Simon Majaro, "Strategy Search and Creativity: The Key to Corporate Renewal," *European Management Journal* (June 1992), pp. 230-238; Noel Capon, John U. Farley, Donald R. Lehman, and James M. Hulbert, "Profile of Product Innovators Among Large U.S. Manufacturers," *Management Science* (February 1992), pp. 157-169; Fariborz Damanpour, "Organizational Innovation: A Meta-Analysis of Effects of Determinates and Moderators," *Academy of Management Journal* (September 1991), pp. 555-590; Larry Dwyer and Robert Mellor, "Organizational environment, New Product Process Activities, and Project Outcomes," *Journal of Product Innovation Management* (March 1991), pp. 39-48; Hans J. Thamhain, "Managing Technologically Innovative Team Efforts Toward New Product Success," *Journal of Product Innovation Management* (March 1990), pp. 5-18; Billie Jo Zirger and Modesto A. Maidique, "A Model of New Product Development: An Empirical Test," *Management Science* (July 1990), pp. 867-883; Charles O'Reilly, "Corporations, Culture, and Commitment," *California Management Review* (Summer 1989), pp. 9-25; Arthur G. Van Gundy, "How to Establish a Creative Climate in the Work Group," *Management Review* (August 1984), pp. 24-28, 37-38.

PART II

IMPROVE
YOUR
ORGANIZATION'S IQ

Chapters 5-12 discuss each of the McKinsey Seven Ss summary questions from the questionnaires in Chapter 4. (Chapter 6 discusses innovation strategy in particular.) These chapters together describe the overall culture of the organization relative to innovation. Chapter 13 provides two fairly lengthy examples of innovative firms: 3M and how it matches the questionnaires, question by question; and Nippon Steel and how it manages innovation. Chapter 13 concludes with a brief plan for starting to achieve high levels of organizational innovation.

DISCUSSION OF THE QUESTIONS

Each of the following chapters, except 6 and 13, discusses the relevant questions from the questionnaires related to that particular S of the Seven Ss. Each chapter opens with a brief review of key concepts. Next the chapter reviews the available evidence and examples for each question. To facilitate discussion, each of the four questions from the questionnaires—a, b, c, and d, have been combined into a single question covering that general issue.

Most of the examples and research studies cited focus on product and process innovations. In many cases, I have extrapolated what we know about these activities to marketing and management innovation. Most of the examples and research cited deal with product innovation and the next most frequently cited examples deal with process innovation. Examples and research on marketing and management innovation are much less frequent, but are still many in number. Most of the examples deal with well-known medium to large sized firms. Generally, the characteristics are applicable to firms of all sizes.

The entire issue of organizational innovation is a complex one. The forty-nine questions examined in the two questionnaires in Chapter 4, are across four different types of innovation and reflect the thinking at this point in time. As our knowledge of innovation evolves, as the available body of research grows, some changes in the questionnaires may be necessary. The information contained in this book helps you decide what to do, why, and how.

Comparing U.S. Firms with Japanese and European Firms

For most questions (where evidence is available) the perspectives or practices of U.S. firms versus those of Japanese and/or European firms is provided. These sections help profile U.S. firms' global competitiveness or the lack thereof. More is known and written about U.S. and Japanese firms' innovation behavior than European ones, and the examples and research reflect that.

Strategies and Operational Planning Form

Chapters 5, 7, 8, 9, 10, 11 and 12 contain a form which, when completed, provides the user with a strategic and or operational plan for improving that person's firm relative to each of the questionnaire items discussed in that chapter.

UNDERSTANDING THE JAPANESE INNOVATION PROCESS

From its position in the 1960s as an economy that relied almost exclusively on an imitation strategy based on the transfer and improvement of externally developed products, services, technologies, and ideas, Japan has emerged as an economy with many firms that have extensive product innovation capabilities and which define the product, service, and technological frontiers in their industries.

The typical Japanese firm pursues an innovation strategy that follows the stages highlighted in Figure II.I.

FIGURE II.I THE JAPANESE INNOVATION PROCESS

In *Tansakii*, the Japanese firm searches for new ideas.

In *Inysei*, the Japanese firm nurtures new ideas, it allows them to incubate.

In *Hassoo*, the Japanese firm generates breakthrough ideas.

In *Kaizen*, the Japanese firm refines its ideas through continuous improvement.

In *Saitiyo*, the Japanese firm recycles old technologies.[1]

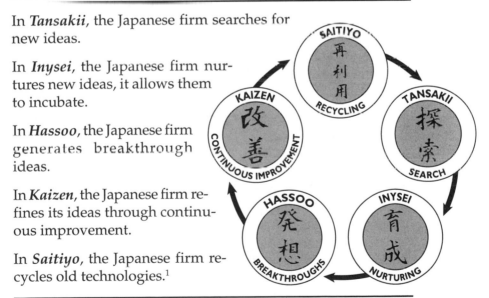

Beginning with Tansakii, the Japanese would be:[2]

1. Searching for world technological trends and assessing the relevant technologies.

2. Next, letting ideas incubate.

3. Using technology teams, they would push for Hassoo. Concurrent engineering, technology fusion, core competence building, and new venture teams would be employed. New businesses would emerge.

4. In Kaizen, continuous improvements would occur.

5. In Saitiyo, old technologies would be recycled.

With Hassoo (breakthrough), Kaizen (continuous improvement), and Saitiyo (recycling), the Japanese are always working on three tiers of innovation at the same time.

Despite the success of this cycle, Japanese managers, government officials, and management associations have called for a strengthening of Japanese innovation efforts. Typical is the three-pronged model suggested by Yuji Nakazono, then director of the Creativity Development Center for the Japan Management Association. First, organizational cultures must be made to facilitate creativity and innovation. Second, managers should set the example by performing creativity activities. Third, all employees should receive training in creative thinking and in understanding the organizational innovation process.[3]

Foreign firms have used a number of approaches attempting to improve their access to Japanese technology and markets, including the establishment of R&D facilities in Japan and the development of complex "strategic alliances" with Japanese firms. Nonetheless, the evidence indicates that too many U.S. firms still view their Japanese R&D operations as oriented largely toward the domestic Japanese market, and are not working to exploit and transfer technologies from Japan into their global R&D networks. U.S. policymakers have yet to address the implications of change in the technological relationship between the U.S. and Japan.[4]

UNDERSTANDING THE EUROPEAN INNOVATION PROCESS

On average, European firms are behind those in the U.S. and Japan in product and process innovation. But as they prepared for the consequences of the Europe 1992 initiative, they often took bold measures to improve their competitiveness. Yet, while some progress has been made, much remains to be done. There really is no single approach to innovation in Europe. Approaches tend to fragment by country. Collectively, Europe is relying on collaboration between countries to fund most of its major science projects. It is ahead in electron accelerators, but behind and making insufficient progress in high-definition TV, information technologies, advanced materials and manufacturing, and communications. $20 billion has been jointly invested in these projects since the 1980s, and there isn't much to show for it.[5] Of major concern is the lack of European industry leadership in high technology fields, especially computers and computer chips, although French-Italian semiconductor maker SGS-Thomson has managed to gain 2.5 percent (1992) of the global market, in contrast to number 1 Intel's 7.8 percent share (1992).[6] Also, European firms have made strides in the supercomputer race as their strengths in software writing have enabled them to be legitimate contenders.[7] Nonetheless, individual countries, for example, Germany, see themselves falling behind in high-tech fields.[8]

REFERENCES

1. Sheridan M. Tatsuno, *Created in Japan: From Imitators to World-Class Innovators* (New York: Harper & Row, 1990), Chapters 5-9.

2. B. Bowonder and T. Miyake, "A Model of Corporate Innovation Management: Some Recent High Tech Innovations in Japan," *R&D Management* (October 1992), pp. 319-335. Their stages have been modified to match Tatsuno's stages.

3. Yuji Nakazono, "Developing Creativity in Japanese Companies: The Situation Today and Current Issues," in *Discovering Creativity: Proceedings of the 1992 International Creativity and Innovation Networking Conference*, Stanley S. Gryskiewicz, editor (Greensboro, North Carolina: Center for Creative Leadership, 1993), pp. 237-245.

4. David C. Mowery and David J. Teece, "Japan's Growing Capabilities in Industrial Technology: Implications for U.S. Managers and Policymakers," *California Management Review* (Winter 1993), pp. 9-34.

5. Jonathan B. Levine, "How Europe Swings the Big Science Tab," *Business Week* (March 22, 1993), pp.62-63.

6. Jane Sasseen, "Chipmaker Comes Out of the Woods," *International Management* (December 1993), pp. 44-46; Jonathan B. Levine, "The Last Hurrah for European High Tech?," *Business Week* (April 29, 1991), pp. 44-45.

7. Richard L. Hudson, "Europeans Begin to Make Their Mark in Supercomputers," *Wall Street Journal* (November 18, 1993), p. B4.

8. Daniel Benjamin, "The Trailing Edge: Some Germans Feel They're Falling Behind in High-Tech Fields," *Wall Street Journal* (April 27, 1994), pp. A1, A6.

S T R A T E G Y

CHAPTER 5

Firms create a competitive advantage by perceiving or developing new and better ways to compete in an industry and bringing them to market, which is ultimately an act of innovation.

> Michael Porter, Consultant,
> Author, Competitive Strategy,
> Professor, Harvard Business School

Strategy is the major set of plans through which an organization achieves its purposes while responding to and proactively changing its environment.[1] Organizational purpose has four components: vision/strategic intent, mission, goals, and objectives. **Vision** is a statement of general direction that serves to motivate the firm and its members.[2] "To be the highest-quality firm in the U.S. auto industry" is a statement of a company's vision. Ford effectively accompanied this vision with the slogan, "Quality Is Job One." **Strategic intent** is an overwhelming purpose that focuses the organization on winning, motivates employees to achieve it, and shows clearly the manner in which resources are to be allocated.[3]

An organization's **mission** describes its business or businesses, its target markets, its geographic areas of operation, and its fundamental operating philosophies, such as those demanding high quality in its products or making innovation a key part of its strategy. **Goals** are general directional statements. Six to eight goals are recommended for every firm; they may include growth, returns to owners, contributions to society, favorable relationships with customers, positive relations with employees, high market share, productivity, and innovation. **Objectives** are specific delineations of goals that are accompanied by a deadline. For example, a firm might aim for a 20 percent market share by the end of the next year, or a 20 percent return on investment by the end of the next quarter.[4]

There are many kinds of strategies for achieving an organization's purposes, but they can all be classified according to one of the three types of strategies mentioned in Chapters 3 and 4: corporate, business, and functional. Innovation can be a corporate, business, or functional strategy or a combination of these, depending on how the firm chooses to innovate.

If a company selects innovation as one of the fundamental ways in which it will operate, this would be a corporate strategy. Hewlett-Packard has focused on innovation as its primary corporate strategy. If a firm pursues a corporate strategy of innovation, it usually has business and functional innovation strategies as well. At Hewlett-Packard, for example, innovation is sought in every action of the firm, from creating new products to developing new ways of managing human resources.

If a firm uses innovation primarily as a way of competing, innovation would be a business strategy for that company. For chip maker Intel, innovation is primarily a way of competing. New products are seen as a means of beating the competition. Intel pursues innovation in other areas as well, but it does not view innovation as a pervasive, overriding philosophy of doing business.

If a firm uses innovation as a way of supporting business strategy, it could be considered a functional strategy. The large number of firms that have adopted continuous improvement as a way of achieving quality as a competitive advantage are using innovation as a functional strategy.

As discussed in Chapter 3, in the future innovation will be the primary basis for achieving a competitive advantage. Innovation is the basis for both differentiation and relative low-cost strategies. It is product and process innovations that enable a firm to achieve these strategies. Innovation is also the basis for superior marketing of products and services, and for superior management of the organization. Both of these activities are aimed at achieving relative differentiation and/or relative low cost. Figure 5.1 presents an overview of the relationships among organizational purposes, the three types of strategy, and innovation.

An innovative organization will have certain stated purposes, policies, and strategies and will function strategically in certain ways. The seven characteristics examined in this chapter represent the key strategic issues that are continually identified as important to successful innovation. In the case of questions 22, 29, 36, and 43, issues identified for product innovation have been extended to process innovations.

FIGURE 5.1 A HIERARCHY OF PURPOSES AND STRATEGIES AND THEIR RELATIONSHIPS TO INNOVATION

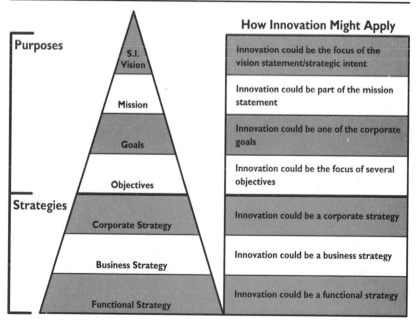

THE CHARACTERISTICS

Exhibit 5.1 contains a set of seven questions on strategy that are summarized from those included in the questionnaires in the preceding chapter. These questions, and those in other chapters, have been generalized to fit the questions on all four types of innovation.[1] After these questions have been discussed, innovation strategy will be examined in more detail in Chapter 6, in which a set of related issues is provided for examining a firm's innovation strategy.

EXHIBIT 5.1 CHARACTERISTICS OF INNOVATIVE
ORGANIZATIONS RELATED TO STRATEGY

To what extent does your organization:

1. Have stated and working strategies for product, process, marketing, and management innovation.

8. Possess a market orientation for product, process, marketing, and management innovation (is close to its customers).

15. Require managers to have objectives for product, process, marketing, and management innovation, and evaluate their performance relative to these.

22. Put every product, process, marketing approach, and management practice on trial for its life every eighteen months to two years.

29. Make commercialization or utilization of new ideas a priority.

36. Use speed strategies and/or objectives that stretch performers' capabilities for product, process, marketing, and management innovation.

43. Know when and how to lead the customer to new products or services and to reduce costs by improving processes, including management practices and do so through innovative marketing.

---

[1] For the sake of brevity, the a, b, c, and d portions of each question have been combined into a single question that expresses the main theme embodied in the individual questions.

1. Have Stated and Working Strategies for Product, Process, Marketing, and Management Innovation.

Regardless of the level involved—corporate, business, or functional—innovation must be an announced and real working strategy if it is to be effective. As part of this approach, the firm must also be committed to both product and process innovation. Research findings indicate that successful firms place a high value on both product and process innovation. For example, an examination of seventy-four companies rated by *Business Month* as being among the five best firms each year during a fifteen-year period reveals six characteristics shared by those firms *(Note item number 3)*:

1. A broad product line accompanied by geographic diversity.

2. An emphasis on planning coupled with sound financial controls and reporting systems.

3. *A high level of commitment to product and process innovation.*

4. Investment in modernization of manufacturing facilities.

5. A reputation for superior quality and customer service.

6. Progressive human resource management practices.[5]

Noted consultant and author Peter Drucker was one of the first management experts to suggest that innovation is an important function of management. He considered it to be one of the eight key results areas for a successful organization, along with such factors as market standing, productivity, and profitability.[6] Consider some examples:

At both Lockheed and Milliken, innovation is viewed as a fundamental route to success. In the 1980s, Lockheed even ran a series of advertisements detailing its strategic reliance on innovation. Milliken's announced corporate strategy focuses on quality and innovation as a means of remaining competitive with Japanese and other foreign firms.[7] Both Lockheed and Milliken have product and process innovation strategies.

At pharmaceutical giant Merck, which for several years many top managers believed to be the best-managed firm in the U.S.,[8] the stated goals are technological innovation and scientific leadership.[9] General Electric has a stated strategy of both product and process innovation, as well as management innovation, and has redesigned its culture and management practices to achieve those ends.[10]

Conseco, Inc., a life insurance and annuities holding company in Carmel, Indiana, has a stated strategy of leading the process of change in the industry by setting new standards for efficiency, product innovation, product profitability, and investment management. This strategy has been extremely successful. For example, Conseco's ratio of general expenses to collected premiums is 3 percent compared to an industry average of 12 percent. Similarly, its average data-processing cost is about $11 per policy, half the industry average. The value of its stock increased about 1,000 percent in five years.[11] A recent study of eighty-six small, innovative Canadian metal manufacturing firms found process innovation to be an important factor in their global competitiveness. These firms also focused on product innovation as well.[12]

One firm for which innovation is a matter of life and death is Rubbermaid. Innovation is not only its strategy but its entire way of life. *Innovate or Evaporate 5.1* examines Rubbermaid's innovative nature.

Here are some more examples. In two decades, Fuji-Xerox grew from a strictly sales-oriented organization, with nineteen employees, to a completely self-sufficient high-tech company with more than 13,000 employees. Much of its growth was due to the high quality of its products and the number of its new products—both results of innovation. In 1988 the company launched its "New Work Way," a program aimed at increasing the level of innovative thinking in all of its employees. The program has produced some dramatic results. For example, a copier marketed under the name Sharaku was developed out of the

RUBBERMAID'S SIMPLE STRATEGY: INNOVATE

In 1993, after being number two in *Fortune* magazine's most-admired-company contest for five of the previous six years, Rubbermaid finally became number one. The company is a veritable juggernaut when it comes to putting out new products: 365 a year—that is, one a day (almost two every work day). Headed by Stanley Gault from 1980 to 1991, the company enjoyed unprecedented growth in profits (an average increase of 14 percent a year) and stock appreciation (an average of 25 percent a year). When Gault retired in 1991, only to move on shortly thereafter to become CEO of Goodyear (he's still chairman of the board at Rubbermaid), he was replaced by Walter Williams, who resigned after eighteen months.

Now the firm is run by Wolfgang Schmitt who has established high objectives for the firm but will continue to pursue its long-established innovation strategy to achieve those objectives. Schmitt wants Rubbermaid to enter a new-product category every twelve to eighteen months (most recently it has introduced hardware cabinets and garden sheds); to obtain thirty-three percent of its sales from products introduced within the past five years; and to obtain twenty-five percent of its revenues from markets outside the United States by the year 2000, an increase of seven percent over the current eighteen percent.

Rubbermaid excels in making mundane items seem interesting and functional, and it also makes them profitable. Each year it improves over 5000 existing products or creates totally new ones. Its product line includes mailboxes, window boxes, storage boxes, toys, mops, dust mitts, snap-together furniture, ice cube

INNOVATE OR EVAPORATE 5.1

continued next page

RUBBERMAID

trays, stadium seats, spatulas, step stools, wall coverings, sporting goods, dinner ware, dish drainers, laundry hampers, and many other utilitarian products. However numdane those items may seem, Rubbermaid's engineers hover over their products as intently as would General Dynamics' engineers over an F-111 fighter. It is this serious approach to what others dismiss as trivial that has helped make the firm so successful.

Most of Rubbermaid's new products come from twenty cross-functional teams, each with five to seven members (one each from marketing, manufacturing, R&D, finance, and other departments, as needed). Each team focuses on a specific product line so that someone is always thinking about key product segments. But innovation doesn't stop with the teams. Individual employees are geared toward creating new products as well.

Rubbermaid has taught its employees to think in terms of letting new products flow from the firm's core competencies—the things it does well. It encourages its managers to find out what's happening in the rest of the company, continually looking at processes and technologies. For example, while running a different Rubbermaid subsidiary, Bud Hellman toured a Rubbermaid plant that made picnic coolers. As he watched the plastic blow-molding equipment, he realized that he could use that process to make a line of durable, lightweight, inexpensive office furniture. Within a couple of years that line accounted for sixty percent of the furniture divison's sales.

Top management often contributes ideas as well. When CEO Schmitt and Richard Gates, head of product development, toured the British Museum in London in 1993, they became extremely interested in an exhibit of Egyptian antiquities. They came away with eleven specific product ideas. Gates says admiringly of the Egyptians, "They used a lot of kitchen utensils, some of which were very nice. Nice designs."

Typical of Rubbermaid's attention to detail is its approach to customer relations. In the Customer Center, which hosts 110 major retail customers a year (including the biggest, Wal-Mart, which accounts for fourteen percent of the firm's sales) the pitch

RUBBERMAID

is always the same: "Let us help you sell more; we've got what consumers want." At the end of each presentation, the customer sees many new products. Then it's on to the War Room, where the deficiencies in competitors' products are demonstrated. Then it's on to the Best Practices Room, where retailers see the best in product mixes and displays. The idea is to establish a store within a store—that is, to put a Rubbermaid store in the retailer's stores.

Rubbermaid does no market testing, although it does hold focus groups. Schmitt doesn't believe in testing. "We don't want to be copied. It's not that much riskier to just roll it out. Plus, it puts pressure on us to do it right the first time," he states. Flops do happen occasionally, but the firm has a remarkable ninety percent success rate with new products and tolerates the few failures that occur in the name of taking risks.

Sources: Alan Farnham, "America's Most Admired Company," *Fortune* (February 7, 1994), pp. 50–54; Brian Dumaine, "Closing the Innovation Gap," *Fortune* (December 2, 1991), p. 57.

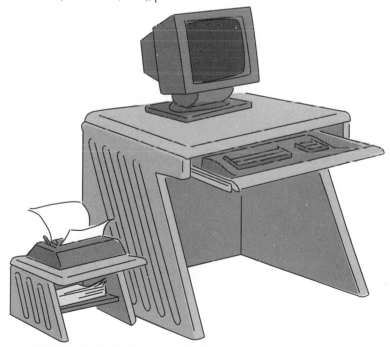

ideas of a few employees addressing some of the problems in the low-end market.[13] Similarly, the Netherlands' Unilever Corporation, a giant consumer products firm, believes that its competitive edge lies in being able to innovate faster than anyone else and then roll out new products under well-known brand names in global markets.[14]

Comparing U.S. Firms with Japanese and European Firms

A 1992 survey by the consulting firm Deloitte and Touche compared the perceived importance of various strategies to 900 U.S. and Japanese manufacturing executives. Overall, Japanese executives placed much more emphasis on product related strategies than did U.S. executives. U.S. and Japanese executives both stressed strategies related to customer service, although the U.S. executives put slightly more emphasis on these strategies. Very telling was the gap of 42 percentage points on the importance of enhancing product features: 83 percent of Japanese executives emphasized this approach, compared to 41 percent of U.S. executives. There was a gap of 30 percentage points on the importance of products with a high R&D component—80 percent of Japanese executives compared to 50 percent of U.S. executives. And there was an 18-percentage-point difference on the need to introduce many new products—68 percent of Japanese executives versus 50 percent of U.S. executives.[15] Figures 5.2 and 5.3 contain the key findings of the study in graphic form.

FIGURE 5.2 RESULTS OF STUDY COMPARING VIEWS OF U.S. AND JAPANESE EXECUTIVES:
1. EMPHASIS ON CUSTOMER SERVICE AND RELIABILITY

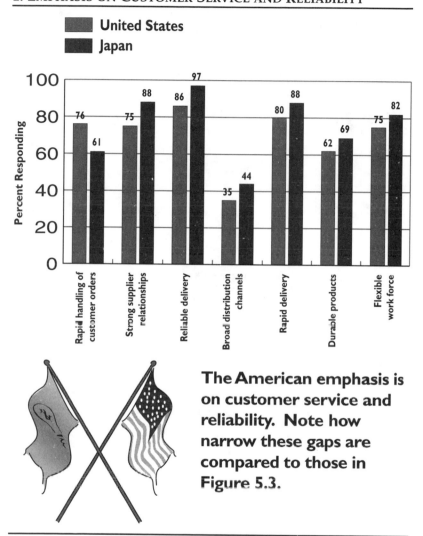

The American emphasis is on customer service and reliability. Note how narrow these gaps are compared to those in Figure 5.3.

Source: Deloitte & Touche, *Winning in Global Markets* (Detroit, MI: Deloitte & Touche, 1992), pp.1, 3.

FIGURE 5.3 RESULTS OF STUDY COMPARING VIEWS OF U.S. AND JAPANESE EXECUTIVES:
2. EMPHASIS ON VARIETY, INNOVATION, AND TECHNOLOGY

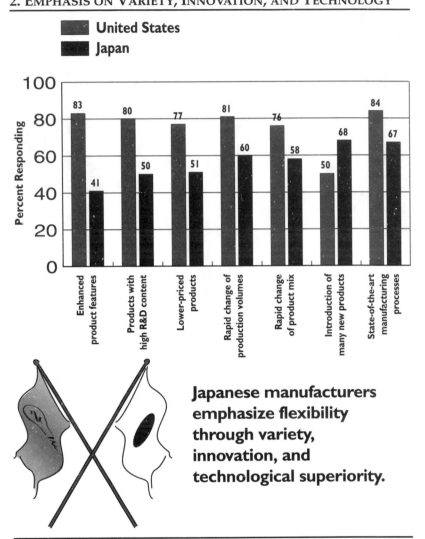

Japanese manufacturers emphasize flexibility through variety, innovation, and technological superiority.

Source: Deloitte & Touche, *Winning in Global Markets* (Detroit, MI: Deloitte & Touche, 1992), pp.1, 3.

8. Possess a Market Orientation for Product, Process, Marketing, and Management Innovation (Is Close to Its Customers).

Closeness to the customer has been a central tenet of American management since Thomas J. Peters and Robert H. Waterman, Jr. wrote about its importance in *In Search of Excellence*.[16] However, Deborah Dougherty of the Wharton School of Business suggests that understanding a market means more than just getting close to the customer. It requires knowledge of at least five areas:[17]

1. Emerging trends or problems.

2. Compatibility with the producer's competencies and goals.

3. Feasibility of the product idea.

4. Detailed understanding of customers' preferences and needs.

5. A real sense of how the product fits into the customer's operation, home life, or other area of focus.

Nonetheless, getting close to the customer is clearly where market orientation begins. Statistical analysis shows that the largest number of good ideas for new products and services come from customers.[18] Listening to the customer is especially critical. Company representatives should go beyond the stated needs and wants of customers and search for unspoken or hidden concerns. Such listening should be used to build a closer relationship with the customer. The skilled listener understands not only the customer but the customer's background.[19] Understanding the customer's needs, wants, and problems should lead to the development of solutions that are more likely to satisfy that customer than those offered by competitors. *Innovate or Evaporate 5.2* reviews the successful efforts of one firm to stay close to it's customers.

At one time Campbell Soup Company emphasized the development of products that were compatible with existing production facilities, as opposed to products that would satisfy

Strategy

Chapter 5

customer needs. This approach resulted in sluggish profits. When Gordon McGovern took over as CEO, he insisted that the company focus on consumer demands and moved not only toward developing more new products, but especially toward developing products that customers wanted.[20] These actions led to a substantial improvement in profits.

The strategy of getting close to the customer gained further support from the findings of a 1993 study on new product innovation by Kuczmarski & Associates, a Chicago consulting firm. In this survey of 77 companies that had introduced over 11,000 new products and services over the previous five years it was found that the most common reason for new-product flops was simple—the company failed to understand the needs of its target market. Firms that launched successful new products understood their customers' needs and provided emphasis on product development, supported by top management, and sufficient funding.[21]

Some companies go to great lengths to find out what their customers want. Honda uses all the standard marketing research approaches, such as customer surveys and focus groups. But in November 1992 it asked its factory workers, the actual bolters and riveters, to call half (47,000) of all recent purchasers of the Accord. This was called the ET Phone Home Project (after the film *ET.*) The goal was to find out whether customers were happy with their cars and to get ideas for improvements. The resulting changes will appear in the company's 1995 models.

Similarly, the United States Automobile Association, an insurer based in San Antonio, annually surveys 500,000 customers (20 percent of its total customer base), of whom an unbelievable 60 percent respond. Through this survey the company not only seeks to keep its customers happy but also searches for new-product ideas. A recent survey led to the launch of a new growth and income mutual fund in June 1993. The new product was an instant success, attracting $76.8 million in assets in less than five months.[22]

From a process perspective, it is the effective integration of new-product requirements with the manufacturing process that enables a firm to seize market opportunities. Process innovations allow the firm to exploit new technologies to create new products.[23] Similar observations could be made about new services.

UNITED STATES SURGICAL CUTS A SWATH THROUGH ITS COMPETITORS

In any ten day period every one of the nation's 5000 hospitals is visited by members of United States Surgical's sales force. They don surgical gowns and stand alongside surgeons using their products and those of competitors. They listen to their customers and understand their needs. Does such extensive effort pay off? Absolutely. U.S. Surgical has garnered 85 percent of the laparoscopy market, the leading edge in surgery. Its sales and profits increased sharply in the early 1990s.

The 30-year-old firm got its start when its founder, Leon Hirsch, redesigned a Soviet-made surgical staple. The improved product worked well, but it didn't sell well. Hirsch concluded that he needed an expert sales force. He therefore began requiring recruits to undergo a stringent six-week course on surgical terms and procedures. Daily quizzes cover important topics such as anatomy, scrub techniques, surgical instruments, and the like. Twenty percent of the trainees are unable to pass the course.

Hirsch's intuition about getting closer to the customer has paid off handsomely. For example, in the case of laparoscopy, a recent graduate of the training course was watching a surgeon perform this technique, using a jury-rigged clip to help remove a gallbladder. The absence of an adequate clip made the process more difficult than it needed to be. The saleswoman reported

INNOVATE OR EVAPORATE 5.2

continued next page

U.S. SURGICAL

this information to headquarters, and shortly thereafter the company had a basic stapler ready for the market. The sales force took both the technique and the instrumentation to customers throughout the nation. The result was a doubling in the percentage of gallbladders removed by laparoscopy, from 30 percent in 1990 to 60 percent in 1991. Three years after introduction, almost 80 percent of all gallbladder operations used surgical staples.*

---

*U.S. Surgical ran into financial difficulties in 1993 and 1994 resulting primarily from an ill advised move into surgical sutures against well entrenched Johnson & Johnson. Changes in the marketplace, for example, hospital cost cutting, also affected their sales.

Source: Ron Winslow, "As Marketplace Shifts, U.S. Surgical Needs Patching Up," Wall Street Journal (February 18, 1994), p. B4; Jennifer Reese, "United States Surgical: Getting Hot Ideas from Customers," Fortune (May 16, 1992), pp. 86-87.

A valuable way of finding out what customers want and need— that is, what improved product features and improvements in organizational processes might be necessary—is the customer complaint. Electronic Controls Company, (ECCO) is a relatively small firm (100 employees) based in Boise, Idaho. ECCO designs, manufactures, and markets amber strobe lights for utility vehicles; it also makes backup alarms for trucks that beep when the driver shifts into reverse. The firm has paid special attention to customer complaints as a way of gathering information about how to improve products and processes. ECCO's specially designed and utilized customer complaint form is discussed in *Innovate or Evaporate 5.3.*

Comparing U.S. Firms with Japanese and European Firms

Firms in different countries follow various approaches to developing a market orientation. U.S. firms spend a great deal of time and money on market research to determine customer needs. Japanese firms spend much less time than U.S. firms on

ECCO'S RIGOROUS CUSTOMER-COMPLAINT FORM

In 1990, then CEO of ECCO Jim Thompson determined that the firm needed to get a better grip on customer complaints, not only to satisfy customers but also to gather information about the most common complaints so that organizational processes and product designs could be improved. ECCO's customer service reps, who fielded most of the complaints, were already authorized to take whatever actions were necessary to alleviate customers' problems. This was fine as far as it went, but Thompson wanted more. No records of complaints were kept, and he wanted to ensure that the valuable information gained from complaints was recorded, analyzed, and acted upon.

The customer-service team devised a form to capture the most relevant information. As the most common types of complaints became clear, questions about these problems were added to the form. The form is continually being modified as product and process changes occasionally result in new kinds of complaints. Top management reviews the past week's complaints every Monday morning. Production and sales teams also review the complaint forms at regular intervals. Everyone in the firm who might talk to customers, including customer service reps, sales personnel, production managers, and even the president (customers sometimes demand *to talk* to the president) is given complaint forms to fill out when the occasion *arises*.

Complaints are tracked in two ways. First, information from completed forms is entered into a database, and a monthly cus-

continued next page

INNOVATE OR EVAPORATE 5.3

ECCO

tomer complaint report is generated from the database which helps management track trends in complaints. Second, the original copies of the forms are filed in one of two binders. Open-and-shut cases go into a "closed cases" file, while complaints that require more action are placed in an "open cases" file until corrective actions have been taken.

This management innovation helps the firm in designing new organizational processes and enhancing existing products. Each quarter, corrective action teams are assigned to the top three problems. Recently, when the firm had received thirty-three complaints in six months about errors in quantities of items shipped, a corrective action team completely redesigned the packing process as well as the packing form.

Source: Jay Finegan, "The Rigorous Customer-Complaint Form," *Success* (March 1994), pp. 101-103.

market research. After some preliminary efforts, they get a trial product into the marketplace. Then they adjust it on the basis of consumer reactions.[24] Moreover, there is a tight integration between R&D and marketing in Japanese firms that is not found in most U.S. firms.[25]

Today many U.S. firms are trying to develop closer, more personal relationships with their customers, not just to learn more about their customers' needs but also in an effort to keep those customers' loyalty. The more customers become dependent on a particular firm, the less likely they are to switch to other suppliers. **Relationship marketing** is one buzzword of the 1990s. This approach involves making a sincere effort to relate to customers and letting them know that the firm cares about them in a genuine, realistic, and holistic way.[26] Relationship marketing is part of a **wraparound marketing strategy**—a strategy aimed at both getting and retaining customers.

There are several levels of relationship marketing, with partnerships with customers being the most extensive of these. Various customer retention tactics can be used at each level.[27] One such tactic involves the use of electronic data interchange (EDI). By sharing databases, and more significantly by providing services that cannot be provided by competitors that don't have access to the customer database, firms can increase customer dependance and loyalty. For example, McKesson Corporation, a San Francisco-based wholesaler, is linked by computer to its customer drugstores. McKesson supplies computerized scanners to the drugstore managers, thereby enabling them to process their inventory needs automatically. Not only does McKesson ship the requested materials almost instantaneously, it also adds pricing stickers with designated profit margins.[28]

15. Require Managers to Have Objectives for Product, Process, Marketing, and Management Innovation, and Evaluate Their Performance Relative to These.

Following the vision/strategic intent, mission, goals, and objectives hierarchy, firms like 3M begin with a vision of innovation, include in it their mission, and then establish corporate goals for innovation, which are parceled out to their managers as objectives. 3M has a corporate-level goal of achieving 30 percent of its worldwide sales each year from products introduced within the last four years. The "3M 30 Percent Challenge" makes product innovation a financial goal and, hence, an individual managerial objective.[29]

At Canon in Japan, managers are given tough objectives across all four types of innovation, such as "making a quality product for half the going price."[30] Canon's semiconductor equipment division, which makes photo lithographic systems, already had a strong focus on commercialization when it was challenged to cut six months off its new-product development time. To achieve this objective, it used computer-aided design, project management, and overlapped product development phases. This streamlined approach cut development costs by 30 percent, time to market by 50 percent, and allowed the division to launch two new generations of products while competitors were launching one.[31]

The noted speaker and consultant Larry Wilson has often observed that "People respect what you inspect, not what you expect." In other words, if it's not on their performance appraisals, they won't accomplish company goals and objectives. If a firm wants innovation, it must make innovation a part of each person's performance appraisal, starting with managers.

Comparing U.S. Firms with Japanese and European Firms

From the 1985 Arthur D. Little study discussed in Chapter 1, we know that compared to European (71 percent) and Japanese firms (82 percent), significantly fewer U.S. firms (51 percent) had executive contribution expectations resulting from innovation in the next five years.[32] From the 1992 study by the same organization, also discussed in Chapter 1, we know that U.S. executives reported that their greatest concern was not that the United States has too few scientists and engineers to do the creative work but that U.S. managers don't know how to manage innovation. I suggest that if innovation were made a key part of their objec-

tives and performance appraisals, they would learn how to manage it.

22. Put Every Product, Process, Marketing Approach, and Management Practice on Trial for Its Life Every Eighteen Months to Two Years.

Noted management consultant and author Peter Drucker was the first to suggest that a product should be put on trial for its life every three years. For many firms this process needs to occur even more often. At 3M, for example, because of the company's 30 percent rule (30 percent of a division's sales must come from products that did not exist four years previously) products are put on trial for their lives all the time.

GENERAL ELECTRIC: THE COMPANY OF TOMORROW, TODAY

General Electric is already the company of tomorrow. In a bold set of management actions aimed at increasing innovation to improve productivity in order to make the company more competitive, GE has set the trends that others will follow into the twenty-first century. CEO Jack Welch, long known for his strategic philosophy of buying and selling firms to gain the number 1 or number 2 position in any industry in which GE is a player, recognizes that maintaining those lofty sales and profit positions depends on improving the management approaches used throughout the company. Welch aims to increase the flow of ideas from all employees by improving the way they are managed.

Three new tools form the core of this management revolution: the workout, best practices, and process mapping. In the **workout**, a manager and his or her subordinates gather for a three-day retreat. Subordinates work on problems with the help of an outside facilitator; the manager does not participate in these sessions. On the third day the manager is asked to respond to solutions proposed by subordinates with a yes, a no, or a deferral for further study. (Managers are encouraged to limit the number of deferrals.) What makes the workout intriguing is that the manager's own supervisor is present on the third day, but the manager is not allowed to witness his or her reactions to the employees' suggestions. The manager faces the group of employees, and the supervisor sits behind the manager, also facing the employees. The intent is to involve employees in decision making, to solve problems, and to change managers' attitudes toward employee involvement.

continued next page

INNOVATE OR EVAPORATE 5.4

GENERAL ELECTRIC

In the **best-practices** technique, the firm compares itself with the firms that are best at performing a particular function or process. GE, for example, has compared itself with the best firms in making appliances and lightbulbs and in performing various financial functions, such as making loans. Once the comparison has been made, GE attempts to improve its performance levels by emulating the best practices of other firms. Significant improvements have been reported throughout GE's many businesses as a result of best-practices analyses.

In **process mapping**, employees complete a flowchart of a process such as making a jet engine. The flowcharts show how all the component tasks are interrelated. Employees then try to see how much time they can cut from the process. In the case of jet engines, which GE has been making for years, the firm was able to cut the manufacturing time in half through process mapping, thereby saving many millions of dollars.

What makes all these approaches work is a change in GE's corporate culture, which has become obsessed with productivity and innovation. Welch has been actively involved in the change by, among other things, attending the sessions in which the new programs were developed. He has laid out the changes he wants and has offered rewards for success. Ever ready to experiment and make things happen, Welch is confidently leading GE into the twenty-first century.

Source: Thomas A. Stewart, "GE Keeps Those Ideas Coming," *Fortune* (August 12, 1991), pp. 41-49.

One firm that has been extremely active in the pursuit of improvement is General Electric. GE is constantly seeking innovation in all aspects of its operations. *Innovate or Evaporate 5.4* discusses some of GE's management innovations and the rationale behind them. The driving force of GE's actions is the need to

achieve increased productivity, which management believes depends on product and process innovations—which, in turn, depend on getting more ideas from all employees.

Comparing U.S. Firms with Japanese and European Firms

Most major Japanese firms have already begun replacing a product the moment it enters the marketplace.[33] U.S. firms tend to keep adding enhancements to old products even if they are past their useful lives.[34] The more innovative U.S. and Japanese firms keep three tiers of product development going at all times: enhancements (from *Kaizen*—continuous improvement), new products from related technologies, and new products from new technologies ("big bang" innovation). Most Japanese firms practice continuous improvement of both products and processes. Many U.S. firms have followed suit. European firms, on average, are just getting into the systematic management of innovation and continuous improvement.

29. Make Commercialization or Utilization of New Ideas a Priority.

Research and development by itself isn't enough. The innovative firm turns the results of R&D into successful commercial products or services. It focuses managers' attention on innovation objectives; its culture reinforces these priorities; and its control systems check to ensure that they have been carried out. At GE, for example, turning ideas into real products is a science. Whereas for the typical U.S. firm only one in ten projects ends up as a successful product, almost 60 percent of projects initiated at GE become successful products.[35] Innovative firms are obsessive about creating new products. Others may be just as obsessive about creating new processes. In firms that want to innovate, top management sets the tone by emphasizing the importance of new-product successes. When French chemical/pharmaceutical giant Rhône-Poulenc determined that it needed more innovation, CEO Jean-Rene Fourtou continuously cited its importance in his internal and external communications.[36] See *Innovate or Evaporate 11.5.*

Some firms have formed new product/research centers (NPRCs), centralized staff product development teams to focus firm efforts on commercialization. Raytheon, for example, used this approach to launch thirty-nine major new products

for eight different divisions over a seventeen-year period. Its emphasis is on R&D, but with a small "r" and a big "D." Raytheon's NPC takes new ideas and concepts and turns them into successful products.[37]

Comparing U.S. Firms with Japanese and European Firms

One of the major differences between U.S. and Japanese firms is that Japanese firms actively focus on commercialization while U.S. firms seem content to do R&D without placing a great deal of emphasis on turning the results into saleable products or services.[38] Japanese firms focus much more intently on the marketability of their research results than do their U.S. counterparts. American researchers tend to be much more interested in research for research's sake, whereas the typical Japanese firm's organizational culture demands greater orientation toward the bottom line.[39] However, U.S. firms are now moving toward greater emphasis on applications.[40]

36. Use Speed Strategies and/or Objectives that Stretch Performers' Capabilities for Product, Process, Marketing, and Management Innovation.

It isn't enough to have a great product or service. It must get to market quickly. While it's true that marketing muscle—that is, advertising dollars—can overcome some of the disadvantages of not being the first to enter a market, most of the time the first to market garners the lion's share. The various speed strategies available to firms can be classified into two general types: those that focus on the supply process and those that speed the product development process. The former requires working closely with suppliers, making speed a priority, and focusing on human resource practices. The latter involves concurrent engineering, parallel processing, simplifying, eliminating delays, eliminating steps, and using new venture units and **skunk works**.[41] This term was first used to describe a select group of creative thinkers at Lockheed Corporation.[42] The term is now used to indicate any number of individuals who work together outside the mainstream of the corporation on creative projects—projects that  may not bear fruit for some time but that the organization is willing to sponsor in the hope that they will eventually bear fruit.

Canon's semiconductor division's speed strategy (discussed previously under #15) gave it a significant competitive advantage in its market. In another example, discussed in Chapter 4, Hewlett-Packard found itself continually behind on new-product development projects. CEO John Young drastically restructured the firm, eliminating cumbersome committee structures in favor of new-product development units headed by "czars" with total authority for making new-product decisions. The committees abolished by Young had been constituted to help form a common computer product interface among autonomous work units as they developed new products. They had accomplished this, but at the expense of major delays in product delivery times caused by bureaucratic factors. The results of the restructuring were breathtaking. HP launched a series of new products, including workstations and palmtop computers, that dominated their markets and returned huge profits. The price of HP's stock more than doubled in less than a year.[43] (*Innovate or Evaporate 4.1* discusses this turnaround in more detail.)

Comparing U.S. Firms with Japanese and European Firms

The Japanese are especially adept at rushing out instant imitations in a process known as **product covering**. They are also excellent at **product churning**, or rushing new products to market without market research. They let customer reaction to the output of the first production run tell them what they should do to improve the product. A 1990 study by McKinsey & Company reveals that Japanese firms develop new products in one-third to one-half the time spent by their Western counterparts, at between one-tenth and one-quarter of the cost.[44]

One study of U.S. and German new-product development (NPD) teams revealed that, on average, the greatest concern of the U.S. teams was staying within their budget and improving product performance. The greatest concern of German NPD teams was meeting product development schedules, followed by improving product performance. The cost of product development was their least important concern. This suggests that many U.S. firms do not yet recognize the need for speed in getting new products to market.[45]

43. Know When and How to Lead the Customer to New Products or Services and to Reduce Costs by Improving Processes, Including Management Practices, and Do So Through Innovative Marketing.

It's becoming increasingly clear that, although it is crucial to be aware of the customer's needs, it is often necessary to lead the

customer along the way toward satisfying those needs. The customer doesn't always know what he or she needs, or even that there is a problem to be solved. Robert Hall, senior vice-president of GVO, an industrial design firm in Palo Alto, California, observes that "To invent products out of thin air, you don't ask people what they want—after all, who would have told you ten years ago they needed a CD player? You ask them what problems they have in the morning when they wake up." Then you figure out how to solve those problems.[46]

This is exactly the reasoning Sony followed in determining the need for the Data Discman. Sony engineers recognized that executives would like to be able to carry large amounts of data with them when they traveled. The Data Discman was created to satisfy that need.[47] Research into the twelve most significant consumer and commercial product breakthroughs from 1960 to 1985 showed that in all cases the customer was led to the

COMPAGNIE BANCAIRE: TOMORROW'S BANK TODAY

In his 1988 book *Breaking Up the Bank*, Lowell Bryan described the bank of the future. It would consist of a group of niche subsidiaries overseen by a holding company. Bryan believed that banks would have to stop trying to be all things to all people and concentrate on niches in which they had a competitive advantage. Most European bankers, hooked on the idea of full-service banking, ignored Bryan's ideas. But one European bank, France's Compagnie Bancaire, had already adopted the strategy and structure envisioned by Bryan.

Compagnie Bancaire has always been an oddity. Founded in 1959 as a collection of miscellaneous firms, it currently has seven major subsidiaries, which are involved in everything from equipment finance (UFB Locabail) and consumer lending (Cetelem) to life insurance (Cardif) and fund management (Cortal). Banque Paribas, a traditional French merchant bank, bought a 48 percent stake in Bancaire in 1969, thereby assuring its independence. In return, Bancaire serves as a cash cow for Paribas.

Bancaire uses innovation as a central strategy. It sees the world differently than most banks. For example, it regards desposit-taking and lending as different businesses rather than as parts of the same business. A better lender than deposit-taker, it has chosen to finance itself from capital markets rather than through a branch network. Only two of its seven subsidiaries take deposits from their customers, insurance and fund management. Bancaire distributes its products through a mixture of other banks, retailers, and direct marketing. François Henrot, the deputy chief executive, explains this strategy by observing that any bank that invests in bricks and mortar has a high overhead.

continued next page

INNOVATE OR EVAPORATE 5.5

COMPAGNIE BANCAIRE

Moreover, the bank believes that no clerk can master the more than 200 products that are available in banks today. So Bancaire has only a few products.

The holding company basically raises capital for its subsidiaries. Beyond that, each subsidiary is free to chart its own course, make its own alliances, create its own products, and develop its own computer systems. Some observers, predisposed to more centralized control, are aghast at the freedom enjoyed by Bancaire's subsidiaries. But CEO André Lévy-Lang justifies this approach because it stimulates innovation. He feels that each part of the bank must learn to live by its wits, rather than merely providing routine products that any competitor could offer. For example, Bancaire was the first French bank to offer floating-rate mortgages and Merrill Lynch-style cash management accounts.

Bancaire is moving rapidly to spread its risks by becoming an international company. It has expanded rapidly in Britain and in Italy and Spain. Lévy-Lang often looks to the United States as a source of innovative ideas. He likes to use American Express as his model. Bancaire's approach to banking helped prepare it for the free-for-all atmosphere of European banking that resulted from the Europe 1992 initiative.

Source: "Compagnie Bancaire," *The Economist* (February 17, 1990), pp. 89-90.

product. None of the products was designed to meet specifications that had been identified through market research; rather, the products were invented and then sold to the customer. Sony's Walkman was one of these breakthroughs.[48] *Innovate or Evaporate 5.5* reviews the innovation strategy of the French bank, Compagnie Bancaire, a firm that leads its customers to new products and to the lower prices resulting from unique process innovation.

Comparing U.S. Firms with Japanese and European Firms

Japanese firms rush their products to market, often without doing any test marketing. The first production run *is* the test market. Sophisticated information systems allow them to make adjustments in product, price, promotion, and distribution within a very short time. (See *Innovate or Evaporate 8.3* on Kao Corporation.) Some U.S. firms, such as Rubbermaid, use a similar approach. (See *Innovate or Evaporate 5.1* on Rubbermaid.)

INTRODUCTION TO THE STRATEGIC AND OPERATIONAL PLANNING GUIDE

In this and each of the remaining chapters that discuss the seven S's, the reader is provided with a form that can be used to create a particular organization's plan of action to improve it's levels of innovativeness. This form, which serves as a guide to strategic and operational planning, can be found on two facing pages at the end of each chapter. On the left facing page is a list of the relevant questions from the questionnaire, plus two blank columns to be completed. On the right side, are three additional blank columns to be completed.

The five columns are based on the three questions underlying all strategic and operational planning: Where are we now, where do we want to be, and how do we get there? The first two questions are reviewed on the left page and the third on the right page; the latter includes three subquestions: What needs to be done, by whom, and by when? Three simplified examples are provided on the next two pages. The examples are intended only to show how the forms are to be used. User situations will be much more complex. The blank forms provided in each chapter are intended primarily for developing a preliminary overview. Most users will require considerably more detailed solutions than can be set forth in the space provided.

Example 1: Question 1

Does your organization have a stated and working strategy of product, process, marketing, and management innovation?

Where are we now?
(Score)

The company has assessed itself as having a score of 2, which suggests that it doesn't have a stated innovation strategy but that some innovation may occur within the firm.

Where do we want to be?
(What are our objectives?)

The organization has indicated that it would like to have innovation included in its mission statement, its statement of corporate philosophy, and its strategy.

How do we get there?
What needs to be done?

A new mission statement must be written that includes innovation as a key component. Innovation must be added to corporate philosophy. It is also quite possible that the firm will add innovation to its goals. This is highly likely because it intends to change its performance management system to include innovation as part of a manager's objectives (question 15). Including innovation as part of strategy will require some effort. This can be done at the corporate, business, and/or functional levels.

By whom?

The firm has determined that the strategic planning office will rewrite the mission and corporate philosophy statements, subject to the approval of the board of directors. It will also help top executives reformulate the company's strategy to include innovation.

By when?

This must be accomplished within two months.

Example 2: Question 8

Does your organization have a market orientation with respect to product, process, marketing, and management innovation?

Where are we now?
(Score)

The firm gives itself a score of 5, which indicates that it does have some marketing orientation but clearly needs a lot more.

Where do we want to be?
(What are our objectives?)

The culture of the organization must support and promote a market orientation. Formalized systems must be developed to achieve this.

How do we get there?
What needs to be done?

The firm believes that in order to change its culture it must establish objectives for a market orientation. It must provide rewards for such an orientation, and it must train and develop its employees to become much more market oriented. More extensive plans would typically be formulated at this point, since changes in organizational culture usually require exhaustive efforts.

By whom?

The firm has determined that the Human Resource Management Department will take charge of this change process but that all functions will be involved so that the entire organization will become market oriented. Top management must show strong support for the proposed changes.

By when?

The firm has determined that it will take one year to create the desired organizational culture.

Strategy

Chapter 5

Example 3: Question 15

Require managers to have objectives for innovation.

Where are we now?
(Score)

The firm's score is zero. It does not set innovation objectives for any of its managers. Some managers might have personal innovation objectives, so their individual scores might be three, four, or five, but there is no corporate program. (Once objectives are set, performance must be compared to these and appropriate actions taken on the differences.)

Where do we want to be?
(What are our objectives?)

The firm wants all its managers to have objectives for innovation.

How do we get there?
What needs to be done?

The firm must change its performance management system so that it includes objectives for innovation and a review of accomplishments related to those objectives.

By whom?

The Human Resource Management Department has again been selected as the controlling agency, but all divisions of the firm must be involved. Top management must show strong support for the proposed changes. (Other firms might choose a cross-functional task force to head up this effort.)

By when?

The firm must establish a new system within six months.

The Examples

INNOVATE
OR
EVAPORATE

PART II

These examples are quite simple; user situations will be much more complex. The purpose of the examples is to indicate how to use the form. Completion of the form and implementation of the actions suggested are essential to success in transforming a relatively uninnovative firm into a highly innovative one.

STRATEGIC AND OPERATIONAL PLANNING GUIDE

Question #	Where are we now? (Score)	Where do we want to be? (What are our objectives?)	How do we get there?		
			What needs to be done?	By whom?	By when?
1. Have a stated and working strategy of innovation	2	Innovation included in mission state-ment corporate philosophy, and strategy	Write new mission statement, add to corporate strategy, philosophy	Strategic planning office, board of directors, top executives	Within 3 months
8. Possess a market orientation	5	Culture of organi-zation supports, pursues a market orientation	Change culture: -objectives -rewards -training -development	HRM and top management in all divisions	Within a year
15. Require managers to have objectives for innovation	0	Managers have objectives for innovation	Change preformance management system; train and develop	HRM and top management in all divisions	Within six months

EXAMPLE

STRATEGIC AND OPERATIONAL PLANNING GUIDE

Strategy Question #	Where are we now? (Score)	Where do we want to be? (What are our objectives?)	
1. Have a stated and working strategy of innovation			
8. Possess a market orientation			
15. Require managers to have objectives for innovation/evaluate results			
22. Put every product and process on trial for its life every 18 months			
29. Make commercialization and/or use of innovation a priority			
36. Use speed strategies to achieve seemingly unobtainable objectives			
43. Know when and how to lead the customer			

How do we get there?		
What needs to be done?	**By whom?**	**By when?**

REFERENCES

1. James M. Higgins and Julian W. Vincze, *Strategic Management Concepts,* (Ft. Worth, Texas: Dryden Press, 1993), pp. 3-5.

2. Noel M. Tichy and Mary Anne Devanna, *The Transformational Leader* (New York: Wiley, 1986), pp. viii-ix, and Chapter 1.

3. Gary Hamel and C.R. Prahalad, "Strategic Intent," *Harvard Business Review* (May-June 1989), pp. 63-76.

4. For a discussion of organizational purposes see James M. Higgins and Julian W. Vincze, op. cit., Chapter 2.

5. P. Rajan Varadarajan and Vasudevan Ramanujan, "The Corporate Performance Conundrum: A Synthesis of Contemporary Views and An Extension," *Journal of Management Studies* (September 1990), pp. 463-483.

6. Peter Drucker, *The Practice of Management* (New York: Harper & Row, 1954), pp. 65-83.

7. Barry K. Spiker, "Total Quality Management: The Mind-Set for Competitiveness in the 1990s," *Manufacturing Systems* (September 1991), pp. 40-45; Sandra Edwards, "Quality Pays Off at Milliken," *Chemical Engineering* (April 1990), pp. 59-61.

8. Jennifer Reese, "America's Most Admired Corporations," *Fortune* (February 8, 1993), pp. 44-47; Alison L. Sprout, "America's Most Admired Corporations," *Fortune* (February 11, 1991), pp. 52-82. Merck won *Fortune's* most admired contest for seven straight years, 1986-1992, until dethroned in 1993 by Rubbermaid.

9. Matthew Lynn, "Merck's Spartan Leadership," *Business* (February 1991), pp. 42-48.

10. Thomas A. Stewart, "GE Keeps Those Ideas Coming," *Fortune* (August 12, 1991), pp. 41-49.

11. Sharon Gifford, "Innovation, Firm Size, and Growth in a Centralized Organization," *Rand Journal of Economics* (Summer 1992), pp. 284-298.

12. E. Lefebvre, L. A. Lefebvre and J. Harvey, "Competing Internationally Through Multiple Innovative Efforts," *R&D Management* (July 1993), pp. 227-237.

13. Yotaro Kobayashi, "Sustaining Entrepreneurship in Large Organizations—The Experience of Fuji-Xerox," *Management Japan* (Spring 1990), pp. 3-10.

14. Alan Mitchell, "The Driving Force Behind Unilever," *Marketing* (April 8, 1993), pp. 20-23.

15. Thomas A. Stewart, "Brace for Japan's Hot, New Strategy," *Fortune* (September 21, 1992), pp. 63-64; Craig A. Geffi and Aleda V. Roth, "Winning in Global Markets," (New York: Deloitte & Touche, 1992), pp. 1-2; Exhibits 1, 5, and 6.

16. Thomas J. Peters and Robert H. Waterman, Jr., *In Search of Excellence,* (New York: Harper & Row, 1982)., pp. 14, 156-199.

17. Deborah Dougherty, "Accelerating Product Innovation," *Newsweek* (October 2, 1989), pp. 24, 26.

18. P. Ranganath Nayak, "Where Do Good Ideas Come From?" *Across the Board* (July/August 1991), pp. 13-14.

19. Fernando Flores, "Innovation by Listening Carefully to Customers," *Long Range Planning* (June 1993), pp. 95-102.

20. Paul A. Engelmayer, "Campbell Plans to Drop Its Tin Soup Can Reflecting New Emphasis on Convenience," *Wall Street Journal* (March 28, 1984), p. 35; Stratford P. Sherman, "Eight Big Masters of Innovation," *Fortune* (October 15, 1984), pp. 66-84.

21. Brian Dumaine, "Payoff From the New Management," *Fortune* (December 13, 1993), pp. 103-110.

22. Terance P. Paré, "How to Find Out What They Want," *Fortune* (Autumn/Winter 1993), pp. 39-41.

23. John Kjeldson, "Tech-ploitation: The New Manufacturing Credo," *Journal of Business Strategy* (July/August 1993), pp. 15-17.

24. Robert J. Samuelson, "Innovation Is Messy," *Newsweek* (June 13, 1988), p. 55.

25. X. Michael Song and Mark E. Parry, "How the Japanese Manage the R&D-Marketing Interface," *Research-Technology Management* (July/August 1993), pp. 32-38.

26. Robert Stacey, "Canada: The Many Benefits of Relationship Marketing," *Direct Marketing* (September 1993), pp. 65-69.

27. Philip Kotler, "Marketing's New Paradigm: What's Really Happening Out There," *Planning Review* (September/October 1992), pp. 50-52.

28. David Wessel, "Marketing Tools: Computer Finds a Role in Buying and Selling, Reshaping Businesses," *Wall Street Journal* (March 18, 1987), pp. 1, 22.

29. "3M Backgrounds—30 Percent Challenge," *3M Public Information Announcement* (1994 Undated).

30. T. Michael Nevens, Gregory L. Summe, and Bro Uttal, "Commercializing Technology: What the Best Companies Do," *Harvard Business Review* (May/June 1990), p. 159.

31. Ibid.

32. Arthur D. Little, Inc., "Management Perspectives on Innovation: Innovation Management Practices in North America, Europe, and Japan (Cambridge, Mass.: Arthur D. Little, Inc., 1985), p. 4.

33. Peter Drucker, "Japan: New Strategies for a New Reality," *Wall Street Journal* (October 2, 1991), p. 12.

34. Michael K. Badaway, "Technology and Strategic Advantage: Managing Corporate Technology Transfer in the USA and Japan," *International Journal of Technology Management* (1991), pp. 205-215.

35. Amal Kumar Naj, "Creative Energy: GE's Latest Innovation—A Way To Move Ideas From Lab To Market," *Wall Street Journal* (June 14, 1990), pp. A1, A9.

36. Patricia Layman, "France's Rhône-Poulenc Looks to Innovation for Growth," *Chemical & Engineering News* (May 3, 1993), pp. 27-28.

37. George Freedman, "R & D in a Diverse Company: Raytheon's New Product Center," *Management Review* (December 1986), pp. 40-45.

38. Otis Port, "The Global Race: Why the U.S. is Losing Its Lead," *Business Week* (June 15, 1990), pp. 32-39.

39. R. B. Kennard, "From Experience: Japanese Product Development Process," *Journal of Product Innovation* (September 1991), pp. 184-188; Alan Murray and Urban C. Lehner, "Strained Alliance: What U.S. Scientists Discover, the Japanese Convert Into Profit," *The Wall Street Journal* (June 25, 1990), pp. A1, A6.

Strategy

Chapter 5

40. John Carey, Neil Gross, Mark Maremont, and Gary McWilliams, "Moving the Lab Closer to the Marketplace," *Business Week—Reinventing America* (Special Issue, Undated 1992), pp. 164-171.

41. Taken primarily from Murray R. Millson, S. P. Raj, and David Wilemon, "A Survey of Major Approaches for Accelerating New Product Development," *Journal of Product Innovation Management* (March 1992), pp. 53-69; and Rene Cordero, "Managing for Speed to Avoid Product Obsolesence: A Survey of Techniques," *Journal of Product Innovation Management* (December 1991), pp. 283-294.

42. Thomas J. Peters and Robert H. Waterman Jr., *In Search of Excellence,* op. cit., pp. 201, 211-212.

43. Catherine Arnst, "Now HP Stands for Hot Products," *Business Week* (June 14, 1993), p. 36; Stephen Kreider Yoder, "Quick Change: A 1990 Reorganization at Hewlett-Packard Already Is Paying Off," *The Wall Street Journal* (July 22, 1991), pp. A1, A8; Barbara Buell and Robert D. Hob, "Hewlett-Packard Rethinks Itself," *Business Week* (April 1, 1991), pp. 76-78.

44. "What Makes Yoshio Invent?" *Economist* (January 12, 1991), p. 51.

45. Ashok K. Gupta, Klaus Brockhoff, and Ursula Wisenfeld, "Making Trade-offs in the New Product Development Process," *Journal of Product Innovation Management* (March 1992), pp. 11-18.

46. Briane Dumaine, "Closing the Innovation Gap," *Fortune* (December 2, 1991), p. 58.

47. Ibid.

48. P. Ranganath Nayak and John M. Ketteringham, *Breakthroughs: Revised Edition* (San Diego: Pfeiffer, 1994), p. 402.

INNOVATION STRATEGY

CHAPTER 6

The global and competitive battles of the 1990s will be won by companies that can get out of traditional and shrinking product markets by building and dominating fundamentally new markets.

Gary Hamel, Consultant and
Professor, London Business School and C. K. Prahalad, Consultant and
Professor, University of Michigan School of Business
"Corporate Imagination and Expeditionary Marketing"
Harvard Business Review

Because innovation strategies are so complex, this chapter reviews the major choices available. These choices are: whether to innovate or imitate; whether to pursue research and development or search and development; whether to focus on product or process innovation; whether to invest in the old or in the new; whether to use "big bang" or continuous innovation; whether to be market or technology driven; whether commitment to innovation should be limited to one area of the firm or should involve the entire firm; and whether to do basic research

Innovation Strategy

Chapter 6

or applied research. Finally, in today's environment firms have no choice but to pursue speed strategies. The following paragraphs analyze these choices, comparing the practices of U.S. firms with those of Japanese and European firms.

INNOVATE OR IMITATE

The initial choice is whether to innovate or imitate. **Innovation**, in this context, includes only product innovation—primarily "big bang" innovation (wherein totally new products are created) as opposed to continuous product improvement. Research has shown that such innovation is necessary to success but is not always sufficient.[1] Rather, as discussed in more detail later in the chapter, product innovation in conjunction with process innovation has been shown to be the most successful strategy.[2]

Imitation strategy offers four distinct possibilities: First, the firm may simply imitate an existing product, making no product or process enhancements. Second, it may make product enhancements. Third, it may make process improvements. Fourth, it may make both product and process enhancements. Passive imitation with no product or process enhancements is tantamount to financial suicide, since it does not produce any competitive advantage based on relative differentiation or low cost. When product enhancement occurs, relative differentiation usually follows. Similarly, when process innovation is the focus of imitation, with the objective of reducing costs, imitation is a viable strategy. Finally, when both product enhancement and process improvement take place, the firm can achieve both relative differentiation and relative low cost.

This combination strategy has long been the basis of the innovation strategies pursued by many major Japanese and other Pacific Rim firms. These firms buy or borrow other firms' technologies and product and service ideas; they then improve on the product and provide the improved product at a lower cost based on process innovations. Researcher Michele Kremen Bolton makes a strong argument that imitation that includes product and/or process improvement is a better strategy than new product innovation for firms operating in:

1. Industries with weak property rights.
2. Technologically interdependent industries.
3. Industries characterized by high market and technological uncertainty.
4. Industries undergoing rapid technological change.
5. Industries with rapid information flow.[3]

This type of imitation strategy requires the commitment of substantial resources for intelligence gathering, benchmarking, and related R&D. It also requires close coordination with suppliers.[4]

Japan's Matsushita is known for its "second mover" strategy. It patiently watches for signs of market creation by a competitor's new product. It then introduces either a product with sufficient enhancements to result in a relative differentiation advantage and/or a product that has a relative cost advantage due to process innovation.[5] Not all Japanese firms are imitators, however. Sony and Hitachi, for example, are exemplary innovators.

Some U.S. firms have become adroit imitators. For example, in the early 1980s, machine tool manufacturer Cincinnati Milacron was faced with a major erosion of its market share by Japanese firms. To counter this threat, it established a company-wide program of benchmarking called Wolfpack. CEO Daniel Meyer appointed "killers" to lead cross-functional teams whose assignment was to target a competitor's product for the team to beat. As a result of the teams' efforts, Cincinnati Milacron recaptured 35 percent of the market for its core line of injection molders.[6]

Although the discussion so far has focused on imitation product strategy, processes may also be imitated. Much of what makes benchmarking successful, for example, is imitating the processes used by other firms.

**The first rule of innovation strategy is:
Innovate and imitate.**

R&D OR S&D

The second choice is how to obtain innovation. For product innovations, the issue is one of internal R&D versus what has been labeled "search and development" or S&D.[7] S&D normally leads to the acquisition of other firms in order to obtain those firms' products or services. It may also lead to joint ventures, in which specific products and services are shared, or to the licensing of other firms' products or services. A study of 113 of the *Fortune* 500 manufacturers found that the most profitable firms were those that invested heavily in R&D. The second most profitable group consisted of firms that pursued innovation through acquisition. The groups that focused exclusively on process R&D performed poorly. However, in the most successful group, process R&D complemented product R&D.[8]

Many major Japanese firms have followed an acquisition S&D strategy in recent years, showing a voracious appetite for research and technology developed in the United States and elsewhere. They have also invested heavily in start-up companies, joint ventures, and licensing arrangements, and have sponsored research in U.S laboratories.[9] As noted previously, of all the high-technology firms that changed hands in the late 1980s and in 1990 in the United States, two-thirds were bought by Japanese companies.[10] Some U.S.-based firms have begun S&D strategies in Japan. American Cyanamid, Hewlett-Packard, Intel, Monsanto, Applied Materials, Texas Instruments, Eastman Kodak, Dow Corning, IBM, Du Pont, Medtronics, W. R. Grace, Procter & Gamble, Upjohn, Dow Chemical, Bristol-Myers, Squibb, Pfizer, and Digital Equipment have either established or acquired research labs in Japan; most of those labs are conducting applied research.[11]

The major question for R&D-based firms is how much to spend on R&D, often stated as a percentage of sales. As noted in Chapter 2, average R&D expenditure by U.S. industry is about 1.9 percent of GNP/GDP, trailing Japan's 3.0 percent.[12] The amount spent on R&D varies widely among different firms. Cypress Semiconductors, for example, spent 23.9 percent of sales on R&D in 1992; Merck spent 11.5 percent in 1992.[13] Unfortunately, U.S. firms' expenditure on R&D (which is largely responsible for product innovation) as a percent of sales has dropped in real terms in recent years, for several reasons. Among these are the short-term focus of performance measurements; the negative impacts of mergers, acquistions, and leveraged buyouts (LBOs) on R&D expenditures; and lack of available capital.

The second rule of innovation strategy is: Practice both R&D and S&D.

PRODUCT OR PROCESS INNOVATION

Historically, R&D spending has been divided unevenly in U.S. firms, with about 80 percent devoted to product and 20 percent to process R&D.[14] Funding for product research and development has long been understood to contribute to competitive advantage, but investment in process R&D has received relatively little attention.[15] This is understandable when one considers the perspective of a society emerging from World War II with vast pent-up demand for products and services and little concern about cost and quality. Judging from the success of firms that emphasize both product and process innovation and of firms that engage in process redesign, principally reengineering, it seems clear that more process innovation is needed to make U.S. and European firms more competitive with Pacific Rim firms.[16] Research has shown that such innovation is necessary for success but that it is not always sufficient.[17] Rather, as discussed in more detail later in the chapter, process innovation in conjunction with product innovation has been shown to be the most successful strategy.[18] U.S. and other North American firms are just beginning to fully appreciate the necessity of process R&D.

Sufficient funding must be allocated to process R&D for it to have an impact. Part of what makes it difficult to manage process R&D is the nebulousness of the concept and its applications. Although it is sometimes difficult to prove the benefits of funds spent on product R&D, at least they are identifiable in the budget. In contrast, process creativity often results from the efforts of individual employees, work groups, and managers to improve their day-to-day operations. Process R&D depends on hard-to-pin-down expenditures such as training and development, empowerment, decentralization, and the like. It's not easy to make a clear connection between the amounts spent and the positive results of that spending, but it can be done. For example, in one five-year period Frito-Lay identified $500 million in savings resulting from daily process redesign efforts using creative problem-solving techniques.[19] The results of reengineering, which involves massive process redesign, are a little easier to track because reengineering usually involves a major project with expectations of major results. "Before" and "after" condition measurements are taken. Cost savings are usually identifiable.

As management innovation becomes more critical to corporate success, more investment will be necessary in this type of process innovation. *Innovate or Evaporate 6.1* describes product and process innovation at the San Diego Zoo. This example is somewhat unique because in service situations, product and process may be one and the same.

The third rule of innovation strategy is: Engage in both product and process innovation .

INVEST IN THE OLD OR THE NEW

Richard N. Foster, a senior partner in the global consulting firm McKinsey & Company, believes that **innovation is the attacker's advantage.** His many years of experience as a consultant have taught him that in the long run successful firms "recognize that they must be close to ruthless in cannibalizing their current products and processes just when they are most lucrative, and begin the search again, over and over."[20]

Foster also observes that products and processes, both of which are seen as being based on technology (including in the case of processes, how things are done), display a relationship between effort (investment) and performance that follows an "S" curve, as shown in Figure 6.1 (page 10). In the beginning, at the bottom of the curve, there must be a relatively large investment before performance (defined as technological progress) can occur. Then, in the middle of the curve, as breakthroughs happen, technological

WHAT A ZOO CAN TEACH YOU

The Zoological Society of San Diego has done more than most businesses to transform itself into a twenty-first century organization. It deserves to be seen for its management as well as for its spectacular collection of beasts and birds.

With 1,200 year-round employees, $75 million in revenues, and five million visitors a year, the San Diego Zoo and its Wild Animal Park make a sizable outfit whose competitors—among them Walt Disney and Anheuser-Busch, owner of nearby Sea World—are real gorillas. Also, as a world-reknowned scientific and conservation organization, the zoo must maintain high technical standards and a Caesar's-wife purity on environmental and other issues.

The zoo is steadily remodeling to show its animals by bioclimatic zone (an African rain forest called Gorilla Tropics, or Tiger River, an Asian jungle environment) rather than by taxonomy (pachyderms, primates). As displays open—three out of ten are finished—they're fundamentally altering the way the zoo is run.

The old zoo was managed through its 50 departments—animal keeping, horticulture, mainte-

continued next page

ZOO

nance, food service, fund raising, education, and others. It had all the traits of functional management, says David Glines, head of employee development. Glines started out as a groundsman, responsible for keeping paths clear of trash. If he was tired or rushed, Glines remembers, "sometimes I'd sweep a cigarette butt under a bush. Then it was the gardener's problem, not mine."

The departments are invisible in the redesigned parts of the zoo. Tiger River, for instance, is run by a team of mammal and bird specialists, horticulturists, and maintenance and construction workers. The four-year-old team, led by keeper John Turner, tracks its own budget on a PC that isn't hooked up to the zoo's mainframe. Members are jointly responsible for the display, and it's hard to tell who comes from which department. When the path in front of an aviary needed fixing last autumn, the horticulturist and the construction man did it.

Seven people run Tiger River; when it started there were 11, but as team members learned one another's skills, they decided they didn't need to replace workers who left. (P.S.: They're all Teamsters Union members.) Freed from managerial chores now handled by teams, executives can go out and drum up more interest in the zoo.

Any effect on business? Southern California tourism took some hits in 1991—first from the Gulf war, then from the recession—but the San Diego Zoo enjoyed a 20 percent increase in attendance. Part of the reason is price: At $12 it costs less than half as much to enter the zoo gates as it does to get into Disneyland.

Zoo director Douglas Myers credits employees' sense of ownership. Says he: "I told them recession's coming; we're going to target our marketing on the local area alone, and we're going to ask all our visitors to come back five times—so each time they'd better have more fun than the time before. The employees came through."

Source: Thomas A. Stewart, "The Search for the Organization of Tomorrow," *Fortune* (May 18, 1992), p. 98. Reprinted with the permission of *Fortune* magazine.

INNOVATE
OR
EVAPORATE

PART II

progress is great and investment relatively small. Eventually, though, the cost of achieving more progress becomes great once again, but the amount of progress is relatively small. It is at the top of the curve that firms must choose when to stop investing in "new improved Tide" and when to create a whole new product or process. It is here that they must decide whether to invest in the old or the new.

It is not just the flattening of the curve that poses a problem. It is the existence of other curves, representing newer technologies created by competitors that may displace the older technologies underlying the firm's products and processes. As shown in Figure 6.2, a firm may face **technological discontinuity**—that is, a gap between its technologies, and those of competitors. Such gaps occurred when steamships replaced sailing ships, when the ballpoint pen replaced the fountain pen, and when PC's began to replace minicomputers for many functions. Technological discontinuity in manufacturing processes exists between Japanese, North American, and European firms in many industries, and between management styles in many Japanese, North American, and European firms. In both cases, the Japanese have taken the lead by replacing old technologies (broadly interpreted) with new ones more quickly than their European and North American competitors.

There are strategies that can be used to extend the life of old technologies; an often-cited example is adding more sails to sailing ships to try to make them faster and thus more competitive with steamships. But inevitably, and often quickly, the newer technology will supplant the older one.[21] One study of U.S. and Japanese firms suggests that U.S. firms too often invest in research in the later stages of the "S" curve, while Japanese firms are quick to move on to new products and processes, albeit in an incremental or continuous fashion.[22]

In 1990 the German automaker BMW found itself facing technological and quality discontinuity. The Lexus and Infiniti had quickly dominated the American luxury car market, previously BMW's primary market. BMW's response was surprisingly (and necessarily) quick and effective. *Innovate or Evaporate 6.2* describes how BMW tackled this problem. Note that BMW's approach doesn't exactly follow the model of constant reintroduction of new products; rather, it emphasizes niche products.

FIGURE 6.1 THE "S" CURVE RELATIONSHIP BETWEEN INVESTMENT AND PERFORMANCE

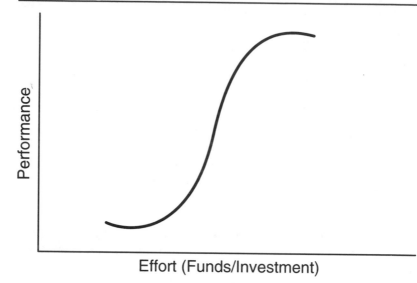

Source: Richard N. Foster, *Innovation: The Attacker's Advantage* (New York: Summit, 1986), p. 31. Copyright 1986 by McKinsey & Company, Inc. Reprinted by permission of Summit, a division of Simon & Schuster.

FIGURE 6.2 TECHNOLOGICAL DISCONTINUITY

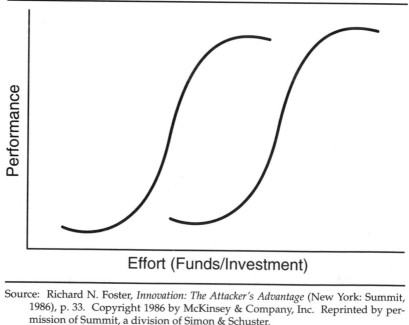

Source: Richard N. Foster, *Innovation: The Attacker's Advantage* (New York: Summit, 1986), p. 33. Copyright 1986 by McKinsey & Company, Inc. Reprinted by permission of Summit, a division of Simon & Schuster.

BMW MAKES A COMEBACK THROUGH INNOVATION

From a peak of 96,000 cars in 1986 to a low of 53,300 in 1991, BMW's sales took a tremendous beating after the Lexus and Infiniti entered the luxury car market. BMW had underestimated just how formidable Japanese firms can be when they combine high quality with low price. Karl H. Gerlinger, the marketing whiz who had been sent to the United States to head BMW's North American operations, launched a counterattack. He felt that the underlying causes of BMW's declining sales were too-high prices and inadequate quality. To lower prices, he had to cut costs on both existing and new models. He also had to improve the quality, design, and features of BMW's cars while launching new, lower-priced models.

One of the major keys to success in all three parts of Gerlinger's strategy—cost, quality, and new designs—was product and process innovation. To improve design and cut costs, BMW combined its purchasing function with R&D and design. Cross-functional teams were formed to create new products; the teams included designers, engineers, purchasing agents, and representatives of the manufacturing department. The makeup of these teams, unique in the automobile industry, allows for close relationships with BMW's 100 systems suppliers. This has enabled the firm to cut costs and improve quality. For example, a sun roof that formerly was assembled from sixty different parts now comes semiassembled in three parts. This integrated approach is resulting in cost savings from 20 percent to 40 percent per car.

In contrast to most auto firms, BMW has resisted the move to shortermodel life cycles, which entail a major capital investment. Instead, it substitutes an agressive variants policy (producing

continued next page

different variations of a model for different niche markets) that helps it catch fickle market trends. For example, the "3" series now has four distinctly different versions. R&D director Wolfgang Reitzle insists on keeping a model on the market for eight years, giving the firm ample time to write off the $1.2 billion that it takes to start a new model.

Source: John Templeman, "BMW's Comeback," *Business Week* (February 1994), pp. 42-44.

The fourth rule of innovation strategy is: Invest in new products and processes as well as old ones.

BIG BANG OR CONTINUOUS IMPROVEMENT

U.S., Canadian, and European firms have generally followed a strategy of *big bang* innovation. This term refers to major new innovations on which new products and processes can be built. Replacements are then introduced periodically—say, every four or five years. This strategy has some disadvantages when compared to that of Japanese firms, which continuously improve existing products (theirs or others') and combine the product improvements with continuous improvements in the processes used to create them. Because they are constantly improving both products and processes, the Japanese do not have to make the major leaps that their competitors must make. Therefore, they can bring new products to market faster, thereby gaining a tremendous advantage in a time of accelerating change in markets, economies, and competitors.[23]

INNOVATE OR EVAPORATE

Innovate or Evaporate 6.3 describes a big bang innovation by Texaco: its Star 2000, combination gasoline and convenience stores, which was followed up by continuous improvement of these and other operations.

PART II

TEXACO REDEFINES THE GASOLINE RETAIL INDUSTRY

Texaco wasn't the first gasoline retailer to combine filling stations with convenience stores, but in 1991 it became the first of the major oil firms to do so when it introduced its Star Marts. Texaco has also been upgrading its refineries and creating both new and improved products, such as cleaner-burning fuels. The results have been nothing less than sensational. From last among the big six oil firms in 1987, by 1993, Texaco had moved into fourth place.

In the late-1980s, following its filing for bankruptcy protection and an unsuccessful run at the company by corporate raider Carl C. Icahn, former CEO James W. Kinnear began a major strategic overhaul of the firm. He slashed the payroll by almost a third, cut other costs, and sold off unprofitable businesses. He boosted Texaco's oil exploration efforts, sought to improve its refining operations, and focused on making the firm's marketing more effective. The latter required both big bang and continuous innovation.

In a stagnant, highly competitive market, where a difference of 1¢ per gallon will cause customers to shift companies, Texaco has steadily been building customer loyalty. The Star Mart stores are a major reason. Other oil firms, seeing Texaco's success, have begun to imitate this concept. But Texaco is ready for them. It is increasing the size of many of its 6000 stores and adding fast-food franchises such as McDonald's and Dunkin Donuts to many of them. It is also testing the addition of quick lube facilities at its stations. "All we want to do is to get you into our stations," notes Donald H. Schmude, president of Texaco Refining & Marketing. To further entice motorists, Texaco offers rebates on gasoline purchases.

continued next page

INNOVATE OR EVAPORATE 6.3

TEXACO

The company is also moving ahead with its refining improvements, planning to invest another $240 million to make its upstream operations nearly self-sufficient in the production of oxygenates, which help limit auto pollution emissions. This adds to the over $2.5 billion in improvements in refinery technology that Texaco and its downstream partner, Saudi Arabian Oil Company, have made since 1988. Texaco is also pursuing an innovative strategy of swapping filling stations with other oil companies in order to get as many stations as possible close to its own seven refineries. (In this industry, where 1¢ a gallon is critical, reduced transportation costs make a huge difference.) Recently, for example, Texaco swapped fourteen outlets in St. Louis for fifteen Amoco stations in the Rocky Moutain region. Its cleaner System 3 fuels are being introduced in international markets, and other innovations are likely to follow.

Source: Tim Smart, "Pumping Up at Texaco," Business Week (June 7, 1993), pp. 112-113.

In Japan, as soon as a product is launched, the firm begins developing its replacement.[24] Ironically, like statistical quality control, so fundamental to the success of Japanese firms, the concept of continuous improvement was introduced to Japanese managers by U.S. consulting firms after World War II.[25]

The future for most U.S. and European firms lies in increasing their levels of continuous improvement.[26] Conversely, the future for most Japanese firms lies in increasing their levels of big bang innovation.[27] As these respective groups of firms overcome their weaknesses, their approaches converge. Joseph G. Moronc, director of the Center for Science & Technology Policy at Rensalear Polytechnic Institute, argues that the key to successfully directing R&D is to align it with the firm's long-term strategy.[28] This often means establishing dual goals of big bang innovation and continuous improvement. At Motorola, for example, the firm's strategy calls for it to be the leading firm in mobile communications. Yet total quality and low costs are obsessions. Thus, Motorola executives must deal simultaneously with two often-conflicting objectives: improving cur-

INNOVATE
OR
EVAPORATE

PART II

154

rent performance—product quality, cost, and features—and attempting to leapfrog the competition with new technologies and new products.[29] See *Innovate or Evaporate 10.1*.

The fifth rule of innovation strategy is: Practice both big bang innovation and continuous improvement.

MARKET OR TECHNOLOGY DRIVEN

For the past twenty years every U.S. business student has learned from marketing texts that new products begin with the customer. But many U.S. organizations seem not to have heeded that dictum. In the 1980s, for example, General Motors made cars that fit its high-technology, low-cost strategy, regardless of whether customers wanted those cars or not. Its management believed that mass marketing could sell them, a strategy that proved to be incorrect.[30] Ford Motor Company, in contrast, surveyed thousands of consumers and incorporated 80 percent of the 400 most desired features into its highly successful Taurus and Sable models.[31]

In their best selling book *In Search of Excellence*, Thomas J. Peters and Robert H. Waterman, Jr., informed readers that "getting close to the customer" is critical to business success.[32] While that may seem obvious now, it came as a revelation to many managers in 1982, when their book first appeared. Fortunately, many firms have sought to do just that—for example, by including customers in their product and process design teams.[33]

But experience and research have shown that getting close to the customer isn't the only avenue to success. Numerous products have been invented that no one even knew they wanted before those products came to market. For example, twelve of the most successful consumer and industrial products of recent years were invented without market research; consumers were convinced of their need for those products through advertising.[34] Sony's Walkman is a classic example. Co-founder Masaru Ibuka happened to come into a lab where engineers were playing a beautiful-sounding portable stereo, a project that had failed because it couldn't be made small enough to satisfy perceived market requirements. Ibuka had just left another lab where engineers were working on light-weight stereo head-phones. He was inspired to wed the two ideas, and with the backing of the former co-founder Akio Morita, he spurred the invention of a new product that became a spectacular success.[35] TVman and Discman soon followed, and consumers were easily convinced that they needed these products as well.

As *Fortune* magazine writer Brian Dumaine notes after examining the innovation situation in the U.S. and Japan, "An essential part of a creative culture is teaching people to lead the consumer, not follow him."[36] Sony's Data Discman was developed after a Sony manager reasoned that executives would like to be able to carry large amounts of data around with them. Robert Hall, senior vice president of GVO, a Palo Alto, California, industrial design firm states that what he calls "needs analysis" is essential. In his words, "To invent products out of thin air, you don't ask people what they want—after all, who would have told you ten years ago that they needed a CD player? You ask them what problems they have when they get up in the morning."[37] And then you provide a solution.

It seems that both market and technology must be considered.[38] The Japanese firms' practice of bringing the product to market in "small starts" and performing market research on the real target market with a real product, as opposed to a questionnaire about a proposed product, enables them to combine both approaches.[39]

The sixth rule of innovation strategy is:
Be both market and technology driven.

SELECTIVE OR TOTAL COMMITMENT

A firm can choose to depend on its R&D unit for all of its innovation, or on both R&D and operations. Or it can involve everyone in the company in efforts to improve products and processes.

By now the choice between these two options should be obvious. In most industries, the firm that obtains a sustainable competitive advantage will involve all of its managers and employees in improving products and processes. For example, in one year employees at Toyota submitted 860,000 suggestions for product and process improvements. Some 94 percent of those ideas were implemented. In Japan, about 66 percent of employees regularly submit suggestions, compared to only 8 percent in the United States.[40] Similarly, at the Cadillac Division of General Motors, employees redesign work, make suggestions, solve problems in teams, and help in new-product design. As a result, Cadillac has brought out highly successful new models and achieved substantial profitability.[41] A small firm that found that it could survive and prosper only through total commitment to innovation is Super Bakery, Inc., a midwestern bakery with $6 million in sales. *Innovate or Evaporate 6.4* profiles this firm's total approach to innovation.

The seventh rule of innovation strategy is:
Be totally committed to innovation as a
strategy.

BASIC RESEARCH OR APPLIED RESEARCH

Firms in the United States have always believed in basic research. The "Ph.D. syndrome" glorifies research for its own sake. Something useful may flow from pure knowledge, but it isn't necessary for research findings to have practical applications. In Japan, organizational cultures downplay basic research, although in the late 1980s this began to change as Japanese firms sought to improve their basic research output in order to become more competitive.[42] One of the major reasons for this is that they are at the leading edge in many technologies and the old imitation strategy won't work as well as it once did unless they want to wait for others to catch up. So now they are willing to do more basic research, but only in areas where applications are anticipated. In Japan, applied research is encouraged. The Japanese always think in terms of how they can use what they have learned or acquired. Their focus is on applications, and this is a major reason for their economic success.[43] Research by strategic consultant and author Michael E. Porter found that generic technology rarely improves competitiveness.[44] Rather, it is necessary for it to have a specific application.

Peter Drucker found on a trip to Japan that Japanese firms are reorganizing their R&D efforts so that teams of engineers, scientists, marketers, and manufacturers work simultaneously on three levels of innovation. At the lowest level, they seek incremental improvements of existing products. At the intermediate level, they try for significant jumps in product design and capabilities (such as Sony's jump from the microtape recorder to the Walkman). At the highest level, the teams seek totally new, big bang leaps in product design and capabilities.[45] This depends on basic research but research focused on potential applications. "The idea is to produce three new products to replace each present product, with the same investment of time and money—with one of the three then becoming the new market leader and producing the innovator's profit."[46] It's clear that both basic and applied research are necessary, and that they can and should be coordinated.

The comments of Nobel Laureate Arno A. Penzias, director of Bell Labs, reflect the trend in the United States toward a more applications-focused approach to research. He told his staff, "I want to still do fundamental research, but I also want you to understand you are doing it for a purpose. If you don't like it, please leave."[47] The trick, of course, is to gain this focus without endangering a lab's free-wheeling atmosphere.

The eighth rule of innovation strategy is: Conduct both basic and applied research in a coordinated way, and make basic research more applications oriented.

SUPER BAKERY, INC
INNOVATING
IS NOT
JUST A
PIECE OF CAKE

Super Bakery, Inc., majority owned by former Pittsburg Steeler star Franco Harris, was formed in Pittsburg in April 1983. The company manufactures donuts and baked goods for the national institutional market—the military, schools, hospitals, nursing homes, prisons. It has chosen to concentrate on the school market. While most managers would shun an industry that is characterized as mature, with numerous local competitors, no real prospects for growth, and little innovation, Super Bakery's managers argue that this attitude provided the firm with an opportunity to gain market share.

In the early 1980s Super Bakery followed the conservative strategy that is typical of its industry: maintaining traditional relationships with customers, suppliers, and employees. But sales grew only slightly from $2.3 million in 1983 to $2.4 million in 1987. Top management realized that the firm had to become more innovative. It created a model with eight parts: Super Bakery, Inc.; competing suppliers; noncompeting suppliers; the customers' competitors, customers' industry; funding sources; government regulations; and customers of its customers. It then formulated and implemented an innovative strategy for each of these areas.

For example, it used relationship marketing with the food distributors, looking for ways to make their jobs easier at every level of interaction between them, as well as between them and their customers. It went into partnership with noncompeting

continued next page

SUPER BAKERY, INC.

suppliers by, for example, putting its donuts into a prepackaged meal. It educated school systems on ways of receiving government funding that they had not thought of before. Finally, it looked to its customers' customers and tried to provide a product that they would demand, thereby pulling Super Bakery's products through the supply chain. All of these actions, and others, which are standard fare for many firms, were innovative activities for this industry.

Super Bakery took many actions to achieve a low-cost position, while simultaneously improving service. Given its scarce resources, it outsourced many selling, manufacturing, and distribution functions. Over time however, it began to assume more of these activities itself. Internally, in 1989 the firm began using cross-functional teams that included sales, order entry, accounting, production, R&D, and marketing personnel plus suppliers. These teams used process management and redesign to help the company cut costs and service customer accounts.

The firm is highly decentralized. Employees are expected to solve problems at all levels, including customers' problems. Cross training is used to give employees an improved understanding of the company's overall operation. The firm works hard at all levels to gather intelligence and operating information. Activity-based costing was used to help make better strategic decisions and to inspire entrepreneurial-type activity. The firm has its own R&D facility, which created the "Super Donut," a reduced-fat, reduced-sugar, protein-enriched and vitamin-fortified product that was a major success from the start. This and a slightly lower-fat donut, the "Ultra Donut," were the first such foods to be approved by the U.S. Department of Agriculture for school breakfasts.

SPEED STRATEGIES

In recent years the speed of product and process development has become a major issue in competitive strategy, especially in industries characterized by rapid technological change. Faster product development is often achieved by the use of cross-functional design teams.

The various speed strategies available to firms can be classified according to whether they focus on the supply process or whether they speed the product development process. The former requires working closely with suppliers, making speed a company-wide priority, and focusing on human resource practices. The latter involves concurrent engineering, parallel processing, simplifying, eliminating delays, eliminating steps, and using new venture units and skunk works (the Lockheed term for R&D centers).[48] A survey of thirty-one firms that had recently completed major product development efforts based on speed strategies found that 84 percent felt their efforts had resulted in a technically successful product; however, only

Innovation Strategy

Chapter 6

55 percent reported that the new product was a financial success. Multifunctional teams were used by 58 percent of the firms, customer involvement by 58 percent, and computer-aided tools by 48 percent.[49]

Many firms are adopting speed strategies. For example, working with the management consulting firm United Research, Vista Polymers Inc. developed a high-speed, team-managed product development and introduction (PD&I) program. In the first nine months of 1990, Vista Polymers introduced four new products and announced a significant technical alliance with a major chemical company. To meet the special challenges associated with implementing fast-cycle PD&I, the Vista Polymers group assembled five-person, five-function integrated work teams representing marketing, sales, engineering, manufacturing, and R&D.[50]

Volkswagen has also adopted speed strategies. Using CAD-based development programs, the firm has cut substantially into the time it takes to bring new models to market. It expects to achieve a 24-month cycle in the near future. A cycle of four years is more typical. As a result of its speed strategies, Volkswagen's designers have reduced tool development time by 65 percent and increased machining productivity by 30 percent, to 80 percent, per casting.[51]

Innovate or Evaporate 6.5 reviews Chrysler's efforts to increase the speed of its product development process. Note that Chrysler's success is due to other factors in addition to speed.

**The ninth rule of innovation strategy is:
Use speed strategies to bring products to
market.**

REINVENTING THE CHRYSLER CORPORATION

In 1989 Chrysler Corporation was faced with a series of problems, including an aging line of cars, a bulging cost structure, and declining profits. Top management, spearheaded by Lee Iacocca, recognized the need for a completely new strategy if the company was to be competitive. Chrysler had to develop new platforms (basic car bodies around which models are built), achieve superior advanced designs, reach the highest levels of quality to entice the typical U.S. buyer of Japanese cars, and cut unnecessary costs—and it had to do all this as quickly as possible. The phrase "reinventing the Chrysler Corporation" became synonymous with the effort to achieve a competitive advantage. It quickly became evident, however, that to make the new strategies effective the firm also had to drastically change its structure, leadership style, management systems, and organizational culture.

CHIMNEYS AND PLATFORM TEAMS

Among the first problems tackled was that of getting new products to market faster with higher quality and higher levels of customer satisfaction. At Chrysler, as at most U.S. corporations, design had historically been isolated from other functional units. The product went from design to engineering to procurement and supply to manufacturing, and finally to marketing and sales. Each of these functional units had its own bureaucracy, which did not communicate with the others unless they balked at proposed plans; then top management had to settle the matter. This structure led to constant bickering. Each functional unit was like a chimney, billowing its own smoke upward to top management. Designs that were created and manufactured in isolation were forced on customers by the sales force, whose job was to sell the product whether

continued next page

INNOVATE OR EVAPORATE 6.5

CHRYSLER

customers liked it or not. Meanwhile the finance department was trying to forecast costs and revenues in isolation from the normal flow of information.

Chrysler decided to adopt cross-functional development teams, called *platform teams*. Four teams were created: large car, small car, minivan, and jeep/truck. Representatives from each of the functional departments, plus customers, were integrated into the product development, manufacturing, and marketing process. Finance was included in the information loop, but the teams were charged with bringing products to market within precise cost levels. The teams were given a high degree of autonomy to achieve their objectives, eliminating the need for management to continually settle disputes.

To facilitate product development, the work of the teams, and the cross-functional nature of their operations, Chrysler officially opened its $1 billion Chrysler Technology Center (CTC) in the fall of 1991. Each platform team has its own floor in the CTC. Team members use shared databases and communication systems. Suppliers are involved throughout the design process. Through focus groups, questionnaires, and interviews, customers are also involved. The CTC includes a manufacturing facility where prototype manufacturing processes can be devised at the same time that a new car is being developed in order to speed manufacturing and improve quality. The platform team works in conjunction with assembly line workers to create the most efficient manufacturing process possible.

CHANGES IN MACRO STRUCTURE, LEADERSHIP STYLE, MANAGEMENT SYSTEMS, AND CULTURE

One of the major changes in structure that occurred during this period was the empowerment of employees to make decisions that were relevant to their jobs. In the past, the supervisor typically made all the decisions. But management recognized that this approach was not entirely effective. In the new structure the supervisor would become a coach and facilitator. Part of the effort to cut up to $4 billion in costs depended on employees making suggestions that would eliminate unnecessary tasks.

The changes in Chrysler's structure, style, and culture are reflected in the company's New Castle, Indiana, plant. Once tar-

CHRYSLER

geted for closing, the plant went from losing $5 million a year in 1988 to saving the firm a net $1.5 million in 1991. This impressive turnaround was accomplished by empowering employees, making sure they knew that change was necessary, and creating a learning environment. Information systems were updated to provide employees with the information they needed in order to make the right decisions.

RESULTS

The results of those changes have been impressive. Chrysler posted significant profits in 1992 and 1993. The price of its stock soared from a low of $10.50 per share in late 1991 to $61.00 per share in February 1994. The profits and stock price reflect Chrysler's tremendous success with the Dodge Viper, an exciting and pricey new sports car; the latest Jeep Cherokee; and the LH series of cars, which entered the medium-price market against European and Japanese competitors and proved extremely successful. Trendy, with many popular features, the cars are so successful that Chrysler's only problem is how to manufacture them fast enough. Additional new models anticipated for 1994 and 1995, including the Dodge Ram truck and the small Neon, are also receiving positive reviews.

Source: The Chrysler Corporation, "Reinventing Chrysler," a videotape, (Detriot: The Chrysler Corporation) 1993; and recent stock market reports.

THE STRATEGIC INNOVATION STRATEGIES: IMPERATIVES, NOT ALTERNATIVES

If you examine the options, you can quickly see that the alternatives discussed in this chapter are really imperatives. Firms have no choice. They must do all of the following:

1. **Innovate and imitate.**
2. **Practice both R&D and S&D.**
3. **Engage in both product and process innovation.**
4. **Invest in new products and processes as well as old ones.**
5. **Practice both big bang innovation and continuous improvement.**
6. **Be both market and technology driven.**
7. **Be totally committed to innovation as a strategy.**
8. **Conduct both basic and applied research in a coordinated way, and make basic research more applications oriented.**
9. **Use speed strategies to bring products to market.**

THE INNOVATION STRATEGY QUESTIONNAIRE

Instructions for Rating Your Firm

The questionnaire in Exhibit 6.1 is designed to help you evaluate your firm in terms of the nine imperatives just listed. Read the question on the left, and indicate the extent to which your firm posesses the stated characteristics. Rate your firm on a scale of 1 (low) to 10 (high).

Scoring the Questionnaire

Add up your scores for the Product and Process columns. A score above 120 for product innovation or above 120 for process innovation is considered satisfactory. Scores below 40 for product innovation and below 40 for process innovation should be seen as a danger signal.

EXHIBIT 6.1

The Innovation Strategy Questionnaire

To what extent does or is your firm...	Product	Process
1a innovate.	1 2 3 4 5 6 7 8 9 10	1 2 3 4 5 6 7 8 9 10
1b imitate, in the sense of borrowing good product and process ideas from others.	1 2 3 4 5 6 7 8 9 10	1 2 3 4 5 6 7 8 9 10
2a practice R&D.	1 2 3 4 5 6 7 8 9 10	1 2 3 4 5 6 7 8 9 10
2b practice S&D.	1 2 3 4 5 6 7 8 9 10	1 2 3 4 5 6 7 8 9 10
3a engage in product innovation.	1 2 3 4 5 6 7 8 9 10	
3b engage in process innovation.		1 2 3 4 5 6 7 8 9 10
4a invest in new products and processes.	1 2 3 4 5 6 7 8 9 10	1 2 3 4 5 6 7 8 9 10
4b invest in old products and processes	1 2 3 4 5 6 7 8 9 10	1 2 3 4 5 6 7 8 9 10
5a practice big bang product innovation and reengineering (big bang process innovation).	1 2 3 4 5 6 7 8 9 10	1 2 3 4 5 6 7 8 9 10
5b practice continuous product and process innovation.	1 2 3 4 5 6 7 8 9 10	1 2 3 4 5 6 7 8 9 10
6a market driven.	1 2 3 4 5 6 7 8 9 10	1 2 3 4 5 6 7 8 9 10
6b technology driven.	1 2 3 4 5 6 7 8 9 10	1 2 3 4 5 6 7 8 9 10
7 commit itself to innovation as a strategy.	1 2 3 4 5 6 7 8 9 10	1 2 3 4 5 6 7 8 9 10
8a sponsor basic research.	1 2 3 4 5 6 7 8 9 10	1 2 3 4 5 6 7 8 9 10
8b sponsor applied research.	1 2 3 4 5 6 7 8 9 10	1 2 3 4 5 6 7 8 9 10
9 use speed strategies to bring products to market.	1 2 3 4 5 6 7 8 9 10	1 2 3 4 5 6 7 8 9 10
TOTALS		

REFERENCES

1. Noel Capon, John U. Farley, Donald R. Lehman, and James M. Hulbert, "Profiles of Product Innovators Among Large U.S. Manufacturers," *Management Science* (February 1992), pp. 157-169.

2. Ibid.; Kornelius Kraft, "Are Product and Process Innovation Independent of Each Other?" *Applied Economics* (August 1990), pp. 1029-1038.

3. Michele Kremen Bolton, "Imitation Versus Innovation: Lessons to be Learned from the Japanese," *Organizational Dynamics* (Winter 1993), pp. 30-38.

4. Ibid., pp. 35-38.

5. Ibid., p. 32.

6. Ibid., p. 33.

7. Marilyn L. Taylor and Kenneth Beck, "Marion Laboratories, Inc.," in James M. Higgins and Julian W. Vincze, *Strategic Management: Text and Cases*, 4th Ed. (Hinsdale, Illinois: Dryden Press, 1989) p. 522.

8. Noel Capon, John U. Farley, Donald R. Lehman, and James M. Hulbert, loc.cit.

9. Stephen Budiansky, "Japan's Research Raid," *U.S. News & World Report* (March 22, 1993), pp. 46-47; Barbara Buell, "Japan: A Shopping Spree in the U.S.," *Business Week* (June 15, 1990), pp. 86-87; Otis Port, "The Global Race: Why the U.S. Is Losing Its Lead," *Business Week* (June 15, 1990), pp. 32-39.

10. Carla Rapoport, "Why Japan Keeps on Winning," *Fortune* (July 15, 1991), p. 76.

11. Susan Moffat, "Picking Japan's Research Brains," *Fortune* (March 25, 1991), pp. 84-96.

12. "U.S. Patents: Big Blue Tops Japan's Firms," *U.S. News & World Report* (March 28, 1994), p. 16; "R&D Scoreboard," *Business Week* (June 28, 1993), pp. 112, 114; Robert Buderi, "The Brakes Go On In R&D," *Business Week* (July 1, 1991), pp. 24-26; Bruce C. P. Rayner, "The Rising Price of Technological Leadership," *Electronic Business* (March 18, 1991), pp. 52-56; Fumiaki Kitamura, "Japan's R&D Budget Second Largest in World," *Business Japan* (November 1990), pp. 35-47; Frederick Shaw Myers, "Japan Pushes the 'R' in R&D," *Chemical Engineering* (February 1990), pp. 30-33.

13. "R&D Scoreboard," loc. cit.

14. Marie-Louise Caravatti, "Why the United States Must Do More Process R&D," *Research-Technology Management* (September/October 1992), pp. 8-9.

15. For a discussion of these issues, including relative amounts spent on the two types of R&D, see Ralph E. Gomory, "From the 'Ladder of Science' to the Product Development Cycle," *Harvard Business Review* (November/December 1989), pp. 99-105.

16. Noel Capon, John U. Farley, Donald R. Lehman, and James M. Hulbert, loc. cit.; also for example, see *Planning Review* (May/June 1993 and March/April 1993). Both issues review reengineering.

17. Noel Capon, John U. Farley, Donald R. Lehman, and James M. Hulbert, loc. cit.; Masaaki Kotabe and Janet Y. Murray, "Linking Product and Process Innovations and Modes of International Sourcing in Global Competition: A Case of Foreign Multinational Firms," *Journal of International Business Studies* (Third Quarter 1990), pp. 383-408.

18. Ibid.; Kornelius Kraft, "Are Product and Process Innovation Independent of Each Other?" *Applied Economics* (August 1990), pp. 1029-1038.

19. Marc Hequet, "Making Creativity Training Creative," *Training* (February 1992), p. 45.

20. Richard N. Foster, *Innovation: The Attacker's Advantage* (New York: Summit Books, 1986), p 21.

21. See Foster, op. cit., chapters six and eight.

22. Michael K. Badaway, "Technology and Strategic Advantage: Managing Corporate Technology Transfer in the USA and Japan," *International Journal of Technology Management* (1991), pp. 205-215.

23. Michael Czinkota and Masaaki Kotabe, "Product Development the Japanese Way," *Journal of Business Strategy* (November/December 1990), pp. 31-36.

24. Peter Drucker, "Japan: New Strategies for A New Reality," *Wall Street Journal* (October 2, 1991), p. 12.

25. Dean M. Schroeder and Alan G. Robinson, "America's Most Successful Export to Japan: Continuous Improvement Programs," *Sloan Management Review* (Spring 1991), pp. 67-81.

26. Roy Amara, "New Directions for Innovation," *Futures* (March 1990), pp. 142-152.

27. Neil Gross, John Carey, and Joseph Weber, "Who Says Science Has to Pay Off Fast?" *Business Week* (March 21, 1994), pp. 110-111.

28. Joseph G. Moronc, *Winning in High-Tech Markets: The Role of General Management* (Boston: Harvard Business School Press 1992), Chapter 1.

29. John Carey, Neil Gross, Mark Maremont, and Gary McWilliams, "Moving the Lab Closer to the Marketplace," *Business Week—Reinventing America* (Special Issue, Undated 1992), pp. 164-171.

30. For a discussion see: James M. Higgins and Julian Vincze, "The Strategic Challenges Facing General Motors in 1992," *Strategic Management Text and Cases*, 5th ed. (Fort Worth, Texas: Dryden Press, 1993), pp. 29-54.

31. James B. Treece, "Can Ford Stay on Top?" *Business Week* (September 28, 1987), pp. 78-86.

32. Thomas J. Peters and Robert H. Waterman, Jr., *In Search of Excellence* (New York: Harper & Row, 1982), p. 14.

33. For example see: Rick Whiting, "Varian Doesn't Debate What Customers Want, It Asks Them," *Electronic Business* (June 1993), pp. 64-66.

34. P. Ranganath Nayak and John M. Ketteringham, *Breakthroughs: The Revised Edition* (San Diego: Pfeiffer, 1994), p. 402.

35. Ibid., pp. 115-137.

36. Ibid.

37. Briane Dumaine, "Closing The Innovation Gap," *Fortune* (December 2, 1991), p. 58.

38. C. Merle Crawford, "The Dual-Drive Concept of Product Innovation," *Business Horizons* (May-June 1991), pp. 13-14.

39. "What Makes Yoshio Invent?" *Economist* (January 12,1991), p. 61; Thomas J. Peters, *Thriving on Chaos: Handbook for a Management Revolution* (New York: Knopf, 1987), pp. 195-208.

40. Rolf C. Smith, Jr. and Raymond A. Slesinski, "Continuous Innovation," *Executive Excellence* (May 1991), pp. 13-14; Michael Czinkota and Masaaki Kotabe, loc. cit.

Chapter 6

41. Leslie King, "The 1990 Baldrige Winners Look Back and Foreward," *Industrial Engineering* (January 1992), pp. 14-15; John Teresko, "America's Best Plant," *Industry Week* (October 21, 1991), pp. 29, 32.

42. Neil Gross, John Carey, and Joseph Weber, loc. cit.; Emily Thornton, "Japan Struggles To Be Creative," *Fortune* (April 19, 1993), pp. 129-134; Stephen Kreider Yoder, "Stifled Scholars: Japan's Scientists Find Pure Research Suffers Under Rigid Life Style," *Wall Street Journal* (October 31, 1988), pp. A1, A6.

43. R. B. Kennard, loc. cit.; Alan Murray and Urban C. Lehner, loc. cit.; Edwin Mansfield, "Technological Creativity: Japan and the United States," *Business Horizons* (March/April 1989), pp. 48-53.

44. Otis Port, op. cit., p. 39.

45. Peter Drucker, loc. cit.

46. Brian Dumaine, op. cit., pp. 58.

47. Robert Buderi, et al., "American Inventors are Reinventing Themselves," *Business Week* (January 18, 1993), pp. 78-79.

48. Taken primarily from Murray R. Millson, S. P. Raj, and David Wilemon, "A Survey of Major Approaches for Accelerating New Product Development," *Journal of Product Innovation Management* (March 1992), pp. 53-69; and Rene Cordero, "Managing for Speed to Avoid Product Obsolescence: A Survey of Techniques," *Journal of Product Innovation Management* (December 1991), pp. 283-294.

49. Necmi Karagozoglu and Warren B. Brown, "Time-Based Management of the New Product Development Process," *Journal of Product Innovation Management* (June 1993), pp. 204-215.

50. Bob Isenhour and Kathryn Payne, "Getting Serious About Product Development," *Management Review* (Vol. 80 No. 4, April 1991), pp. 19-22.

51. Mathew Moore, "Driving Volkswagen Into the '90s," *CAE* (August 1992), p. 30.

S T R U C T U R E
CHAPTER 7

Above all the innovative company organizes itself to abandon the old, the obsolete, the no longer productive.

> Peter Drucker,
> Consultant & Author,
> "The Innovative Company," Wall Street Journal

An organization may have sound objectives and strategies for innovation, but these alone are not enough to ensure that innovation is achieved. It must also have the structure necessary to bring about innovation. **Organization structure** has five principal aspects: how each job is designed, how authority is delegated to accomplish each job, how jobs are grouped together in a logical fashion, the manager's span of control, and the coordination of work. Changes are occuring in each of these five components as organizations struggle to find the "right" structure. While it is generally understood that structure has to be matched to strategy for an organization to succeed, there is now substantial research evidence to support this belief.[1]

Perhaps more than any of the other Seven S's, structure is in a state of flux. What is right today may not be right tomorrow. Restructuring and rightsizing, common actions in the 1980s and early 1990s, have been viewed as important contributors to increased innovation. But management researchers have found that innovation does not necessarily follow these actions. A consulting firm, the Wyatt Company, surveyed 1,005 companies that had undergone major restructuring over the past five years and employed a total of more than 4 million people. Only 7 percent of the firms reported an increase in innovation that could be attributed to downsizing.[2] Restructuring by simply eliminating jobs isn't enough. At the very least, the employees who remain must be empowered to be innovative. On a more pragmatic level, the kind of restructuring that is accomplished by **reengineering**, in which organizational processes are redesigned, is more likely to increase innovation than most restructurings involving downsizing. Moreover, reengineering is itself an activity whose results are expected to be process innovations.

Two small surveys, one of managers, and the other of front-line employees, reveal perceived structural problems that may hinder innovation in U.S. corporations. When managers were surveyed by United Research Company, a consulting firm, over half of those surveyed reported that they believed that their corporate structures hindered innovation. Only a third saw these structures as helpful. The rest gave them mixed reviews, indicating that there was little momentum for changing the status quo. Studies conducted by an industrial-psychology firm, Standard & Associates, suggest that part of the problem may lie with front-line management. Front-line workers indicated that there was considerable concern with improving productivity (here construed to be related to innovation) among top managers, but less than half felt that their immediate supervisors shared this concern.[3]

Most bureaucratic structures hinder creativity and innovation. These **mechanistic structures** are characterized by highly specialized tasks, little coordination of tasks, specific role definitions, rigidity, hierarchical control, vertical lines of communication, and information retention at the highest levels which leaves other managers and workers with little opportunity to

be creative problem solvers. Conversely, **organic structures,** which are characterized by empowerment, decentralization, flexibility, fluidity, open communication, and participative decision making, are generally believed to be more innovative.[4]

Over the industry or product life cycle, firms tend to move from organic to mechanistic structures as efficiency becomes more important for survival than innovation. The paradox, of course, is that as environments grow more turbulent, both innovation and efficiency must be achieved simultaneously. The structural elements discussed in this chapter are intended to allow the organization to have the best of both worlds.[5] Interestingly, in contrast to U.S.-based firms, which tend to be either mechanistic or organic, many major Japanese firms possess a mixture of

Structure

Chapter 7

these two characteristics. They operate very organically in some situations, but high levels of formalization, detailed schedules, and elaborate controls suggest a mechanistic structure.[6] Of course, the example of Hitachi in Chapter 1 describes a firm that is extremely organic. Honda, too, is very organic.

From the standpoint of innovation, the issue is whether or not the firm has structural mechanisms to assist in achieving strategic objectives for innovation. These mechanisms must foster new products and product enhancements as well as new processes and process improvements. The major concerns are the use of structural mechanisms to facilitate innovation activities, such as intrapreneurship; the use of cross-functional teams to improve interdepartmental coordination; structuring of new-product development/research centers and process innovation activities; inclusion of customers and suppliers in product and process design efforts; the use of alliances to obtain innovation; development of flexible structures; and the nature of procedures for evaluating innovations.

THE CHARACTERISTICS

Exhibit 7.1 lists the seven summary questions related to the characteristics of structure examined in the questionnaires in Chapter 4.

EXHIBIT 7.1 CHARACTERISTICS OF INNOVATIVE
ORGANIZATIONS RELATED TO STRUCTURE

To what extent does your organization:

2. Develop structural mechanisms to facilitate intrapreneurship, process redesign initiatives, marketing innovation, and management innovation.

9. Require cross-functional and/or customer/supplier new-product teams, process redesign teams, marketing and/or management innovation teams.

16. Have new product/research, process redesign, marketing innovation, and management innovation centers.

23. Have open communication between product, process, marketing, and management centers/teams and the rest of the organization.

30. Structure for flexibility, in order to adapt and seize the opportunity

37. Use alliances to obtain product, process, marketing, and management innovations.

44. Have an efficient and effective structure for creating new products or services, process redesign, marketing/or management innovation.

---

2. Develop Structural Mechanisms to Facilitate Intraprenuership, Process Redesign Initiatives, Marketing Innovation, Management Innovation.

Companies that seek innovation must develop specific structural mechanisms. They must sponsor special units, profit centers, divisions, even separate companies in order to encourage entrepreneurial activity within the firm. The general thrust of such actions is to provide sufficient authority to employees with an entrepreneurial bent to enable them to in effect run their own businesses within the firm. These approaches are often referred to as intrapreneurship, a term coined by Gifford Pinchot III, president of the New Directions Group, Inc., an intrapreneurship consulting firm.

Intrapreneurship seeks to merge the entrepreneurial spirit of a small organization into the culture of a larger, more established business organization. An **intraprenuer** is a company employee who is allowed to act like an entrepreneur but does so for the company rather than striking out on his or her own. The company encourages and subsidizes individuals to develop and implement their ideas. Intrapreneurship results in enormous flexibility. It enables a corporation to be highly responsive, to turn on a dime.[7] The major consequence of intrapreneurship is innovation.[8]

Intrapreneurship is often implemented in the form of virtually independent business units, commonly referred to as **strategic business units (SBUs)**. Each SBU has different customers and products than the firm's other SBUs. They are given the autonomy necessary to meet the demands of their customers. United Airlines, IBM, 3M, Texas Instruments, Northwestern

Bell, Kodak, and many other major companies have extensive intrapreneurship programs. IBM's original PC was created as a result of an intrapreneurship approach in which the company established an SBU that was geographically remote from its Armonk, New York, headquarters and the accompanying bureaucracy.[9] At 3M, virtually all divisions operate as separate companies.[10] This is also true of Johnson & Johnson's 166 businesses. (See *Innovate or Evaporate 11.2*).[11] And as noted earlier (*Innovate or Evaporate 4.1*), when Hewlett-Packard redesigned its product development process so that development teams were headed by czars with complete autonomy, rather than being directed by committees, the results were amazing.[12] New products flowed rapidly and profitably, giving HP a new lease on life. More recently, Percy Barnevik, CEO of European giant Asea Brown Boveri (ABB), established 5000 profit centers in a firm with 218,000 employees—a massive change in organizational structure.[13]

Colby H. Chandler, then CEO of Kodak, attributed much of Kodak's turnaround in the late 1980s, which included a proliferation of new products and a drastic reduction in costs, to the restructuring of the firm into divisions that functioned as individual companies with the authority to make the decisions they considered necessary to compete in their specific environments. This organic approach was in direct contrast to the mechanistic structure that had long dominated the firm in which no one but the CEO could make a decision.[14] Kodak also underwent a major downsizing, but it was not enough. In mid-1990 Chandler was replaced by Kay R. Whitmore, who in turn was replaced in October 1993 by George M. C. Fisher, then CEO of Motorola. Massive downsizing at Kodak may give way to more reengineering, as Fisher plots a new strategy emphasizing multimedia, and less simple cutting of jobs and more planning for the right structure as opposed to simply a structure with fewer positions.[15] See *Innovate or Evaporate 7.1* for a description of Kodak's Zebras, a reengineered unit of the firm.

There are several other ways of encouraging entrepreneurial activity. For example, at highly successful Intuit, maker of Quicken and other software, an Innovation Ideas Committee headed by Suna Kneisley helps the company relentlessly pursue customer satisfaction. The committee collects and follows up on every creative product improvement idea emanating from the firm's customers and its technical support staff.[16] At Du Pont, employees can apply for up to $50,000 of SEED money (**$** {**D**ollars} to **E**ncourage **E**ntrepreneurial **D**evelopment) to pursue new product ideas.[17] At Flow International Corporation, any employee who comes up with a convincingly good idea is given the seed money necessary to start his or her own company within or for the firm.[18]

New-venture teams are popular with many firms. A **venture team** is a small, semi-autonomous group that operates as a unit to create and develop a new idea. 3M and Security Pacific are among the many firms that have used venture teams successfully.[19] Signode Industries, Inc., a privately held corporation formed by a leveraged buyout, is the nation's leading manufacturer and distributor of steel and plastic strapping systems; it also produces construction products, fastening tools, and bar coding systems. Signode developed the venture team concept in order to broaden its product line and move into new product/market areas more rapidly. The teams become part owners of the products they create.[20]

Another example of this approach can be seen in Thermo-Electron Corporation. As its labs produce new ideas, the company spins-off new companies. Stock is sold to the public, but Thermo retains a majority for itself. In effect, the company sells its core technologies. Its profits have soared as a result. Employees can also score well at Thermo. If they dream up a good new idea, they don't just get a pat on the back; they may get to run their own company. As a result, Thermo isn't just one company but fifteen, and its still growing.[21]

It follows that mechanisms must be provided for process innovation as well. These may include, but would not be limited to, reengineering and continuous improvement. Centers are focal points of process innovation, but smaller units such as task forces, teams, and committees might also direct such efforts. Cross-functional teams are especially common. Process redesign teams often include customers and suppliers in addition to employees.

Research on the new-product development efforts of twelve mainframe computer manufacturers reveals that the ones that launched new products most successfully had formed "integration teams," a type of cross-functional team. These teams investigate the impact of R&D efforts on manufacturing processes and smooth the integration of new products into existing processes and/or help create new processes. A good integration team figures out how to adjust new technologies to what the company already does. Thus, product development occurs parallel with product design and production efforts, rather than sequentially as has been the case in the past. Less successful firms still follow the sequential model—that is, conduct R&D first and then worry about design and how to make the product. Of twenty-six total major innovations, eleven of the lowest-cost and quickest-to-market products resulted from integration efforts. Only two of these products resulted from the traditional approach.[22]

At Quantam Chemical Corporation, manufacturing technology centers (MTCs) help the company improve its technology and cut costs. MTCs consist of employees with skills in certain technologies who meet to share their expertise in tackling specific problems. MTCs continually evaluate manufacturing processes, noting problems, recommending solutions, and spearheading implementation efforts. After picking a particular problem to solve, each MTC draws up a project plan. The MTC oversees implementation and champions the innovation or practice chosen by the team. MTC personnel interact with management, engineering, R&D, and representatives of other departments. Excellent ideas are recognized, implemented, and rewarded.[23]

Process innovation initiatives may require the use of teams, centers, or other special units. The major process innovation thrusts today are continuous improvement and process redesign (reengineering). Process redesign initiatives usually result in new structures, but those structures are based on carefully thought out changes, in contrast to the percentage changes in all functional areas that are typical of downsizing programs. As in intrapreneurship, one key to process innovation efforts is autonomy. *Innovate or Evaporate 7.1* discusses Kodak's reengineering efforts. This is the type of process innovation that can help a firm become more competitive.

KODAK'S ZEBRAS

The concept of *reengineering* involves substantive re-design of work processes. In fact, work is often designed around processes, not traditional functional departments such as marketing, finance, operations, and human resources. Rather, firms organize themselves around the six to eight key processes that bind the organization together—for example, order generation and fulfillment process. In this approach, marketing, finance, operations, logistics, and human resources designate members of a cross-functional team (which could be composed of several teams) to carry out that process. Organizing around processes allows for more self-management and the elimination of a substantial number of managerial positions. It can also result in higher levels of customer satisfaction.

Kodak began its reengineering efforts in 1989. The company wanted to improve productivity in its black-and-white film business, which accounted for $2 billion in sales from over 7000 products marketed throughout the world. The 1500 employees who make black-and-white film—inevitably called "zebras"—don't work in departments; instead they are part of "the flow." A team of twenty-five leaders watches over the flow. Within the flow are streams of products related to customers. The self-managed cross-functional teams providing these products are evaluated on the basis of customer satisfaction measures such as on-time delivery. For example, one stream provides products for the Health Sciences Division and works closely with it to schedule production and develop new products. (Two functions, accounting and human resources, remain outside of this structure.)

When the flow began, the black-and-white film business was running 15 percent over budgeted costs, was late on delivery one-third of the time, took up to forty-two days to fill an order, and had the lowest morale of any unit in Kodak. In 1992, after a little over two years of reengineering, the unit came in 15 percent under budgeted costs, had cut its response time in half,

continued next page

INNOVATE OR EVAPORATE 7.1

Comparing U.S. Firms with Japanese and European Firms

Historically, most Japanese firms have not encouraged intrapreneurship. Some, like Hitachi, however, have allowed managers to essentially run divisions as if they were their own firms.[24] Many U.S. firms have accepted the concept and taken steps to implement it. Japanese firms have built-in mechanisms for process redesign—for example, wide-spread use of continuous improvement. U.S. firms are beginning to follow their lead. One of the unique characteristics of Japanese organizations is the extent to which knowledge is shared among individuals, groups, and departments. Furthermore, more than one individual, group, or department may be working on the same problem at the same time, sometimes from a different perspective, sometimes in direct competition. This approach has its pros and cons. It produces large numbers of new ideas, often very quickly. However, it is an expensive duplication of effort, exhaustive, and prone to group think.[25]

European firms are moving rapidly to restructure in order to become more competitive.[26] Typical is Ciba-Geigy, a diversified Swiss pharmaceutical, industrial, and agricultural firm. In the late 1980s the company's chairman, Alex Krauer, concluded that the firm was too bureaucratic. He downsized the company and simultaneously created fourteen highly autonomous divisions. New-product development took off, and profits zoomed upward in the early 1990s.[27] Similarly, Perstorp AB, a large Swedish specialty chemical maker with major businesses

INNOVATE OR EVAPORATE

PART II

in polymers, laminates, and biotechnology, uses several techniques, including intrapreneurship, to foster innovation. *Innovate or Evaporate 7.2* examines intrapreneurship and other structural factors at Perstorp.

9. Require Cross-Functional and Customer/ Supplier New-Product Teams, Process Redesign Teams, Marketing and/or Management Innovation Teams.

If you are going to get close to the customer and use a speed strategy, what structural mechanisms can you implement to ensure that these will actually occur? In a study of fifty U.S. organizations John Eutie found that they often instituted special management arrangements to ensure that design, operations, and marketing worked together. For example, they often asked front-line workers to help in product design.[28]

Today many organizations are turning to **cross-functional teams,** in which representatives from several functions, such as design, marketing, operations, and finance, join together to accomplish a particular objective. And with increasing frequency customers and/or suppliers are included in the teams to develop new products; improve quality; and cut process times, complexity, and cost.[29] Such teams dramatically improve coordination.

Consider an example. Honeywell, facing stiff competition across all product lines, created "tiger teams" to develop products faster. Representatives from marketing, design, and engineering worked together in a tiger team to develop a new climate-control device for a customer who had threatened to take the work to a competitor if Honeywell couldn't produce the new product quickly. The team was given permission to break all the rules in order to cut product development time from four years to one. They did break all the rules, and they did succeed in cutting development time to one year—thereby keeping the customer.[30]

One of Milliken's very successful innovation strategies has been to form teams with customers to develop new products and services. This has proven especially effective in making the firm more competitive with foreign firms, which almost always have an advantage in the form of lower labor costs. For example, Milliken loads the trucks it sends to Levi Strauss plants in such a way that the materials can be unloaded in the order in which they are needed. The trucks thus become mini-warehouses for Strauss, which does not have to establish its own inventory of raw materials.[31]

 **Comparing U.S. Firms with Japanese and European Firms**

U.S. firms have begun adopting the cross-functional approach as they have come to realize that it is critical to their survival. Japanese firms have long used the approach, and European firms are moving to adopt it as well. For example, European chemical firms producing adhesives and sealants are including both customers and suppliers in cross-functional product innovation efforts, and this has spurred new-product development at those firms.[32]

16. Have New-Product/Research Centers, Process Redesign Programs, Marketing Innovation Programs, and Management Innovation Programs.

There must be a center, a program, or an initiative for accomplishing the work of innovation. Chrysler's Technology Center, Bell Labs, Xerox's Palo Alto Research Center (PARC), and Disney's Imagineering Division are examples of these kinds of structural entities. In addition to developing such entities, companies often assign their most creative people to skunk works. However, if the center, program, initiative or skunk works is an organization's only form of innovation, it is unlikely to be a very innovative organization. It takes more than a research unit to make a company creative.

PERSTORP AB, CHAMPION OF <u>INTRA-</u>PRENEURSHIP

Perstorp AB has been a champion of intrapreneurship and internal joint venturing in Europe for many years. Both internally developed and externally acquired innovation are critical to Perstorp's strategy. President Karl-Erik Sahlberg comments, "Because we earn most of our profits from relatively mature products that need constant rejuvenation, we have had to develop a commitment to innovation. We think that we have had some success in creating an environment where ideas can thrive and bring us into new business areas."

In the 1980s Sahlberg globalized the firm through acquisitions focusing on niche businesses. About 80 percent of the firm's revenues now come from markets outside Sweden. Sahlberg also focused the firm on internal innovation activities. Perstorp discontinued its corporate research laboratory in favor of having divisions do their own R&D, thus moving research efforts closer to the customer. A major disadvantage of this approach was that the divisions experienced a conflict between meeting their short-term objectives and taking the actions necessary to ensure long-term profits.

Two funding mechanisms were developed to encourage a longer-term perspective. First, the President's Fund supports new-product development projects focusing on long-term research efforts that divisions would not normally undertake because of their size and impact on short-term profits. Second, the Research Foundation funds special projects done in collaboration with universities or other external R&D organizations. Perstorp's general manager of corporate development may also

continued next page

INNOVATE OR EVAPORATE 7.2

use a discretionary fund to provide grants for special projects with innovative potential. Requests for funds above a certain amount are reviewed by Perstorp's executive management committee.

Another mechanism that encourages innovation is Perstorp's new business development company, Pernovo AB. Pernovo is a subsidiary that serves as an internal venture capital company, providing funding, in trade for equity, to small, highly innovative firms with products for international niche markets. Over 1000 firms are reviewed each year; of these, about ten are given the funding to move forward. Those that succeed become subsidiaries of Perstorp AB.

Source: Jules Arbose, "How Perstorp Persuades Its Managers to Innovate," *International Management* (June 1987), pp. 41-47.

Noting the success of other firms, many companies are redesigning their research centers or creating totally new ones. In August 1993, for example, Mazda, feeling pressure from Toyota at home and from Toyota, Honda, GM, Ford, and Chrysler in the United States, announced the creation of a cross-functional design center—the Product Development Center (PDC)—to oversee the efforts of three product centers in terms of commonization and standardization of components and systems among the three product groups.[33]

Innovate or Evaporate 7.3 describes how an important skunk works project at Ford Motor Company produced the new Mustang.

One of the most famous research centers is Disney's "Imagineering" unit. Engineers in this unit, who use their imaginations and hence are called **imagineers**, are credited with many of the new ideas that have resulted in Disney's recent financial success, especially in its theme parks. They, for example, developed the exciting Star Tours ride at Disneyland. They also came up with a similar ride for Disney World.[34]

FORD'S SKUNK WORKS

Ford Motor Company developed the 1994 Mustang using a skunk works approach. Four hundred people (not very many by industry standards), working on a very tight budget, broke all the rules of new-product development and redesigned a legend. "Team Mustang" developed the car in three years at a cost of $700 million—that is, in 25 percent less time and at a 30 percent lower cost than any other recent Ford model. One of the team's founders, John Colletti, and other team members toured competitors' factories to determine why they could produce new models faster and at a much lower cost than Ford. After Colletti and program manufacturing boss Dia Hothi had taken a close look at some German auto plants, the plans for the new model and the necessary operations began to gel. The plan called for putting everyone involved under one roof, with drafters sitting next to financial managers, and engineers next to designers. Dia Hothi was given full autonomy, and thus the car was designed to be built using the factory tools on hand. All this went against Ford's traditional culture. But Alex Trotman, executive vice-president of Ford's North American automotive operations, supported the idea. The team became a sort of "Mustang Car Company" that just happened to be financed by Ford.

INNOVATE OR EVAPORATE 7.3

continued next page

FORD

The overall team was broken into "chunk teams," with each group responsible for a "chunk" of the car. Suppliers were brought in from the very beginning. The best available were selected on that basis, rather than through competitive bidding. This saved a considerable amount of time.

The effort was not without some hitches. The convertible, for example, had some stabilization problems. The first redesign didn't work, and several months later the car was still unstable; it shook noticeably at certain speeds. Computer simulations weren't providing any clues. A special team of fifty people was assigned to solve the problem. Eventually, by disassembling a Mercedes-Benz convertible, they found the solution. A 25-pound steel cylinder was welded to a spot behind the front fender. The cylinder acted like a finger on a tuning fork to reduce vibration.

Colletti notes that saving the Mustang was critical, but so was pride. Colletti and others at Ford were tired of hearing how Japanese automakers could do everything better than U.S. firms. "They're not superhumans," he declared.

Source: Joseph B. White and Oscar Suris, "New Pony: How a 'Skunk Works' Kept Mustang Alive—On a Tight Budget," Wall Street Journal (September 21, 1993), pp. A1, A12.

23. Have Open Communication Between Product, Process, Marketing, and Management Centers/ Teams and the Rest of the Organization.

Essential to coordinating the innovation process is open communication between the people who develop ideas and the rest of the organization. Hewlett-Packard's Colorado Springs Division has no internal walls; by this means physical and status barriers are removed so that communication can be totally open.[35] Rosabeth Moss Kanter, author of *The Change Masters*, notes that in innovative companies entrepreneurial managers use a process of bargaining and negotiation to build coalitions that provide the necessary information, support, and resources to proceed with an innovation.[36] She observes that innovation requires coalition building, which in turn requires persuasion. There must be open communication and a network of discussants. Most of the entrepreneurial companies described by Kanter actively encourage face-to-face communication. [37]

Arnoud De Meyer of INSEAD in Fontainebleau, France, arrived at similar conclusions after examining a series of case studies. Echoing Kanter, he suggests that in larger organizations the innovator must "leverage" the rest of the organization. This means enlisting the support and participation of everyone who will have a stake in the success of the innovation.[38]

Comparing U.S. Firms with Japanese and European Firms

Japanese firms have long engaged in open communication despite the hierarchical arrangements that are typical in most Japanese companies. Knowledge is shared among employees at all levels. Consensus must be established for plans to go forward. U.S. firms are moving rapidly to develop more open communication, but European firms vary widely, depending on their cultural environment. French and German companies, for example, tend to have closed communication because management is viewed as the source of knowledge and decisions are made in a top-down fashion. Firms in Scandinavian countries, in contrast, are more participative and tend to have more open communication.

30. Structure for Flexibility, in Order to Adapt and Seize the Opportunity.

In the turbulent environment faced by organizations today, flexibility is critical. Firms must be able to adjust, to seize opportunities as they present themselves. Under these conditions, it has become increasingly clear that smaller organizations are more innovative than larger ones. For example, they invest more funds as a percentage of sales than larger firms do.[39] What about GE, Hewlett-Packard, and other large firms that are very innovative, you may ask. They emulate smaller firms to some degree by creating numerous smaller, self-managed units with the

Structure

Chapter 7

authority to take action—in other words, with the authority to be innovative.[40] In a world where rapid product/process development and manufacturing/service flexibility are essential, it is easier to transform a smaller organization than a larger one.[41]

Since the future belongs to the nimble and quick, firms must structure accordingly. Hewlett-Packard, for example, has almost always relied on smaller organizational units to increase its rate of innovation. Some consultants recommend that organizational divisions should contain no more than 500 employees.[42] A visionary study on manufacturing done at the Iacocca Institute at Lehigh University, drawing upon the comments of participants from seventy-seven U.S. firms, concludes that "We stand at the threshold of a new era in manufacturing." Going beyond mass production and the "lean and mean" approach, firms are entering an era of "agile production" in which factories are small and modular, and machinery and layout are flexible and reprogrammable to allow for an almost infinite variety of products and quick response to very specific customer requirements.[43] In such a flexible system, the concept of "mass customization" becomes a reality.[44]

Flexibility is just as important in service operations as it is in manufacturing operations. *Innovate or Evaporate 7.4* discusses how one service firm, Barnett Banks, meets the challenge of innovation at least partly through its flexible structure.

Comparing U.S. Firms with Japanese and European Firms

Most major Japanese firms, by their own admission, have become too mechanistic and not nearly as responsive to market forces as they would like to be. However, the same could be said for most U.S. and European organizations. There are firms in all three global arenas that are highly flexible, and many others that are trying to become more so. As mentioned earlier, typical of those leading the charge in Europe is Asea Brown Boveri (ABB). ABB's CEO, Percy Barnevik, has divided the 218,000-person firm into 5,000 profit centers, perhaps the most extensive delegation of authority in the history of business. He believes that a profit orientation increases employee motivation.

BARNETT BANKS INNOVATES

One of the most innovative firms in its industry is Barnett Banks. A major regional bank headquartered in Jacksonville, Florida, Barnett is generally recognized, along with Banc One of Columbus, Ohio, as one of the two most innovative banks in the industry. Barnett possesses most of the characteristics that have been identified as important for innovation. First and foremost, it manages its culture. It has a stated strategy of innovation; it sets objectives that can be achieved through innovation; it rewards performance; it encourages risk taking; and it has an outstanding record of new-product and service innovation. But perhaps what sets it apart most from its other competitors is its flexibility. It treats each of its thirty-three regional banks as an independent company, capable of adapting to local market conditions. In Naples, Florida, for example, Barnett's products cater to an older, frequently retired, and often affluent clientele. But a totally different mix of services is available in other branches. Loan officers have tremendous authority to change the provisions of loan contracts. For example, when one potential borrower objected to a standard clause in the contract, the loan officer read it, determined that it wasn't critical, crossed it out, initialed the change, and made the loan.

Barnett's recent innovation activities include an attempt to establish electronic home banking services with multimedia capabilities, an integrated retail banking system, expanded uses of electronic imaging, videobanking, and marketing mutual funds to mature customers.

Sources: Richard Mitchell, "Home Banking's Scramble for Success," *Bank Management* (September 1993), pp. 45-48; Karen Kahler Holliday, "Marketing Mutual Funds to Mature Customers," *Bank Management* (December 1992), pp. 42-49; Jim Jaben, "Barnett Branches Out," *Bankers Monthly* (November 1992), pp. 8-9; Stuart A. Matlow, "Lights, Camera, Videobanking," *Bankers Monthly* (September 1992), pp. 23-25; Thomas E. Ricks, "Branching Out: Attentive to Service, Barnett Banks Grows Fast, Keeps Profit Up," *Wall Street Journal* (April 3, 1987), pp. 1, 27.

INNOVATE OR EVAPORATE 7.4

37. Use Alliances to Obtain Product, Process, Marketing and Management Innovations.

A **strategic alliance** is an agreement between two organizations to carry out a strategy jointly. The most common type of alliance is a **joint venture**, which is basically a partnership between two corporations whose purpose is to meet specific, limited objectives.[45] Strategic alliances are very important in rapidly changing environments and in situations in which knowledge is critical to competitiveness. The partners may have market and/or technical knowledge. They may also share knowledge and the expenses of gaining knowledge. Alliances are an excellent route to global expansion. They can also be used to set industry standards that others must follow. For example, IBM and Microsoft made MS-DOS an industry standard.[46] Strategic alliances help spread the risk and at the same time provide access to knowledge that would otherwise be unobtainable.[47] Apple Computer, for example, has alliances with IBM, Sony, and Sharp Electronics: each of these alliances allows Apple to participate in market segments that would otherwise be closed to it. Establishing strategic alliances is viewed as important for gaining access to markets and technology in both Japan and Europe.

Strategic alliances can turn a relatively small firm into a global enterprise. Nokia, for example, has grown from a medium-sized Finnish consumer goods conglomerate to a world-class communications and electronics company. It has operations in thirty-three countries and production in sixteen, largely through strategic alliances. Nokia has alliances with Tandy and AT&T in mobile phones; with Philips, Thomson, and Bosch in the European high-definition television project; and with Technophone Ltd. in the cellular market in the United Kingdom.[48]

Alliances can also be formed for less complex or extensive purposes that are nonetheless important to the participants. In 1991, Becton, Dickinson & Company, a medical supplies and equipment firm, and Preston Trucking Company, Inc., a regional carrier, established a partnership with the objectives of improving service and quality, cutting costs, and streamlining logistics. The partnership received the total commitment of both firms' top managers, who came together in a series of meetings in which they drew up a list of sixty-five shared goals and objectives and the actions required to accomplish them. The two companies work together to create process innovations that will be mutually beneficial. The improved performance delivered by the partnership enabled Becton Dickinson to win the 1993 LTL Shipper of the Year Award. The company saved $100,000 in the first year of the partnership. Preston Trucking benefitted by creating a service that helped lock in Becton Dickinson as a customer and by developing a new service to offer other customers.[49]

A new form of alliance, the **transnational strategic alliance** (TSA), is characterized by the sharing of complementary resources and capabilities across borders, and greater sharing of costs and risks than is typical of joint ventures. The shared objectives and the relationships between the partners are much more encompassing. Among the typical objectives of TSAs are (1) rationalization (implementation) of joint production and marketing efforts, (2) cost-effective procurement on a global basis, (3) technology sharing and co-production, and (4) enhancement of abilities to take advantage of a particular opportunity. Grupo Vitro (Mexico) and Corning (USA) have formed a TSA; so have Tyson Foods (USA), C-Itoh (Japan), and Provemex (Mexico).[50]

Comparing U.S. Firms with Japanese and European Firms

Japanese firms clearly lead U.S. and European firms in developing strategic alliances. Japanese firms have used alliances for a much longer time than firms in other parts of the world. Much of their nation's competitive structure is based on networks of supporting firms.[51] Some U.S. and European firms, however, are recognizing the need for strategic alliances and are taking steps to establish them.[52] For example, **inter-company innovation problem solving** is common in Europe, and U.S. firms are showing some interest in this process. In this approach, participants join together to fund research and/or tackle common problems. Inter-company networks may also be formed for the purpose of exploring a new technology.[53]

European firms are increasingly active in strategic alliances. For example, the pharmaceutical division of Switzerland's Ciba-Geigy and the Elan Corporation of Ireland have both engaged in several joint ventures with other pharmaceutical firms.[54]

44. Have an Effective and Efficient Structure for Creating New Products, Process Redesign, Marketing and/or Management Innovation.

If the implementation of an innovation strategy is to produce genuine innovations, a major issue is, "How should the R&D unit be structured to make that effort as effective as possible?" Each firm must find its own answer to that question, but it's clear that there must be a formalized process, that there should be several levels of innovation, and that the different levels of research need to be coordinated.

3M has separated its R&D function into three structural divisions based on different planning time horizons. Its division-level researchers develop products for current markets. Sector-level laboratories develop products five years before they are scheduled for introduction. They also research applied mathematical, chemical, and physics problems. Corporate research departments are involved in leading-edge research exploring primary technologies. This R&D structure has led to unprecedented successes in product development for 3M.[55]

Another major issue is the overall corporate structure—does it facilitate or hinder innovation? Inappropriate structure and culture have often caused major firms to lose their innovativeness and their responsiveness to the market. General Motors, for example, in the late 1980s and early 1990's, suffered through a period of falling market share and some substantial losses. Two of the major causes of these problems were too little innovation and poor market responsiveness. These resulted from an unwieldy organization structure and a lethargic culture. Together, they combined to stifle both process and product innovation. IBM is another large firm whose structure and culture have prohibited market responsiveness and innovation in recent years (despite IBM's exceptionally strong patent filing record discussed in chapter 2). Louis Gerstner, IBM's CEO, tackled these problems head on, something his predecessor John F. Akers had attempted to accomplish, but never quite did. *Innovate or Evaporate 7.5* reviews the structural situation at IBM and the actions that have been taken to correct it. *Innovate or Evaporate 11.6* reviews the cultural changes that Lou Gerstner is attempting to instill at IBM.

IBM RESTRUCTURES IN ORDER TO REINVENT ITSELF

In 1988, CEO John A. Akers enacted a major reorganization. He took control of the firm away from a six-person management committee and reorganized the firm into six strategic business units. That reorganization was met with considerable positive customer response. In December 1991, Akers announced the second major restructuring in three years. He planned to divide the firm into thirteen autonomous units, nine manufacturing and development lines of business, and four geographically based marketing and services companies to sell what the nine manufacturing units produced.

The three largest manufacturing and development businesses were Enterprise Systems which made mainframes, related processors and software; Adstar which made storage devices, tape drives and related software; and Personal Systems which made PC's, workstations, and related software. The four geographic

continued next page

IBM

sales units were: IBM Europe/Middle East/Africa, IBM North America, IBM Asia Pacific, and IBM Latin America. Critics heralded this reorganization as long overdue. It was generally believed that the increased autonomy would lead to greater market responsiveness and increased product innovation. IBM's bureaucracy had long been recognized as thwarting innovations. Its mainframers had managed to stave off those who wanted to move ahead with smaller, ever more powerful personal computers, workstations and client servers for fear of cannabalizing mainframe sales. The reality of course was that competitors did it for them. This restructuring was accompanied by a major downsizing. Including the cuts announced at this time, Akers had reduced IBM's work force from 407,000 in 1986 to 302,000 at the beginning of 1992.

In April, 1992, Louis Gerstner came to IBM from RJR Nabisco. Seven months later, he scrapped the plan to break the firm into 13 separate companies. He had discovered two sets of compelling reasons for doing so. Externally, several thousand customers that Gerstner had talked to did not want the company broken up into separate companies. Rather, they wanted IBM to deliver an overarching, cohesive perspective that solved their business problems, as opposed to the myriad of vendors with distinct products that couldn't function together. Internally, the firm was about to launch the most pervasive strategic technology thrust in its history. Gerstner's actions were taken because he believed that this new technology, labeled "Power," could best be sold through a unified firm. In his actions, Gerstner clearly sought a structure that would support the firm's innovation strategy.

Sources: David Kirkpatrick, "Gerstner's New Vision for IBM," *Fortune* (November 15, 1993), pp. 119-126; Joel Dreyfuss, "Reinventing IBM," *Fortune* (August 14, 1989), pp. 36-39; Michael W. Miller, "IBM's Customers Know About Problems Akers is Dealing with in Reorganization," *Wall Street Journal* (February 1, 1988), p. 14.

Comparing U.S. Firms with Japanese and European Firms

Japanese firms—and, increasingly, U.S.-based firms as well—are moving toward three-tiered programs of innovation like 3M's. At the first level, they seek incremental improvements in existing products. At the second level, they try for a significant jump like Sony's jump from the microtape recorder to the Walkman. At the third level is leading-edge innovation. These three levels of innovation often occur simultaneously under the direction of a single cross-functional development team.[56] A two-tiered approach consisting of continuous improvement and big bang innovation is also common.[57]

Finding the right structure for the R&D unit isn't easy. DuPont has reorganized its product development unit five times in the past six decades. Its current structure parallels that of Japanese organizations described earlier.[58]

Firms from Europe, Japan and the U.S. are all striving to create macrostructures that improve innovation.

STRATEGIC AND OPERATIONAL PLANNING GUIDE

Structure Question #	Where are we now? (Score)	Where do we want to be? (What are our objectives?)	
2. Develop structural mechanisms for innovation			
9. Require cross-functional customer/ supplier innovation teams			
16. Have innovation centers			
23. Have open communication between teams and rest of firm			
30. Structure for flexibility to seize opportunity, adapt to change			
37. Use alliances to obtain innovation			
44. Have effective and efficient evaluation structure			

How do we get there?		
What needs to be done?	**By whom?**	**By when?**

REFERENCES

1. Mohammed H. Habib and Bart Victor, "Strategy, Structure, and Performance of U.S. Manufacturing and Service MNCs: a Comparative Analysis," *Strategic Management Journal* (November 1991), pp. 586-606; Roderick E. White, "Generic Business Strategies, Organizaional Context and Performance: An Empirical Investigation," *Strategic Management Journal* (March-April 1986), pp. 217-231; for a review of the literature and systhesis of the two fields, see James W. Frederickson, "The Strategic Decision Process and Organizational Structure," *Academy of Management Review* (April 1986), pp. 280-297.

2. Amanda Bennett, "Downsizing Doesn't Necessarily Bring an Upswing in Corporate Profitability," *Wall Street Journal* (June 6, 1991), pp. B1, B8; also see Ronald Henkoff, "Getting Beyond Downsizing," *Fortune* (January 10, 1994), pp. 58-64.

3. "Labor Letter-Creativity is Tough Where Companies Resist Change," *The Wall Street Journal* (May 3, 1988), p. A1.

4. The classic study of this phenomenon, substantiated by numerous later research can be found in Tom Burns and George M. Stalker, *The Management of Innovation* (London: Tavistock, 1961), pp. 119-122; also see Robert D. Russell, "Innovation in Organizations: Toward an Intellectual Model," *Review of Business* (Fall 1990), pp. 19-26, 47; which reviews the results of a study on organic organizations and related innovation.

5. This is a simplified version of the discussion of this issue made by Paul Strebel, "Organizing for Innovation Over an Industry Cycle," *Strategic Management Journal* (March/April 1987), pp. 117-124.

6. Jeffery L. Funk, "Japanese Product Development Strategies: A Summary and Propositions About Implementation," *IEEE Transactions on Engineering Management* (August 1993), pp. 224-236.

7. Gifford Pinchot III, *Intrapreneurship* (New York: Perennial Library, 1985), pp. xi-xiii.

8. Michael A. McGinnis and Thomas P. Verney, "Innovation Management and Intrapreneurship," *Advanced Management Journal* (Summer 1987), pp. 19-23; Gifford Pinchot III, op. cit., pp. xv-xxi, 3-65.

9. Richard J. Ferris, "Capturing Corporate Creativity," *United* (January 1987), p. 7; John Naisbitt, "Helping Companies Hatch Offspring," *Success* (May 1987), p. 14; Colby H. Chandler, "Eastman Kodak Opens Windows of Opportunity," *Journal of Business Strategy* (Summer 1986), pp. 5-8.

10. Joyce Anne Oliver, "3M Vet Enjoys Taking Risks, Knocking Down Barriers," *Marketing News* (April 15, 1991), p. 13.

11. Joseph Weber, "A Big Company That Works," *Business Week* (May 4, 1992), pp. 124-132.

12. Catherine Arnst, "Now H-P Stands for Hot Products," *Business Week* (June 14, 1993), p. 36; Robert D. Hof, "Suddenly Hewlett-Packard is Doing Everything Right," *Business Week* (March 23, 1992), pp. 88-89; Stephen Kreider Yoder, "Quick Change: A 1990 Reorganization at Hewlett-Packard Already is Paying Off," *Wall Street Journal* (July 22, 1991), pp. A1, A8; Barbara Buell and Robert D. Hof, "Hewlett-Packard Rethinks Itself," *Business Week* (April1, 1991), pp. 76-79.

13. Gail Schares, "Percy Barnevik's Global Crusade," *Business Week* (October 22, 1993), pp. 204-211.

14. Peter Pae, "Kodak to Again Restructure Operations," *The Wall Street Journal* (August 18, 1989), p. B2; Leslie Helm, "Why Kodak is Starting to Click Again," *Business Week* (February 23, 1987), pp. 134-138; Leslie Helm and James Hurlock, "Kicking the Single-Product Habit," *Business Week* (December 1, 1986), pp. 36-37;

15. Mark Maremont, "TO: George Fisher—RE: How To Fix Kodak," *Business Week* (November 8, 1993), p. 37; Joan E. Rigdon, G. Christian Hill and Gautam Naik, "New Focus: Hiring Fisher, Kodak Gambles on a Future in Multimedia World," *Wall Street Journal* (October 29, 1993), pp. A1, A7; Thomas A. Stewart, "The Search for the Organization of Tomorrow," *Fortune* (May 18, 1992), pp. 92-98, which discusses Kodak's reengineering efforts.

16. John Case, "Customer Service: The Last Word," *Inc.* (April 1991), pp. 89-93.

17. Constantine S. Nicandros, "The Innovation Imperative" *Vital Speeches of the Day* (September 1990), pp. 13-20.

18. Amy Bermar, "Getting the Goods," *CIO* (August 1990), pp. 87-89.

19. Philip D. Olson, "Choices for Innovation-Minded Corporations," *Journal of Business Strategy* (January/February 1990), pp. 42-46.

20. Robert J. Schaffhauser, "How a Mature Firm Fosters Intrapreneurs," *Planning Review* (March 1986), pp. 6-19.

21. John R. Wilke, "Innovative Ways: Thermo-Electron Uses an Unusual Strategy to Create Products," *Wall Street Journal* (August 5, 1993), pp. A1, A7.

22. Matco Iansiti, "Real-World R&D: Jumping the Product Generation Gap," *Harvard Business Review* (May/June 1993), pp. 138-147.

23. Joseph P. Rotellor, "Break the Barriers to Innovation," *Chemical Engineering* (October 1993), pp. 137-142.

24. Takeo Imori, "Hatachi: Too Little Too Late?" *Tokyo Business Today* (December 1992), pp. 12-13; Neil Gross, "Inside Hatachi," *Business Week* (September 28, 1992), pp. 92-98, 100.

25. Ikujiro Nonaka, "Redundant, Overlapping Organization: A Japanese Approach to Managing the Innovative Process," *California Management Review* (Spring 1990), pp. 27-38.

26. Stewart Toy, "Europe's Shakeout: The Race to Restructure is Getting Frantic," *Business Week* (September 14, 1992), pp. 44-51.

27. Joseph L. McCarthy, "Alex Krauer: Ciba-Geigy," *Chief Executive* (July/August 1992), pp. 20, 22.

28. Herb Brody, "America's Technology Champions," *High Technology Business* (June 1988), p. 23.

29. For examples, see: Jane Carbone, "Chrysler Tries the Partnering Route," *Electronic Business Buyer* (November 1993), pp. 97-99; Karen Holtzblatt and Hugh Beyer, "Making Customer-Centered Design Work for Teams," *Communications of the ACM* (October 1993), pp. 92-103; Robert J. Hershock and David L. Braun, "Cross-Functional Teams Drive Change," *Executive Excellence* (July 1993), pp. 16-17; Paul O'Connor, "Managing Product Teams," *R&D* (July 1993), p. 67; Rick Whiting, "Varian Doesn't Debate What Customers Want, It Asks Them," *Electronic Business* (June 1993), pp. 64-66; Susan Ciccantelli and Jason Magidson, "From Experience: Consumer Idealized Design— Involving Consumers in the Product Development Process," *Journal of Product Innovation Management* (September 1993), pp. 341-347.

30. John Bussey and Douglas R. Sease, "Speeding Up: Manufacturers Strive to Slice Time Needed to Develop Products," *Wall Street Journal* (February 23, 1988), pp. A1, A24.

31. Thomas J. Peters, "The Home Team Advantage," *U.S. News & World Report* (March 31, 1986), p. 49.

32. Michael Roberts, "Major Challenges Force Changes in Europe," *Chemical Week* (March 10, 1993), pp. 30-31.

33. "Madza Motors' Organizational Changes Announced," *Japan 21st* (September 1993), pp. 13-14.

34. Stephen J. Somavelt, "Creating Fantasies Using Disney's Imagineers to Build Space Attraction," *The Wall Street Journal* (January 6, 1987), pp. 1, 25.

35. Karen Fitzgerald, "Encouraging Risk-Taking, Sanctioning Failures are Helping Spur Creativity," *IEEE Spectrum* (October 1990), pp. 67-69.

36. Rosabeth Moss Kanter, *The Change Masters* (New York: Simon & Schuster 1985), pp. 217-240.

37. Ibid., pp. 160-162.

38. Arnoud De Meyer, "Organizational Leverage Effect in Innovation," *European Management Journal* (December 1991), pp. 397-402.

39. For example see: Michael Selz, "Smaller Firms Invest in R&D In a Big Way," *Wall Street Journal* (February 18, 1992), pp. B1-B2.

40. For example see: James Brian Quinn, "Managing Innovation: Controlled Chaos," *Harvard Business Review* (May/June 1985), p. 28.

41. Garrett H. DeYoring, "Managing Technology at Warp Speed," *Electronic Business* (January 21, 1991), pp. 53-57.

42. For examples see: Thomas J. Peters, "Rethinking Scale," *California Management Review* (Fall 1992), pp. 7-28; Paul Geroski, "On Diversity and Scale-Extant Firms and Extinct Goods?" *Sloan Management Review* (Fall 1989), pp. 75-81; Steve Kaufman, "Going for the Goals," *Success* (January/February 1988), pp. 38-41; John A. Byrne, "Is your Company Too Big?" *Business Week* (March 27, 1989), pp. 84-94.

43. Thomas A. Stewart, "Brace Yourself for Japan's Hot New Strategy," *Fortune* (September 21, 1992), pp. 63-64.

44. B. Joseph Pine II, "Making Mass Customization Happen: Strategies for the New Competitive Realities," *Planning Review* (September/October 1993), pp. 23-24; B. Joseph Pine II, "Mass Customizing Products and Services," *Planning Review* (July/August 1993), pp. 6-13.

45. For a discussion of their uses see: David Lei, "Offensive and Defensive Uses of Alliances," *Long Range Planning* (August 1993), pp. 32-41.

46. J. G. Wissema and L. Euser, "Successful Innovation Through Inter-Company Networks," *Long Range Planning* (December 1991), pp. 33-39.

47. John Carey, "Moving the Lab Closer to the Marketplace," *Business Week— Reinventing America* (Special Issue: Undated 1992), pp. 164-171.

48. Carol Kennedy, "How Nokia is Going High-Tech," *Long Range Planning* (April 1992), pp. 16-25.

49. Jim Thomas, "1+1= Innovation," *Distribution* (September 1993), pp. 44-48.

50. Philip F. Banks and Jack Baranson, "New Concepts Drive Transnational Strategic Alliances," *Planning Review* (November/December 1993), pp. 28-31.

51. Michael Porter, *Competitive Advantage of Nations* (New York: Free Press, 1990), pp. 69-130.

52. Kevin Kelly and Otis Port, "Learning From Japan," *Business Week* (January 27, 1992), pp. 52-60.

53. J. G. Wissema and L. Euser, loc. cit.

54. D. Jane Bower, " New Product Development in the Pharmaceutical Industry: Pooling Network Resources " *Journal of Product Innovation Management* (November 1993), pp. 367-375.

55. Alicia Johnson, "3M: Organized to Innovate," *Management Review* (July 1986), pp. 38-39.

56. Peter Drucker, op. cit.

57. For example see: Harry S. Dent, Jr., "Growth Through New Product Development," *Small Business Reports* (November 1990), pp. 30-40.

58. Gene Bylinsky, "Turning R&D Into Real Products," *Fortune* (July 2, 1990), p. 72.

S Y S T E M S

CHAPTER 8

In today's business world, information is the only source of competitive advantage. The company that develops a monopoly on information, and has the ability to learn from it continuously, is the company that will win, irrespective of its business.

Dr. Yoshio Maruta
CEO, Kao Corporation

Even if an organization has formulated an effective innovation strategy and created the proper structure to carry it out, it still needs to develop the necessary systems to ensure the strategy's success. **Systems**, as defined in the Seven S's, include the flows and processes that enable an organization to function on a day-to-day basis. Systems of all types are necessary to formulate, implement, and control an innovation strategy.

Typical systems include those that provide marketing research, help design products, record sales, advertise products, help determine prices, distribute products and services, provide quality control, inventory products, schedule work, allocate resources, manage materials, provide funds, budget for capital assets, report on operations, report the firm's financial condition, recruit employees, compensate employees, provide performance evaluation, provide for employee health and safety, give executives and other managers needed information, and provide expert advice. In addition, the traditional functional areas of marketing, finance, operations, and human resources—also consist of flows and processes, and hence can also be referred to as systems. Various flows and processes that don't carry the label "system" include such things as obtaining and filling orders, integrating logistics, and commercializing technology invented by the firm.

Experts on innovation agree that certain types of systems are critical to successful innovation (assuming that other organizational systems are operating satisfactorily). The key systems are reward systems, formal mechanisms for celebrating success, management information systems focusing on innovation, formal idea evaluation systems that separate creation from evaluation and that look beyond simple financial analysis, systems for getting products from the lab to the market, information exchange systems, and effective suggestion programs.

THE CHARACTERISTICS

Exhibit 8.1 lists the seven summary questions related to the characteristics of structure as examined in the questionnaires in Chapter 4.

EXHIBIT 8.1 CHARACTERISTICS OF INNOVATIVE ORGANIZATIONS RELATED TO SYSTEMS

To what extent does your organization:

3.   Reward product, process, marketing, and management innovation.

10. Celebrate successes in product, process, marketing, and management innovation.

17. Have innovation management information systems—for example, to scan the environment for new opportunities, monitor and benchmark competitors' actions, determine best practices, keep abreast of new technologies, monitor market conditions, and exchange information internally.

24. Have formal idea assessment systems for product, process, marketing, and management innovation. Such systems should seperate creation from evaluation and look beyond simple financial analysis.

31. Have a system for getting products from the lab to the marketplace, and a system for implementing process innovations.

38. Use both formal and informal information exchanges on product, process, marketing, and management ideas.

45. Have effective suggestion programs for product, process, marketing, and management innovation.

---

3. Reward Product, Process, Marketing, and Management Innovation.

Reward systems for innovation involve two distinct groups: first, systems for researchers, scientists, engineers, and other professional innovators; and second, systems for anyone else within the firm who innovates. Generally, rewards for innovation include providing the freedom to be creative and honoring successful innovators. The latter can be done via financial rewards and promotions as well as through organized recognition programs.[1]

Until recently many experts believed that researchers, scientists, engineers, and other professional innovators were best motivated by the work itself—by technical challenge, the opportunity to create, and autonomy. And in many if not most instances this is still true. But corporations such as General Motors, Kodak, General Electric, Hughes Aircraft Co., and Phillips Petroleum Co. have discovered that their professional innovators are very receptive to financial and other nonintrinsic rewards.[2] Ramani Mani of General Electric observes that the payoff for scientific work often is not immediately evident. Therefore, recognition, especially financial recognition, may be very important in the short run.[3]

Companies vary in their approaches to nonfinancial rewards. According to George S. Howie, former director of IBM's technical personnel programs, "IBM has a program which is called the IBM Fellows. The fellows are typically engineers who have worked for the company 15-20 years and who have been extremely creative and productive. They are given executive

Systems

Chapter 8

salaries and five years to work on what they want to with the resources needed to support that research."[4] IBM does not do this in the hope of making new-product breakthroughs. Rather, "It is primarily for recognition of outstanding work."[5] Similarily, 3M's Golden Step Award (in the shape of a winged foot) is its version of a Nobel Prize for employees. Several Golden Steps are given out each year to employees whose new products have reached significant revenue and profit levels.[6] At Kodak, managers are taught in a company leadership class to find ways of rewarding creative and innovative people.[7]

Other types of rewards include promotions, not just to management positions, but on a dual ladder involving both management and professional achievement. 3M has a dual-ladder promotion program that consists of one ladder for management and another for professional success. Former CEO Allen Jacobson once said of 3M's system, "Some innovative people would rather face mustard gas than budget forecasts. What these people need is a system that rewards them for their innovative abilities without forcing them into a manager's desk where they'll be miserable."[8] Art Fry, inventor of the famous Post-It Notes, was promoted through the dual ladder, eventually attaining the position of corporate scientist, the highest rung on the technical side of the company.[9]

Rewards for nonprofessional innovators' contributions vary, but they usually focus on financial compensation, as well as on recognition. Because few organized innovation programs, except for suggestion programs, exist outside R&D, design, and marketing, little information about these programs is available. Getting to keep one's job seems to be the most typical reward. Process innovation often seems to be considered a normal part of a person's job. However, some firms use suggestion programs extensively and tie financial incentives to these programs.

Rewards are an increasingly complex issue as firms make greater use of teams to innovate and improve quality. Team rewards are atypical, but they will need to be utilized more often and more effectively in the future. Gain sharing is an appropriate reward, but it should often be team based. For example, at the IBM plant in Austin, Texas, employees earn $50 every time they serve on a quality improvement team (which can create process innovations). They may serve on a maximum of eight teams per year. Additionally, at the end of the year, rewards are given for the best results produced by teams during that year. Up to three teams are rewarded with $15,000 to be divided among the team's members.[10]

Comparing U.S. Firms with Japanese and European Firms

Unfortunately, the average American company does not reward its employees for their innovations, or does so in a very modest way. The most that employees can typically expect is continued compensation for doing their jobs. Most companies require employees to sign a waiver in which they give up their rights to any inventions or significant process improvements they may make during their tenure with the company. A few companies provide some financial rewards, but seldom more than a few hundred dollars.

Consultant Neal Orkin suggests that both companies and employees would benefit if companies paid employees for their inventions. As indicators of a serious problem in the U.S. economy (too few new ideas), he cites reductions in the growth rate of the gross national product and a decrease of about 50 percent in the number of patents issued in proportion to the total population over a ten year period. He feels that the solution lies in legislation. Western European countries and Japan have laws governing payments to inventors by their companies. Such payments are typically required in Western Europe, with the amounts determined by a mandatory negotiation process.

Orkin cites a Japanese law as a good example of how such payments stimulate application for patents. Statistics revealed a 300 percent increase in patent applications in Japan during the first ten years that the law was in force.[11] Not all Japanese firms provide such payments; highly innovative Sony, for example, seldom does (see *Innovate or Evaporate 2.2*).[12] Orkin also cites the high level of creativity in the video game industry as a reason to reward employees for innovation. Because inventors of games virtually always share in the profits from their games, the rate of innovation in this industry is very high.[13] Because

Systems

Chapter 8

207

many innovators believe they are not adequately compensated for their efforts, royalty compensation is becoming increasingly common. It provides both monetary reward and feedback from the market to the innovator about the impact of his or her innovation on the marketplace.[14]

10. Celebrate Successes in Product, Process, Marketing, and Management Innovation.

A specific type of reward that has a significant positive impact on the rate of innovation is the celebration of successful innovations. This occurs most commonly for individual or group innovators, but sometimes an entire corporation may celebrate its combined efforts.

Milliken has an Innovator's Hall of Fame in which pictures and brief descriptions of the contributions of leading Milliken innovators are displayed.[15] 3M has a similar form of recognition for its scientists, the Carleton Society, which honors those who have made long-range contributions to 3M's product and technological leadership.[16] Toyota, Mazda, and Honda stage annual contests for the most innovative new cars and features so that their engineers can receive acclaim from their peers. Innovators are rewarded with public displays of their efforts. One Toyota winner was a car that could be collapsed from a longer version, for use in the countryside, to a smaller city version. Another winner featured front seats that became minicars. The mother vehicle could be parked and the minicars could then be used to get about in a crowded city like Tokyo.[17] Another winner, from Mazda, was a vehicle that could be collapsed into a suitcase.[18]

Apple Computer announces its new products and programs through its developers instead of through the public relations office, thereby giving employees a sense of ownership of their innovations.[19] Elf Acquitaine, a $30 billion oil, chemical, and pharmaceutical conglomerate based in France, conducts a wide variety of research and has numerous reward and recognition programs. Among the more significant of these is an annual innovation awards ceremony in which major project successes from the company's three major subsidiaries are celebrated.[20]

The Harris Companies are independent contract-research laboratories operating in Europe, the United States, and Japan. Nearly 500 of Harris's approximately 600 employees are scientists and technologists, who conduct a total of about 4 million tests a year for a client base of over 6000. The information provided by these tests is used to help improve the environment, food, and health of people throughout the world. One of the firm's most important activities is rewarding its employees for their achievements and celebrating their successes. The company's Scientific Achievement Day is described in *Innovate or Evaporate 8.1*

17. Have Innovation Management Information Systems—for example, to Scan the Environment for New Opportunities, Monitor and Benchmark Competitors' Actions, Determine Best Practices, Keep Abreast of Technologies, Monitor Market Conditions, and Exchange Information Internally.

Innovation management information systems (IMIS) include systems that scan the environment for new opportunities, market conditions, technological changes, best practices, and competitors' actions; they also help members of the organization exchange information internally. An IMIS should be both formal and informal in nature and should be part of the organization's overall MIS. It's important to understand that specific resources must be dedicated to the innovation effort and specific objectives established for that effort. It isn't enough just to have an MIS: part of it must be dedicated to innovation. True, information may be shared by both systems, but an active effort must be made to obtain information that is relevant to the company's innovation efforts.

Competitor analysis is concerned with what competitors are doing, what they are going to do, and how these actions will affect the firm. Typical of such issues are a competitor's current and future strengths, weaknesses, opportunities, and threats (SWOT); its purposes (vision/strategic intent, mission, goals and objectives); its strategies; and how well it implements its strategies.[21] More specifically, with respect to innovation

Systems

Chapter 8

the firm should determine competitors' SWOT's relative to innovation; benchmark their innovation activities;[22] determine which of the major types of innovation strategies they are following (see Chapter 6) and how they implement these; and what successes—that is, product and process innovations—their strategies have produced. Analyses of probable product and service line extensions should also be made. Signals of technological leaps should be carefully monitored. Benchmarked items might include patents filed, product and process R&D expenditure levels, and capital expenditures. A firm would analyze this information to see what weaknesses existed and where it might be able to gain an advantage over a competitor.

Innovations do not have to come from within the company. Creative concepts and products can be borrowed from others and enhanced or turned into innovations. Many American firms actively shop international markets for new products and/or use product ideas obtained this way. For example, Ford Motor Company's very successful Taurus and Sable models, introduced in 1985, relied on European technologies. These cars resembled the German-made Audi, and to a large extent they were based on European designs that Ford had used previously, in combination with test data from studies conducted with the goal of designing a more wind-resistant car. Similarly, Procter & Gamble introduced a new liquid Tide in 1984. The ingredient that helped suspend dirt in wash water came from the company's Cincinnati headquarters, but the formula for the surfactants—that is, the cleaning agents—was developed by the company's technicians in Japan. Goodyear Tire & Rubber Company developed its radial tires for the U.S. market on the basis of a design that had been used by its European subsidiary.[23]

In another example, TRW purchased a European seatbelt manufacturing company in the belief that European firms have historically been leaders in seatbelt design. It then purchased a U.S. seatbelt manufacturing facility and put to use the technology it learned in Europe. It then developed a new belt that it hoped would catch on in the United States (it did). The new belt, then standard on all Mercedes Benz models, tightens around the wearer just before a crash. An electronic sensing device in the car senses sudden deceleration and sets off the

HARRIS'S SCIENTIFIC ACHIEVEMENT DAY

Scientific Achievement Day is a very special celebration for the Harris Companies. While processes, systems, and technology are all viewed as important to the firm's success, Harris wants its employees to know that it still views their outstanding performances as the underlying reason for that success. The awards criteria, which are reviewed each year include: (1) work that has been positively recognized by clients for scientific/technical factors, (2) significant enhancement of market-procedure development/validation or implementation, (3) recognized technical trouble-shooting, (4) leadership in technical ideas, (5) publication of major presentations at internal or external scientific meetings, (6) leadership in professional technical organizations, (7) accomplishment in training and/or mentoring of technical associates, and (8) major technical or scientific suggestions.

Scientific Achievement Day is devoted to awards, speakers, and presentations. The day begins with a breakfast for award recipients and their spouses, after which awards are presented to scientists and technicans. The awards ceremony starts off with welcoming remarks from one of Harris's leading scientists, who notes the contributions made by all the staff. Company officers then present gold, silver, or bronze medallions to honorees. Next comes a luncheon honoring the award winners, which includes an address by a speaker from the scientific community. The third feature of Scientific Achievement Day is the display of projects by individuals and teams. Most Harris associates enter posters describing what they do, which are presented to the assembled scientists with explanations by the individuals or teams involved. This provides not only a high level of visibility and recognition for those involved but also an opportunity for the exchange of information among members of the firm.

Source: Christine M. Harris, "A Celebration of Scientific Achievement," *HRMagazine* (February 1993), pp. 51, 53.

INNOVATE OR EVAPORATE 8.1

seatbelt retractor. TRW has also transferred other auto technologies from England to the United States and has found that
being alert to changes in the technologies used by firms in other
countries is critical to its success. [24]

Major sources of ideas outside an organization are professional associations whose members share similar research
interests. Other sources include professional clubs and other
organizations in the local area as well as national and international associations.

Bell Laboratories brings in outside speakers, who speak on topics that are often totally unrelated to the specific research being
conducted by its staff. The speakers are brought in because
there is always a possibility that new insights may be gained
from what they have to say.[25]

Comparing U.S. Firms with Japanese and European Firms

Japanese firms are adept at borrowing technology from U.S. firms and turning it into
salable products. In addition, Japanese
firms actively monitor even the most ob-
scure research efforts of competitors. For example, a Japanese
firm had replicated the AT&T experiment that led to the further
development of superconductivity *before* AT&T corporate officials
knew about the success of their own company's efforts. The research had been reported in an obscure European scientific journal; intelligence officers for the Japanese firm immediately reported it to their scientists, who then replicated the experiment.[26]
Japanese firms often buy small U.S. high-tech firms to acquire
their technology and apply it to create a marketable product.

Many U.S. firms are beginning to obtain information about research by Japanese and other firms outside the United States.
Some, such as Texas Instruments, Dow Corning, IBM, DuPont,
and W. R. Grace, have opened research labs in Japan in the hope
of utilizing the talents of Japanese researchers.[27] American firms
can also buy smaller U.S. firms or enter into joint ventures with
them. DuPont, for example, has a joint venture with Biotech Research Laboratories, which has one of the few diagnostic kits for
AIDS on the market. Both firms benefit from this relationship.[28]

Similarly, many Japanese and European firms have established R&D operations in the United States. In recent years thousands of Japanese managers have traveled to the United States to study the technologies of U.S. firms.[29] This may be one of the main reasons why Japanese firms have been more successful than U.S. firms in using borrowed technologies to create marketable products.

One of the advantages of Japanese firms over their global competitors is the way they treat corporate information. They believe they can improve performance by providing their employees with all the information they need to do their jobs better. U.S. and European firms tend to view most internal data as proprietary, information only on a need-to-know basis. An exception to the norm is Levi Strauss, described in *Innovate or Evaporate 8.2*. *Innovate or Evaporate 8.3* describes Kao Corporation, a firm that typifies the Japanese approach to information management.

24. Have Formal Idea Assessment Systems for Product, Process, Marketing and Management Innovation. These Systems Should Separate Creation from Evaluation and Look Beyond Simple Financial Analysis.

An organization needs an effective and efficient system for managing innovation. There must be a way for ideas to move up the organizational hierarchy or be approved at lower levels. Most innovative firms have a series of steps through which ideas pass, gain support, and acquire funding. 3M uses a multilayered idea review process, with each layer establishing different criteria for approving ideas and passing them along to the next layer.[30] This formal process, known as a **stage-gate system**, helps separate creation from evaluation. Ideas must pass through various "gates" before moving to later stages in the development process. Figure 8.1 portrays such a system, which is described in more detail in Exhibit 8.2.

FIGURE 8.1 OVERVIEW OF A TYPICAL STAGE-GATE SYSTEM

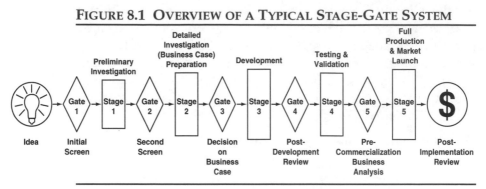

Source: Reprinted by permission of the publisher from ("New Product Process at Leading Industrial Firms," Robert G. Cooper and Elko J. Kleinschmidt), *Industrial Marketing Management* (May 1991), p. 138. Copyright 1991 by Elsevier Science Inc.

EXHIBIT 8.2 CHARACTERISTICS OF STAGE-GATE SYSTEMS

1. Stage-gate systems break the innovation process into a series of standard stages (typically three to seven). Each stage consists of a set of prescribed activities, such as:

    *   conducting a user needs-and-wants market study;

    *   performing an extended, controlled user field trial;

    *   undertaking a patent search;

    Often hundreds of identifiable activities are defined and assigned to various stages.

2. The stages cut across functional and departmental boundaries: They are multifunctional and multidisciplinary, including R&D, manufacturing, marketing, quality control, and other functions within any one stage. No stage is dominated by any single group; there is no "marketing stage" or "R&D stage."

3. Decision points, or "gates," separate the stages, providing opportunities to review the project at the completion of each stage. They include a set of inputs or goals—that is, what the project leader must accomplish or deliver before passing through the gate. Gates control the innovation process; it is here that go/ kill decisions, establishment of priorities, and evaluation of quality of execution occur according to a preset list of criteria.

4. The project is undertaken by a multifunctional team headed by a team captain or project leader. The team and leader see the project through the entire process, from initial idea to post-launch

INNOVATE
OR
EVAPORATE

PART II

continues on page 14

214

LEVI STRAUSS & CO. TAKES ITS INFORMATION SYSTEMS SERIOUSLY

Levi Strauss & Co. makes Levi's jeans, Dockers, and other apparel. It has manufacturing or sales operations in many countries and competes in a mature market. To accomplish its vision and mission, it has empowered its employees through autonomous teams, training and development, and information systems.

Each of Levi's 2500 employees has a workstation and access to information in the firm's mainframe computer. Bill Eaton, the chief information officer, explains that to empower employees it was necessary to create an open systems architecture with complete systems access. Employees are trained in the skills needed to access various networks to obtain specific types of information. Customers and suppliers are linked to the firm

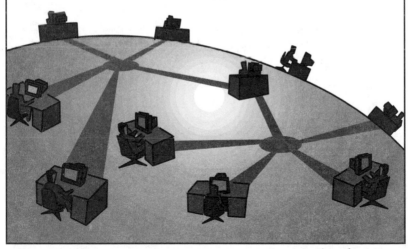

continued next page

LEVI

through LeviLink, a network electronic data interchange system. Levi's employees even have access to their personnel files. Through OLIVER (On-Line Interactive Visual Employee Resource), an interactive computer network, they can look at up to 500 screens of personal information. Using OLIVER, employees can check their total compensation, disability, health care, pension, employee investment plan, survivor benefits, beneficiary, and other personal information.

All the information systems at Levi Strauss, from purchasing to personnel, can communicate with each other. In fact, the capability for such communication is considered in all of the company's technology purchases. Levi Strauss has also created a special position, Director of Quick Response, to deal with electronic services to retailers and suppliers. Expert systems are used in several areas, such as inventory management. Finally, the globalization of its business has caused the firm to install international communication networks that enable its far-flung operations to keep in touch with each other.

Sources: David Brousell, "Levi Strauss's CIO on: The Technology of Empowerment," *Datamation* (June 1, 1992), pp. 120-124; Jennifer J. Laabs, "OLIVER: A Twist on Communication," *Personnel Journal* (September 1991), pp. 79-82; and Larry Stevens, "Systems Development vs. the Tower of Babel," *Bobbin* (June 1992), pp. 22, 24.

EXHIBIT 8.2 CONTINUED

activities. Senior managers watch the gates, making the appropriate decisions at each of these checkpoints.

5. The process is designed for speed and quality of execution: Parallel activities (that is, activities taking place concurrently within a stage, rather than sequentially) and efficient, timely gate decisions keep the project moving along; project evaluations focus resources on the most meritorious projects; and quality control checks ensure that the project is executed well.

Source: Robert G. Cooper and Elko J. Kleinschmidt, "New Product Processes at Leading Industrial Firms," *Industrial Marketing Management* (May 1991), p. 138.

INNOVATE
OR
EVAPORATE

PART II

KAO CORPORATION'S INFORMATION SYSTEM SUPPORTS ITS INNOVATION STRATEGY

Japan's Kao Corporation, begun as the Kao Soap Company in 1890, is a diversified company with interests in two primary areas: household products (with divisions for personal care cosmetics, laundry and cleansing, and hygiene) and chemical products (with divisions for fatty and specialty chemicals, and floppy disks). The firm was founded on the principle of equality as expressed by seventh-century statesman Shotoku, whose philosophy profoundly influenced Yoshio Maruta, Kao's CEO from the late 1970s through the early 1990s. Two of Shotoku's precepts are: "Human beings can live only by the Universal Truth, and in their dignity of living all are absolutely equal," and "If everyone discusses on an equal footing, there is nothing that cannot be resolved." Kao's corporate philosophy thus reflects belief in individual initiative and rejection of authoritarianism.

Because work is viewed as something flexible and flowing, Kao is designed to be run as a "flowing system" that spreads ideas and stimulates interaction. To give free rein to creativity and initiative, organizational boundaries and titles have been abolished. The result is a learning organization in which sharing of information is essential and information systems are critical to the company's success.

continued next page

217

KAO

Every employee at Kao seeks to learn and help others learn. Every manager knows Maruta's fundamental assumption: "In today's business world, information is the only source of competitive advantage. The company that develops a monopoly on information, and has the ability to learn from it continuously, is the company that will win, irrespective of its business." In some U.S. firms, executive information systems allow only top managers to gain access to key data; at Kao, the MIS extends to everyone. The equality perspective makes information available to everyone in the company. The task of Kao's managers is to take information from the environment, process it, and by adding value, turn it into knowledge. Every piece of information is viewed as potentially providing insight into product positioning, product improvement, or the development of a new product.

Nowhere is the advantage of this philosophy more evident than in Kao's flexible manufacturing program designed, according to systems developer Masayuki Abe, "to maximize the flexibility of the whole company's response to demand." The firm obsessively collects and distributes data, which are entered into a single system that links together sales and shipping, production and purchasing, accounting, R&D, marketing, hundreds of shopkeepers' cash registers, and thousands of salesmen's hand-held computers. Kao boasts that its management information system is so complete that it can turn out an annual report one day after the end of the year.

Kao can tell whether a new product will be successful within two weeks of the product launch. It does so by using focus groups, consumer calls, and point-of-sale information from 216 outlets in a system known as Project Echo. This approach obviates the need for market surveys. It also helps explain how Kao could enter the highly competitive cosmetics industry in Japan and become the number two player in that industry in less than ten years—to put it succinctly, the company can adjust quickly to meet customer demands. When, for example, Mrs. Wanatabe buys a bar of soap, the purchase is instantly recorded. With this information Kao can increase variety while cutting inventory levels. In addition, through its wholesalers Kao can deliver an order within 24 hours to any of 280,000 shops that, on average, order only seven items at a time. No other company in the world can match Kao's flexibility.

Sources: Thomas A. Stewart, "Brace for Japan's Hot New Strategy," *Fortune* (September 21, 1992), pp. 62-73; and Sumantra Ghoshal and Charlotte Butler, "The Kao Corporation: A Case Study," *European Management Journal* (June 1992), pp. 179-191.

Kodak utilizes a system like the one just described. Any new idea must pass through a series of evaluations at several levels of the organization. As a result, judgment on the new idea is suspended until it has had a chance to be developed.[31] Figure 8.2 portrays Kodak's system as it existed in 1988. Today the system remains quite similar, although there is no longer a formal chart, and early coordination with potential implementers, such as manufacturing, has been improved.[32]

FIGURE 8.2 A SYSTEM FOR EVALUATING IDEAS

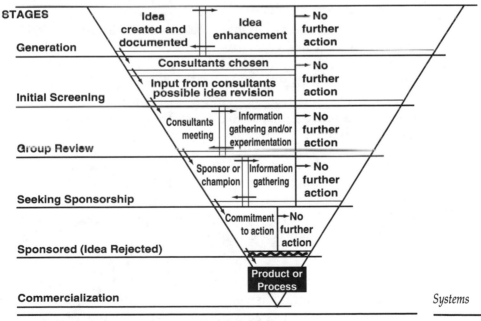

Source: Reprinted courtesy of Eastman Kodak Company.

Most major U.S. firms use some type of net present-value or cash-flow analysis to evaluate new products. A key element of successful new-product introduction is going beyond simple financial analysis to understand what the product can do for the company besides bringing in more profits.[33] It is also important to examine the underlying assumptions regarding costs and the associated risks.[34]

Companies like Parker-Hannifin Corporation, a $2 billion industrial parts maker, are increasingly looking beyond traditional financial analyses in evaluating ideas. Assistant controller John D. Campi feels that traditional cost accounting shouldn't be used in judging whether or not to implement a new idea. He continually seeks new approaches to these decisions. Chairman Patrick S. Parker agrees. "We don't think that what the customer wants can be told by traditional analyses," he says.[35] Parker-Hannifin therefore encourages its managers to use their intuition in making decisions on such matters as whether to add new products to an existing product line.[36]

Young and Rubicam, one of the best-known advertising agencies in the United States, found that it had to become more creative in order to be more competitive. Accordingly, it changed its organizational culture. One of the key changes was the development of a "Risk Lab" headed by Stephanie Kugelman, a fifteen-year Y&R veteran who became known as "Dr. Risk". Kugelman and five staff members move throughout the organization, listening to employees' creative ideas and giving them feedback. The Lab also conducts consumer feedback studies. The purpose of the Lab is to offer evaluative feedback to creative thinkers before they take their ideas to the boss or a client.[37]

Even firms that have formal assessment systems sometimes find that they need improvement. Eastman Chemical Company, a subsidiary of Eastman Kodak until it was spun off in January 1994, found that it wasn't getting enough productivity from its innovation system. It reinvented the system, as described in *Innovate or Evaporate 8.4.*

Creativity is encouraged by many local and state governments through formal mechanisms. In fact, most innovation in government occurs at the state and local levels. Tying welfare to

EASTMAN CHEMICAL REINVENTS ITS INNOVATION PROCESS

Although Eastman Chemical Company (ECC) had long recognized the importance of product and process innovation, it was not until 1988 that the firm became acutely aware that its innovation process was not sufficiently productive. A major study was launched to determine what improvements were needed; the firm then began developing strategies for implementing those improvements.

Before 1988, ECC's innovation process began with identification of a customer's needs. This effort included not only external customers but also internal customers such as manufacturing. This step was followed by several others: discovery-driven research, R&D efforts to develop potential solutions, a desirability/feasibility/capability study, designation of the project as an innovation concept, an applied research project, and finally commercialization of a new product.

From the beginning of the process to the end, innovation was seen as an R&D function, not as something involving the whole company. More specifically, this meant that the resource allocation process was especially burdensome and that the new-product development process managed effectively. There was little participation by marketing and manufacturing and little reward for such participation when it did occur. Technology transfer from the lab to the market was often weak. There was too little interaction between R&D and the firm's

continued next page

INNOVATE OR EVAPORATE 8.4

EASTMAN CHEMICAL

business centers in determining market needs. Project managers were not well trained in project management or innovation management.

ECC set out to change these conditions. It established seven goals. The first aim was to make everyone at ECC an active participant in the innovation process. The second was to increase the participation of business centers. Third, ECC wanted to make certain that all functions gave their commitment to innovation from the beginning of a project. The fourth goal was to move projects through the process more quickly and with a higher success rate than in the past. Fifth, the need for a particular project was to be revalidated throughout the project's life. Sixth, ECC would identify new business opportunities and create projects to take advantage of them. Finally, a system for managing and continually improving the innovation process would be created.

To achieve these objectives, ECC divided the innovation process into four parts:

1. **Needs identification** included systems for identifying, validating, and communicating product and process needs.

   - Multifunctional teams would be used in separate product/market categories to carry out these steps.

   - Business centers would review and support high-impact and other significant validated needs.

   - A futures technology and market research function would be established.

2. **Concept development** involved generating ideas and developing viable concepts to be implemented.

   - Informal multifunctional teams devoted to concept development early in the innovation process would be formed.

EASTMAN CHEMICAL

3. **Innovation concepts/applied research** comprised ECC's system for new product and process concepts being commercialized via a structured project management system.

   - An improved project management system would be implemented.

   - A company-wide system for assigning prioritites to innovation projects would be implemented.

   - A full-time project manager would be appointed for high-priority projects.

4. **Market development** included market evaluation, introduction, and sales development for the new product.

   - For new-product projects, a market development team consisting of representatives from appropriate marketing organizations would be formed.

   - Appropriate measures of innovation would be established for each functional and business area.

   - Certain administrative processes would be streamlined.

   - A process facilitator would be appointed to oversee the entire innovation process.

After three years the program had scored several significant measurable improvements, notably in project completion cycles, the value of products produced, and the success rate of new products. From a qualitative standpoint, much of the change was in the way the process was managed—for example, in the involvement of all major functions and in the systems for assigning priorities and allocating resources to projects.

Source: Jerry D. Holmes, Gregory O. Nelson, and David C. Stump, "Improving the Innovation Process at Eastman Chemical," *Research-Technology Management* (May/June 1993), pp. 27-35.

work and training, using circuit-riding city managers, using private enterprise to provide public services, and tax amnesty programs are among the ideas generated by state and local governments. These programs involve formal assessment procedures.[38]

Comparing U.S. Firms with Japanese and European Firms

Japanese firms have approached the problem from a more strategic perspective than their U.S. or European counterparts have. Japanese managers don't ask, "Judging from today's knowledge, can we sell a new product for this price and make a profit?" They say, "Judging from our predictions for the future, we have to offer this product, and we will have to produce it at this cost in order to make a profit. Now, Mr. Manufacturing Vice-President, find a way to produce it at this cost."[39]

31. Have a System for Getting Products from the Lab to the Marketplace and a System for Implementing Process Innovations.

As mentioned in Chapter 2, U.S. firms excel at basic research compared with their Japanese counterparts, but in general they are not nearly as successful in turning basic research discoveries into marketable products. Japanese firms, on the other hand, excel at applied research and at turning basic research results into successful products. A few U.S. firms, such as Hewlett-Packard, 3M, and GE, have also learned how to do this. By examining these and other successful innovators, we can see that it isn't enough to put a bunch of brilliant scientists in a laboratory and wait for them to produce brilliant ideas, only some of which may have commercial potential. Studies have shown a strong link between a firm's competitiveness and its ability to commercialize ideas.[40] American firms must therefore learn how to capitalize on their discoveries more effectively.

INNOVATE OR EVAPORATE

——

PART II

But it isn't easy to turn discoveries into products. Frank Carrubba, formerly Hewlett-Packard's lab chief, once described the process as follows: "You're standing there with a handful of darts aiming at a bull's eye on a suspended dart board swinging in the wind. You hope to hit the bull's eye. But you're lucky if you hit the dart board at all."[41] Despite the frustration implied by this description, it is easier to manage this process than most executives believe. Hewlett-Packard is one firm that seems to have the answer. It estimates that a full 60 percent of the research conducted in its labs ends up as product applications.[42] Anywhere from 50 percent to 70 percent of the firm's sales may be derived from products that have been introduced within the previous three years.[43] Also consider 3M, a renowned leader in new-product development. Division managers at 3M are highly motivated by the dictum that 30 percent of sales and 25 percent of profits must come from products that didn't exist five years earlier. They either achieve these ends or they are likely to be replaced.

How do companies like Hewlett-Packard and 3M achieve such outstanding results? The specifics of the system vary from one firm to another,[44] but the most successful programs are quite similar. Beyond the stage-gate system described earlier, there is a set of required actions. Commercialization is given high priority. Innovation performance objectives, such as those found at 3M, are used to help managers focus on results. Such objectives require careful benchmarking of competitors' innovation efforts, such as their R&D expenditures, new products and processes, and capital expenditures. Perhaps the most important ingredient is a lab manager who is able to balance the needs for a firm's long-term basic research against its short-term needs for applied research to keep the company profitable. The lab manager must also understand how to balance the desires of scientists to do basic research against the company's need to sell products. Top management must also be active in the commercialization process, not necessarily on a day-to-day basis, but by being visible in the lab, giving support, and making sure that programs are on target.

Many U.S. firms that are adept at technology transfer use a hub-and-spoke approach to R&D. Corporate labs do R&D with a capital "R" and a small "d," while division labs do R&D with a small "r" and a capital "D." Corporate labs work on projects with time horizons of three to seven years or more, while division labs work on projects with one- to two-year time horizons.

Successful companies monitor the technology transfer from the corporate level to the division level to make certain that the expense of the corporate lab is justified. Many firms are also having most of their R&D done at the division level so that customer needs are met more quickly and better.

DuPont's approach is somewhat different. The company formerly used the hub-and-spoke approach, but in 1985, it instituted collaborative "centers of excellence." Each center is devoted to a specific technology, such as advanced ceramics or microbiology. Scientists doing basic research collaborate with product experts from the divisions. When one considers the diversity of approaches to long- and short-term integration, it helps to realize that even successful firms change systems to keep in step with changing times. DuPont, for example, has taken five distinctly different approaches to managing the lab since 1937.[45]

Increasingly, cross-functional teams are the key structure in the product design process. These teams help move products from the lab to the marketplace because marketing and manufacturing get involved early in design making the transition smoother. Naturally, these teams must develop cross-functional skills, but the organization as a whole must also operate cross-functionally. At Hewlett-Packard, for example, the entire organization is based on cross-functional teams that run their own businesses. HP keeps its divisions small and gives them a great deal of autonomy and accountability.[46]

In fact, most successful innovative firms give their divisions the autonomy they need to respond to the market or create new markets. These firms also provide for both formal and informal exchanges of information. Innovative firms recruit researchers who are oriented toward commercial applications, beginning their recruitment processes long before the prospective scientists and engineers finish their college careers. And they pay top dollar, including signing bonuses. Once on board, these employees are compensated well. Innovative firms share information with alliance partners and, on occasion, even with competitors. Finally, these firms are much more focused on customers than was typically the case in the past. Customers often take part in the design process. In the best firms, even basic researchers actually visit customers at their locations.

The characteristics just discussed overlap those mentioned elsewhere, both in this chapter and in others. This is so because these characteristics are managed in a coherent and cohesive fashion in successful firms. In many firms, these characteristics might appear but are not so well managed. In the most successful firms, they are approached as a system rather than as separate issues. GE is an example of a firm that knows how to manage its innovation systems. *Innovate or Evaporate 8.5* describes how GE manages its systems for both product and process innovation.

38. Have Both Formal and Informal Information Exchanges Within the Company for Product, Process, Marketing, and Management Ideas.

The importance of formal and informal information exchanges cannot be overstated. Firms must encourage such exchanges if they are to benefit fully from their knowledge. For example, at AT&T researchers are required to share their technology with other AT&T researchers on a regular basis.[47] The same is true at 3M.[48] GE's successes also result partly from the sharing of ideas across organizational boundaries. Walter Robb, head of GE's R&D program since 1986, has taken great pains to ensure that ideas are shared among his engineers and scientists. As noted in *Innovate or Evaporate 8.5*, he has instituted a Friday evening beer-and-pretzel get-together at which scientific speakers discuss their findings. Among the results is a patent on a plastic that can conduct electricity, an innovation which resulted from the work of a chemist and an engineer who exchanged comments about a Friday evening presentation. The development of three-dimensional medical imaging technology probably wouldn't have happened without the Friday get-togethers. Four years and much hard work later, it shows considerable promise.[49] Also, GE teams which have been successful at process innovation tour other GE businesses giving seminars on how they achieved their successes.

The Japanese copier company Ricoh, provides areas where employees can meet and share ideas. In the center of Ricoh's R&D Center near Yokohama is an eight-spoked "tree of imagination." The spokes, or limbs, are shaped like trees with the top half cut off. Employees meet at these "branches" to share ideas.[50] Hewlett-Packard, Steelcase, and Herman Miller also provide areas where employees can meet and exchange ideas.

Comparing U.S. Firms with Japanese and European Firms

On average, Japanese firms tend to share more information with their employees than their United States and European counterparts. As indicated earlier in the discussion of Kao Corporation, Japanese managers view information as something to be shared, not kept secret. It is only natural, therefore, that they would promote formal and informal exchanges of information to a greater extent than U.S. managers, who tend to view most information as proprietary.

45. Have Effective Suggestion Programs for Product, Process, Marketing, and Management Innovation.

A suggestion program, if properly managed, can be extremely beneficial in producing creative money-saving and money-making ideas. Programs in which the person who proposes an

GENERAL ELECTRIC: SYSTEMATIC INNOVATION

Today many firms are developing systems for ensuring that products get from the lab to the market. Many others are developing systems for ensuring that process innovations occur and are implemented. Very few firms have been able to do both, but GE is an exception.

As noted in Chapter 1, GE has an exceptional record for commercialization. The consulting firm Booz-Allen found that in one five-year period GE undertook 250 major technology projects. Of these, 150 produced important product applications. GE's system for getting products to the lab begins with the high priority given to commercialization, even commercialization that could cannibalize the company's current products. Annual targets must be met. Next, GE has a lab director who understands the need for long-term research and has increased GE's long-term R&D funding levels by 50 percent.

The corporate culture promotes social and professional interaction. Art exhibits and classical music concerts are frequent; Friday evening beer-and-pretzel parties increase cross-functional exchange of ideas; and informal as well as formal contacts among researchers are encouraged.

Researchers who come to a dead end in one department are permitted to move to another to develop their ideas. Each year about 35 of the R&D center's 1800 staff members are transferred to new departments. In addition, researchers present their ideas to managers throughout the company, not

INNOVATE OR EVAPORATE 8.5

continued next page

GENERAL ELECTRIC

to just those in their own division. Much of GE's success in creating new products can be attributed to this insistence on a cross-functional perspective.

As discussed in *Innovate or Evaporate 5.4*, GE has set the trends in process innovation that others will follow into the twenty-first century. CEO Jack Welch aims to increase the flow of ideas from all employees by improving the way they are managed. Three tools form the core of this management revolution: the workout, best practices, and process mapping. Information in process redesign successes are shared throughout the company as teams from successful units tour other GE companies providing seminars on "how they did it."

Sources: Thomas A. Stewart, "GE Keeps Those Ideas Coming," *Fortune* (August 12, 1991), pp. 41-49; Amal Kumar Naj, "Creative Energy—GE's Latest Invention: A Way to Move Ideas from Lab to Market," *Wall Street Journal* (June 14, 1990), pp. A1, A9.

idea gets a share of the resulting profits seem to work best. In such programs, there is a pot of gold at the end of the rainbow that follows the brainstorm.[51]

Susan Stanton, a Federal Express van driver, noticed that packages sometimes slid around in the van and ended up out of order, delaying delivery and increasing the company's costs. To solve this problem, Stanton designed racks. These racks, which were subsequently installed in hundreds of trucks, save Federal Express about $8 million a year. The company rewarded Stanton with a check for $25,000. This seems like a large amount, but a smaller reward might have left her feeling cheated.[52]

A survey by the American Society for Quality Control and the Gallup Organization identified the following characteristics of successful suggestion programs:

1. Their employees know what is important to corporate success.

2. All their employees know where they fit in the system and how they can contribute to it.

3. They stay in touch with their customers.

4. They invest a large amount of money in training programs.

5. They emphasize teamwork.

6. They train their employees to make suggestions.

7. Suggestions are acted upon quickly.

8. Recognition for ideas is part of the daily lives of their workers.[53]

Eastman Kodak has a very effective employee suggestion program, called the Innovation Network, that could serve as a model for other employers. Kodak's program includes autonomy in the development of ideas, constructive feedback, recognition for successful innovations, and financial rewards.[54]

Not all suggestion programs are effective. When Hallmark Cards experienced difficulties with its Creative Thinking Suggestion Program, the company decided that it needed to offer different types of rewards and broader forms of team recognition.[55] Sometimes a suggestion program can be improved by adding a little extra push. For example, American Airlines has a highly effective suggestion program called IdeAAs in Action that saved the company $83 million its first two and a half years.[56] To make the program even more successful, American launched its IdeAAdvocate Program. AAdvocates are volunteers who help raise levels of employee participation, improve the quality of ideas, and provide feedback to those who make suggestions.[57] Similarily, Pacific Gas & Electric decentralized the approval process:

Systems

Chapter 8

for suggestions that would result in savings of less than $50,000, the originating unit can make an award without first obtaining higher-level approval.[58]

Most well-managed suggestion programs are very effective. Significant cost reductions, quality improvements, and new products and enhancements result. For example, Evart Products Company combines gainsharing with a structural suggestion program. One result has been a reduction in the rate of defects from 437 parts per 10,000 to *only two* parts per 10,000.[59]

Not all suggestion programs have to be continuous. Black & Decker's Household Products Division ran a program for only one year—1989. The program produced suggestions that resulted in $580,000 in savings that year and another $3 million in the next few years.[60] Similarly, when United Telephone of Indiana wanted to make a quick improvement in its corporate productivity, it held a thirty-day campaign during which its 1083 employees (including management) contributed a total of 1300 ideas.[61]

Comparing U.S. Firms with Japanese and European Firms

While Kodak, Federal Express, Lockheed, McDonnell-Douglas, American Airlines, and many other U.S.-based firms have effective suggestion programs, few if any of those programs can match the productivity of programs in major Japanese firms, which take suggestion programs very seriously. The former Akio Morita, co-founder of Sony, commented, "We insist that all our employees contribute their thoughts and ideas, not just their manual effort. We get an average of eight suggestions a year from each employee. We take most of these ideas very seriously."[62] Toyota receives about 860,000 suggestions a year, of which 94 percent will be implemented. About 66 percent of Japanese employees submit suggestions, compared to 8 percent of U.S. employees.[63]

Ford Motor Company recently launched a comprehensive new suggestion program, called the Continuous Improvement Recognition System (CIRS), aimed at increasing the rate of employee participation to 75 percent. Red Maynard, corporate manager for CIRS, traveled around the world studying numerous firms' suggestion programs before settling on the CIRS model, which has already resulted in substantial savings for Ford. CIRS offers hourly and salaried employees, including members of cross-functional teams, a chance to earn points every time their suggestions are approved. The points earned may be redeemed from a catalog of over 2,000 items, including electronic goods, furniture, sporting equipment, Ford products, and travel prizes. Modest ideas are awarded points immediately, while ideas which claim to save over $500 must be approved by departmental committees. Committee members also earn points if they respond quickly. Since recognition is an important part of the suggestion program, Ford distributes a monthly video that highlights successful efforts of work groups. Ford also runs success stories in its in-house publications.[64]

A KEY ASSUMPTION

The underlying, but to this point unstated assumption, is that organizations should have an effective system for measuring their innovation performance. This measurement system should incorporate not only their own successes and failures, but also those of their competitors. Key questions the firm should be asking itself for all four types of innovation include: What are our innovation successes and failures? What key industry (or broader) business innovations have we missed and why? Are we getting a sufficient return on our research and development expenditures? What percentage of our innovations have been very successful, somewhat successful, or not very successful? How proficient are we at converting our ideas into innovation? Are we leading the industry or following it?

Such an assessment needs to occur periodically, ideally every year. Firms that do not have such a measurement system, need to immediately develop and implement one. Otherwise, how will they know if they are properly spending, thousands, millions, or billions of dollars?

STRATEGIC AND OPERATIONAL PLANNING GUIDE

Systems Question #	Where are we now? (Score)	Where do we want to be? (What are our objectives?)	
3. Reward innovation			
10. Celebrate innovation successes			
17. Have innovation management information systems			
24. Have assessment systems going beyond financial analysis			
31. Have a system for getting from lab to market and for implemention			
38. Use formal and informal information exchanges			
45. Have effective suggestion programs			

	How do we get there?		
	What needs to be done?	**By whom?**	**By when?**

REFERENCES

1. Ashok K. Gupta and Arvind Singhad, "Managing Human Resources for Innovation and Creativity," *Research-Technology Management* (May/June 1993), pp. 41-48.

2. Paul H. O'Neill and Paul L. Smith, "The Quality Struggle From Two Angles: A CEO's View, A CFO's View," *Financial Executive* (May/June 1991), pp. 51-60, discusses Kodak; the rest are discussed in Alan Farnham, "How to Nurture Creative Sparks," *Fortune* (January 10, 1994), pp. 94-100; and in Mark Alpert, "The Care and Feeding of Engineers," *Fortune* (September 21, 1992), pp. 86-95.

3. Michael Gates, "Scientists Speak Out: Spurring Innovation," *Incentive* (October 1989), pp. 49-51.

4. Walter Kitchell, III, "Managing Innovators," *Fortune* (March 4, 1985), p. 182; and as voiced in discussions with IBM personnel May 13, 1994.

5. Ibid.

6. "3M Backgrounds—3M Award Programs," (Internal 3M News Memo, undated 1993); Alicia Johnson, "3M: Organized to Innovate," *Management Review* (July 1986), pp. 38, 39.

7. Paul H. O'Neill and Paul L. Smith, loc. cit..

8. "3M Backgrounds—Policy: The 3M Dual Ladder System," (Internal 3M news memo, undated 1993).

9. "3M Backgrounds—Person: Art Fry," (Internal 3M news memo, undated 1993).

10. Rebecca Sisco, "Put Your Money Where Your Teams Are," *Training* (July 1992), pp. 41-45.

11. Neal Orkin, "Rewarding Employee Invention: Time for Change," *Harvard Business Review* (January/February 1984), pp. 56-57.

12. Brenton R. Schlender, "How Sony Keeps the Magic Going," *Fortune* (February 24, 1992), p. 79.

13. Neal Orkin, loc. cit.

14. Shari Caudron, "Motivating Creative Employees Calls for New Strategies," *Personal Journal* (May 1994), pp. 103-106.

15. "Milliken: Quality Leadership Through Research" (Spartanburg, SC: Milliken & Company, 1986), p. 5.

16. Ronald A. Mitsch, "Three Roads to Innovation," *Journal of Business Strategy* (September/October 1990), pp. 18-21.

17. A. T. III, "Japan's Fantasy Cars," *Fortune* (December 14, 1992), p. 16; Sally Solo, "Japan Reinvents the Wheel," *Fortune* (November 20, 1989), p. 11.

18. Rick Tetzelli, "Suitcase Cars," *Fortune* (May 4, 1992), p. 13.

19. Jim Braham, "A Rewarding Place to Work," *Industry Week* (September 18, 1989), pp. 15-19.

20. Robert Cassidy, "Elf's R&D Goes Beyond Oil," *R&D* (December 1991), pp. 46-47.

21. John M. Kelly, *How to Check Out Your Competition* (New York: John Wiley & Sons, 1987); William E. Rothschild, "Competitor Analysis: The Missing Link in Strategy," *Management Review* (July 1979), pp. 22-39.

22. Michael Kenward, "The Fathers of Innovation," *Director* (September 1993), pp. 34-40.

23. Paul Ingrassia, "Global Reach: Industry is Shopping for Good Ideas to Provide Products," *The Wall Street Journal* (April 29, 1985), pp. 1, 16.

24. Ibid.

25. "Bell Labs: Imagination, Inc.," *Time* (January 25, 1982), pp. 56-57.

26. Author's personal knowledge.

27. Susan Moffat, "Picking Japan's Research Brains," *Fortune* (March 25, 1991), pp. 84-96.

28. John Case, "Sources of Innovation," *Inc.* (June 1989), p. 29.

29. Ibid.; Robert Ronstadt and Robert J. Kramer, "Getting the Most Out of Innovation Abroad," *Harvard Business Review* (March/April 1982), pp. 94-99.

30. Russell Mitchell, "The Masters of Innovation," *Business Week* (April 10, 1989), pp. 58-64; Alicia Johnson, loc. cit.; Thomas J. Peters and Robert H. Waterman, Jr., *In Search of Excellence* (New York: Harper & Row, 1982).

31. Leslie Helm, "Why Kodak is Starting to Click Again," *Business Week* (February 23, 1987), pp. 134-139.

32. Telephone discussion with personnel from the previous Office of Innovation, (January 10, 1994).

33. Joseph Guiltinan, "A Strategic Framework for Assessing Product Line Additions," *Journal of Product Innovation Management* (March 1993), pp. 136-147; Don Frey, "Learning the Ropes: My Life as a Product Champion," *Harvard Business Review* (September/October 1991), pp. 46-56.

34. Timothy M. Devinney, "New Products and Financial Risk Changes," *Journal of Product Innovation Management* (September 1992), pp. 222-231.

35. Zachary Schilles, "Numbers Don't Tell the Story," *Business Week* (June 6, 1988), p. 105.

36. Ibid.

37. Eileen Prescott, "An Agency's Turn to Madcap Ads," *New York Times*, Section 3—Business (June 7, 1987), pp. 1, 36.

38. Joseph P. Shapiro, "Why States Can Do What Uncle Can't," *Business Week* (December 28, 1987/January 4, 1988), pp. 35-38.

39. Ford S. Worthy, "Japan's Smart Secret Weapon," *Fortune* (August 12, 1991), pp. 71-75; Toshiro Hiromoto, "Another Hidden Edge—Japanese Management Accounting," *Harvard Business Review* (July/August 1988), pp. 22-26.

40. T. Michael Nevens, Gregory L. Summe, and Bro Uttal, "Commercializing Technology: What the Best Companies Do," *Harvard Business Review* (May-June 1990), p. 155; see also E. J. Kleinschmidt and R. G. Cooper, "The Impact of Product Innovativeness on Performance," *Journal of Product Innovation Management* (December 1991), pp. 240-251.

41. Gene Bylinsky, "Turning R&D Into Real Products," *Fortune* (June 2, 1990), p. 72.

42. Ibid., p. 73.

43. Ibid; Alan Deutschman, "How HP Continues to Grow and Grow," *Fortune* (May 2, 1994), pp. 90-100; Jonathan B. Levine, "Has Philips Found Its Wizard?" *Business Week* (September 6, 1993), pp. 82-84.

44. Most of this commentary is taken from Gene Bylinsky, op. cit., pp. 72-77; T. Michael Nevens, Gregory L. Summe, and Bro Uttal, loc. cit.; and Amal Kumar Naj, "Creative Energy—GE's Latest Invention: A Way to Move Ideas From Lab to

Market," *Wall Street Journal* (June 14, 1990), pp. A1, A9.

45. Gene Bylinsky, op. cit., p. 74.

46. Alan Deutschman, op. cit., p. 98.

47. Gene Bylinsky, "The New Look at America's Top Lab," *Fortune* (February 1, 1988), pp. 60-64.

48. Russell Mitchell, loc. cit.

49. Amal Kumar Naj, loc. cit.

50. Akira Okamoto, "Creative and Innovative Research at Ricoh," *Long Range Planning* (October 1991), p. 169.

51. Lisanne Renner, "Idea Bonuses—Pot of Gold at the End of a Brainstorm," *Orlando Sentinel* (September 2, 1985), p. C1.

52. Ibid.

53. D. S. Ramelli, III, and Clifton Cooksey, "How to Run a Suggestion Program," *Incentive* (October 1991), pp. 103-108, 218.

54. Michael Gates, "Managing Creativity," *Incentive* (September 1989), pp. 181-185.

55. Tricia Kelly, "Keep On Keeping On," *Quality Progress* (April 1993), pp. 19-22.

56. Peggy Stuart, "Fresh Ideas Energize Reward Programs," *Personnel Journal* (January 1992), pp. 102-103.

57. Steven E. Groffman, "American Airlines Employee Suggestion Program Takes Off," *Human Resources Professional* (Summer 1992), pp. 13-17.

58. Louanne Klein, "P G & E Awards $2 Million for Employees' Bright Ideas," *Human Resources Professional* (Spring 1991), pp. 20-25, 60.

59. Timothy L. Ross and Larry Hatcher, "Gainsharing Drives Quality Improvement," *Personnel Journal* (November 1992), pp. 81-89.

60. Regina Eisman, "Employee Motivation: Workers Iron Out Motivation," *Incentive* (June 1990), pp. 86-87.

61. Keith Beiser, "United Is Looking for a Few Good Ideas," *Telephony* (March 12, 1990), p. 68.

62. Akio Morita with Edwin M. Reingold and Mitsuko Shinomma, "Made in Japan," *Macmillan Executive Summary Program* (#1, 1987), p. 1.

63. Rolf C. Smith, Jr., and Raymond A. Slesinski, "Continuous Innovation," *Executive Excellence* (May 1991), pp. 13-14.

64. Geoffrey Brewer, "Ford," *Incentive* (February 1993), pp. 22-23.

CHAPTER 9

The management revolution means respecting, fostering, and optimizing a person's potential as a human. And creativity is the unique ability that makes us human... Every human being has a heart, and the most crucial test for management is whether it can inspire human hearts.

Tadahiro Sekimoto
President, NEC Corporation

A firm must not only have a strategy, create a structure, and operate systems, but must also employ the appropriate leadership style so that all of the Seven S's function in a coordinated way to achieve innovation. And, while everyone agrees that leadership is essential to achieving innovation, precisely what is meant by leadership is frequently debated. There are almost as many definitions of leadership as there are people using the term.[1] Most experts would agree, however, that leadership involves influencing others, and all would agree that a leader is a person who has followers. Most would also agree that leaders are followed because they take certain actions and behave in certain ways. **Leadership**, then, is the process of making choices about how to treat people in order to influence them and then translating those choices into actions.[2]

Management is typically viewed as the creative problem-solving process of planning, organizing, leading, and controlling the work of others to achieve an organization's objectives.[3] But managers are not necessarily leaders,[4] although it is usually expected that they will lead.[5] Thus, the leadership component of management requires special attention. Some organizations, such as GM, spend millions of dollars training their managers in leadership skills.[6] Moreover, as employees increasingly manage themselves, the role of the manager is becoming oriented more toward leadership and less toward administrative skills.[7] The administrative side of management is about coping with complexity; the leadership side is about coping with change.[8] As administrators, managers set objectives, make plans for reaching them, and allocate the necessary resources; they make it possible for their plans to be carried out by organizing and staffing; and they ensure that their plans are achieved by controlling and problem solving. As leaders, managers establish direction through vision, align people with that vision through communicating with and empowering those who can help achieve it, and motivate and inspire those individuals.[9]

Most successful managers *are* leaders. They have sound human relations skills and thus are able to influence others to carry out the work of the organization. If managers cannot become leaders, they soon find that work is not getting done. Some managers try to do all the work themselves, which is neither managing, nor leading.

Over the years, the study of leadership has focused on **small-group or transactional leadership,** which can be applied throughout the organization. More recently, it has focused on transformational leadership, which is found primarily at the upper levels of most organizations but should be present throughout the organization if total transformation is to occur. **Transformational leadership** involves transforming an organization from one major state or condition into another.[10] For example, when Lou Gerstner took over at IBM he was charged with transforming the firm from an overweight, punch-drunk fighter into a lean, mean fighting machine.[11] The quintessential transformationalist, of course, is Lee Iacocca, who rescued Chrysler from oblivion. It takes both sound small-group leadership skills and transformational skills to implement an innovation strategy successfully.

THE CHARACTERISTICS

This chapter discusses the basic issues of organizational leadership relative to achieving innovation. Innovation succeeds or fails through the manager's management/leadership style at all levels of the organization. **Management style** is the manager's consistent pattern of management over time. **Leadership style** is the leader's consistent pattern of leadership over time. The appropriate management and leadership styles should start at the top and descend the organizational hierarchy. Very specific leadership actions are necessary to result in innovation, but in general, the style described here would be appropriate for most organizations in the 1990s, not just for those focusing on innovation. Exhibit 9.1 lists the summary characteristics relative to leadership style that are found in innovative organizations.

EXHIBIT 9.1 CHARACTERISTICS OF INNOVATIVE ORGANIZATIONS RELATED TO LEADERSHIP STYLE

To what extent does your organization:

4. Create a vision/strategic intent.

11. Allow people to make mistakes.

18. Suspend judgment on new ideas.

25. Empower subordinates: delegate sufficient authority to allow people to be innovative.

32. Use a problem-solving management style.

39. Use transformational leadership.

46. Use special approaches in managing innovative personnel.

While much of this chapter describes how R&D managers, and managers in general, should manage creative personnel, the top R&D manager sets the tone for everything the firm does.

Innovate or Evaporate 9.1 examines the Netherlands' N. V. Philips' new top R&D manager's leadership style, and explains why Philips pursued him so doggedly.

4. Create a Vision/Strategic Intent.

As discussed in Chapter 5, vision establishes a general direction *and* the motivation to follow in that direction. (As used here, vision also encompasses strategic intent.) Typically, the best vision statements are one, two, or a few sentences long. "Quality is job one," not only describes what Ford Motor Company wanted but also motivated its employees to achieve high levels of product quality. Apple Computer's 1983 annual report describes the firm's vision as "to bring technology to individuals... We want to translate highly advanced technology into top-quality, affordable, and easy-to-use products. We are in essence tool builders for individuals... What we can and will do is to continue to innovate."[12] This vision statement reflected the thinking of Steven Jobs, one of the firm's co-founders and then chairman of the board. Jobs's vision guided the firm through its development of the Macintosh personal computer.

Creating an effective vision doesn't stop with a clever slogan or statement. It requires appropriate implementation efforts. The corporate vision must be conveyed to every employee by his or her manager. For many managers, who have not been asked to translate corporate vision into work group actions, this may entail learning a new skill. Each firm will develop its own style, and so will each individual manager. For example, the stated vision of Amgen, a biopharmaceutical firm based in Thousand Oaks, California, is "To be the world leader in developing and delivering important, cost effective therapeutics based on advances in cellular and molecular biology."[13] It inspires its employees to focus on how Amgen products affect people throughout the world. For example, one of the firm's products is Neupogen, a genetically engineered drug that helps prevent infections in cancer patients. On bulletin boards that employees pass each day, Amgen posts letters from grateful parents whose children used the drug and are now back in school. This helps create a sense of vision accomplished. Amgen also airlifted the first batch of Neupogen to its distributors (at a cost of $150,000) so that customers could have the product in a

CAN FRANK CARRUBBA LEAD PHILIPS TO THE PROMISED LAND?

When Dutch giant N. V. Philips lost $2.2 billion in 1990, Jan Timmer, its new CEO, saw that he had to take decisive action. Twice his head-hunters had contacted Frank Carrubba, widely believed to be the best R&D manager in the world, and twice they had been rebuffed. So in the summer of 1991 Timmer himself called Carrubba and offered him total control of every link in the product chain, from research to manufacturing. Such responsibility is rarely given to anyone, especially in a firm the size of Philips, which has forty diverse businesses with sales totaling $31 billion in 1992. When Carrubba left Hewlett-Packard, 72 percent of HP's sales came from products introduced in the past three years. At Philips, the rate was less than half that, and several new products had failed to meet expectations. Since Carrubba had a reputation for team management and knowing how to get the most out of people, he was charged with rallying the troops, a difficult task in a firm that was suffering losses and had eliminated 70,000 out of a total of 300,000 employees over a three year period.

Carrubba had to keep the firm's profits flowing by achieving successful applications research and at the same time cranking up the long-term innovation machine to ensure Philips's future. While Timmer was busy lowering costs, downsizing, and reengineering, Carrubba was putting together a system that

continued next page

PHILIPS

would secure Philips's future. Part of Carrubba's skill is based in his own attitudes about people. He comes across not as a brash, eat-'em-up manager that Europeans believe characterizes so many U.S. managers, but as very human. One senior Philips executive comments, "People love Carrubba—not like him, love him."

Carrubba believes in open communication and is known for the "town square" approach he used at Hewlett-Packard. Recalling the parks in Waterbury, Connecticut, where he grew up, he created a town square atmosphere in labs and lounges so researchers could help each other solve their problems. Joel S. Birnbaum, Carrubba's boss at HP, also praises his ability to spot winners. "He has a very good intuition for which technologies will, in the end, work out. He can survey the scene and pick out the winners," recalls Birnbaum.

Among the actions Carrubba has taken in his two years at Philips are the following:

1. When he found that there were barriers between R&D, product groups, and factories that prevented the right prducts from reaching the market, he created a five-year plan on a system that requires coordination among these functions. This approach, known as concurrent engineering, though widespread in the United States and Japan, is still relatively rare in Europe.

2. Because the firm had sold off several units and had downsized, critical software skills were lacking. Carrubba formed cross-divisional task forces to develop new products and businesses. He personally heads a task force to spread software knowhow throughout the firm. He also established a training and prototype center for ultracompact products in order to teach employees miniaturization skills.

3. A 30 percent cut in R&D staff left the firm short in several areas of research. Carrubba has therefore contracted with external sources such as MIT to perform the needed research.

4. Since internal R&D was fragmented, open in scope, and inefficient, Carruba established R&D milestones linked to corporate strategy.

few days rather than the two to three months most drug companies take to get products to market once they have gained FDA approval.[14] This gesture demonstrated to employees the firm's commitment to its vision.

Comparing U.S. Firms with Japanese and European Firms

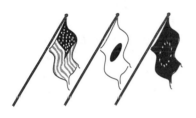

U.S. and European firms have only fairly recently begun to understand the contribution a shared vision can make to innovation. Throughout this book we have talked about how managers and employees in Japanese firms share information, how they share corporate goals and insist on consensus. To understand the bond between the Japanese professional/managerial employee and his or her firm, one need only look at the way employees are introduced to the firm: the employee swears allegiance to the firm and the firm swears allegiance to the employee in a ceremony that resembles an exchange of wedding vows.[15] Thus, the corporate vision is instilled in all employees from the beginning.

11. Allow People to Make Mistakes.

Apple Computer brought us the Apple II, the Macintosh, and the Power Macintosh. But it also brought us Apple III and Lisa, products that missed the mark, and Newton, a product whose sales have been disappointing. Ford has produced the Taurus, Sable, Continental, and Thunderbird, successes all, but it also bombed with the Edsel. Disney has scored big hits with "The

Style

Chapter 9

Lion King," "Alladin," "Three Men and a Baby," and "Down and Out in Beverly Hills," but it has also produced less noble films like "My Father the Hero" and "Blank Check," and of course, Disney also brought us Euro Disney which continues to be a cash drain. If firms want innovation, they have to be willing to accept a certain number of mistakes. Not even highly productive innovators can be a 100 percent successful. Of course, stockholders get nervous when products fail, and rebellious if too many fail. We naturally want to have as few failures as possible, but inevitably some will occur. However, innovative firms recognize that people who strive to innovate should not be punished if their new products or new processes fail.[16]

At Johnson & Johnson, a mistake can be a badge of honor. CEO Jim Burke has encouraged risk taking, and that policy has kept the new products flowing. In the 1960s Burke himself failed with the first major product he tried to launch for the company, but he was subsequently responsible for many successes. Even when he failed, he was congratulated for taking a risk, a lesson he learned from then chairman General Robert Wood Johnson, a lesson he has never forgotten.[17] *Innovate or Evaporate 9.2* describes how AT&T coped with an apparent failure.

Comparing U.S. Firms with Japanese and European Firms

An important element in comparing U.S. firms with those in other nations is cultural differences. Japanese culture, for example, places great emphasis on saving face. Individuals are seldom admonished publicly. Groups shoulder much of the responsibility for what goes on in a firm. The team, not the individual, succeeds or fails.

18. Suspend Judgment on New Ideas.

Managers in most successful firms are willing to wait a long time and through numerous failures before a breakthrough occurs, as long as the effort looks promising. They also allow individual initiatives to continue. At GE in the late 1970s, for example, researchers constantly hit roadblocks in developing a substitute for Xenon gas for use in X-ray machines. In 1980

BELL LABS: RESEARCH FOR FUN AND PROFIT

For twelve years, physicist Linn F. Mollenauer had been trying to develop "perfect" light pulses for sending messages by under sea cable. But in 1988 lab director and Nobel Laureate Arno Penzias ordered Mollenaur to give up and devote his research efforts to something else. Furious and defiant, Mollenauer continued, knowing that he was close to a breakthrough. His persistence eventually paid off. In 1990 he sent his special pulses 6000 miles through a cable without regeneration, ten times the commercial distance record.

Penzias later admitted that he had made a mistake in ordering Mollenauer to stop, apologized to him, and in a talk to the lab's top researchers, praised him for his persistence. In another firm Mollenauer's rebellion might have been crushed, but AT&T allowed the research to continue even after twelve years and many dead ends, showing that it understands that research takes time and mistakes will often be made.

But at AT&T, as at most other major firms, the price of R&D continues to climb and mere genius is no longer enough. Research efforts must pay off more quickly with innovations that lead to successful products. "The costs of R&D keep going up,"

continued next page **247**

INNOVATE OR EVAPORATE 9.2

BELL LABS

says Jan H. Suwinski, head of Corning Inc.'s Opto-Electronics Group. "Every company is trying to improve its hit rate [and] one of the hardest things is figuring out what [research] to stop." Charles V. Shank, director of Lawrence Berkeley Laboratories (who once supervised Mollenauer at Bell Labs), observes that pressures to innovate "will mean that work like Mollenauer did may never be done again at Bell Labs."

Penzias responds: "My motto is research for fun and profit. If you just have fun you doom the organization to irrelevance... and who'd want to work here?" He goes on to say, "We allocate our resources as best we can. Occasionally I allow researchers to overrule me when I'm wrong and people in the organization convince me my call wasn't right."

Source: John J. Keller, "R&D Hardball: Defying Boss's Orders Pays Off for Physicist and His Firm, AT&T," *Wall Street Journal* (June 25, 1991), pp. A1, A13.

---

they gave up. But physicist Dominic Cusano did not. He was allowed to transfer to another department, where he continued his research. He joined forces with Charles Greskovich, another researcher, and after three more years of hard work, the pair eventually found the substitute. By 1990 their product was adding $100 million a year to GE's revenues.[18]

Similarly, Honda began its research on lean-burn engine technology in 1984. Not until 1991 did the research bear fruit with the revolutionary engine introduced in the company's 1992 Civic model. The new technology improved gas mileage by 35 percent, to over 55 miles per gallon.[19]

Wayne Sanders, CEO of Kimberly-Clark, had faith in a secret project called Omega. Despite the fact that the company had to take a $12 million write off on the project, Sanders, then head of the diaper business, told scientists to keep working. Eventually researchers found the secret they sought, and Huggies Pull-Ups were born. This popular product has high margins and low costs, thus serving as a major cash cow. Sanders's patience paid off, both for him and for the company.[20]

Comparing U.S. Firms with Japanese and European Firms

Besides allowing sufficient time for ideas to germinate, there is another issue to consider: the desirability of suspending judgment. One of the most common problems in product development is that, by the time a product finally reaches the market, it often bears little resemblance to the original idea. At every stage of development people try to make changes. To avoid such meddling, Japanese managers and researchers spend more time up front reaching consensus on the product's characteristics; then they stick to the specifications that have been established. A study, by the consulting firm A. T. Kearney, showed that because they spend more time planning products, Japanese firms experience far fewer interruptions during development and fewer problems after launch than do U.S. firms. Chrysler is one U.S. firm that has adopted this approach to planning.[21]

25. Empower Subordinates: Delegate Sufficient Authority to Allow People to Be Innovative.[22]

A participative organizational climate is not absolutely necessary, but it is highly desirable. Ignoring the front line often causes problems, as managers at LOTUS Development Corporation discovered. The company suffered a series of software development delays and profit squeezes because marketers made product decisions without involving front-line programmers. Frank King, then senior vice-president of the company's Software Products Group, changed the approach to product development, making it more participative. As a result of the change, the development process was speeded up and better products were created.[23] Today, cross-functional teams dominate Lotus' product development process.[24]

At the furthest extreme of participation is **empowerment**, by which we mean giving employees the greatest possible amount of power to do their jobs.[25] The more employees are empowered, the more likely they are to innovate and take the initiative to solve their problems. A study of product development managers conducted by the manufacturers' Alliance for Productivity and Innovation and the Wyatt Company, a consulting firm, revealed that empowerment leads to the perception of a more innovative organizational culture.[26] Researchers surveyed firms to determine the effects of empowerment on product and/or service improvements. They found that organizations that empower employees in total quality management programs are twice as likely as other firms to report significant improvements in products or services.[27]

Eaton Corporation, despite flat sales, has increased productivity by increasing the level of innovation occurring on the front line. It has accomplished this largely by empowering employee teams.[28] At Microsoft, employees are expected to ask questions and make decisions.[29] At AT&T, employees have been directed to participate and have been empowered to do so. To enable the company to respond quickly to changing market situations, CEO Robert Allen has changed AT&T's structure making it more organic and has incorporated empowerment into the company's culture.[30]

Perstorp AB is a Swedish specialty chemicals manufacturer whose intrapreneurial approach to managing a large number of small, diverse, high-tech businesses has made it extremely successful financially and productively in terms of innovations. (*See Innovate or Evaporate 7.2.*) President Karl-Erick Sahlberg attributes much of the success of these businesses to the delegation of authority to their top managers, who may do what is necessary to compete effectively in their respective markets.[31]

Beech Aircraft Corporation, faced with a declining market and increasing competition, restructured, eliminating numerous positions. The remaining employees were given considerable authority to improve processes and create product enhancements. In short, Beech tapped its employees' inherent creativity by giving them the authority to be creative.[32]

An important step taken by Jack Welch, CEO of GE, has been to change GE's culture at all levels so that subordinates are empowered. He feels that this is vital to the corporation's success.[33] Similarly, Hewlett-Packard managers are given substantial amounts of power, which they pass along to their subordinates.[34] *Innovate or Evaporate 4.1* describes HP's approach. *Innovate or Evaporate 9.3* describes how one CEO attempted to

SAMSUNG GROUP SEEKS MORE INNOVATION

Lee Kun-Hee, chairman of Korea's Samsung Group, is proud of his firm's sales of $54 billion a year, but he also wants Samsung to become a nimble global competitor. Believing that it has to achieve greater innovation and quality, he is grafting many Western management ideas onto the firm's Confucian-based hierarchy. His actions, dubbed the Second Foundation, constitute a remarkable change in organizational design, culture, and leadership style. Lee wants Samsung to become one of the world's ten largest technological powerhouses as well as the world's fifth-largest electronics firm, by the turn of the century. Only if the Second Foundation succeeds will the firm achieve those goals. Some observers feel that all of South Korea's competitiveness may be at stake, as other Korean firms will either emulate Samsung's successes or avoid its failures.

Samsung Group already boasts Korea's most industrious and able management teams, but the Confucian organizational culture perpetuates an authoritarian management style that often stifles creativity and innovation. Lee wants to change that style by delegating more authority, encouraging more risk taking, rewarding innovation, transforming the organization. In effect, he wants to turn the hierarchy upside down, abandoning the inward-looking approach to management established by his late father, Lee Byung-Chull. "I am telling them to change everything except how they treat their families," says the 51-year-old chairman.

continued next page

SAMSUNG

Recognizing that change begins at the top and that he himself had to set the example, Lee slowly began delegating authority to his subordinates. To force managers to make decisions, he often worked at his guest home, refusing to take their calls or accept their visits. Still they resisted the changes. In 1993 Lee took his entire top management group to Los Angeles to show them how customers ignored Samsung's products. Still there was little change. Later that year on a flight to Frankfurt, Germany, a trusted Japanese consultant reported that the Samsung Design Center was being poorly run and no one at the lab seemed to care about changing it. The normally mild-mannered Lee hit the ceiling. He called Seoul and in a taped conversation, yelled at his senior executives for an hour. He then ordered copies of the tape distributed to all top managers. Shortly thereafter he issued what came to be known as his Frankfurt Declaration: "Quality first, no matter what." He summoned hundreds of managers in groups of twenty to forty to Frankfurt for round-the-clock meetings. Eventually, all of the company's top managers went through sessions with him. Lee used the opportunity to demonstrate the poor market response to the company's products, but he spent most of the time discussing competiveness, marketing, quality, and training. Lee also imposed numerous changes on the firm, such as dramatically changing work hours.

His message is that everyone in the firm must learn things that may be alien to its culture: otherwise Samsung is doomed to failure. He expects results, but he knows they'll be slow in coming. He is determined to make his firm more innovative and quality oriented in order to make it more competitive, but he recognizes that not all of his top managers will be able to handle change well. He expects that 5 percent will leave the company; 25 to 30 percent will have reduced responsibilities; and only 5 to 10 percent will receive increased responsibility.

Sources: Lakmi Nakarmi and Robert Neff, "Samsung's Radical Shakeup," *Business Week* (February 28, 1994), pp. 74-76; Ed Paisley, "Management: Innovate, not Imitate," *Far Eastern Economic Review* (May 13, 1993), pp. 64-68.

increase the level of participation in his corporation. Note how a corporate culture, enmeshed in a different set of cultural factors from those encountered in the United States, responds to the need to be innovative on a global basis.

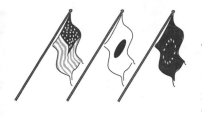

Comparing U.S. Firms with Japanese and European Firms

U.S. management style tends to focus on tasks, whereas Japanese management style focuses on people. An advantage of the Japanese style is that by encouraging participation the firm makes better use of its employees' collective capabilities. Moreover, empowerment keeps people motivated. The typical U.S. management style does little to utilize employee capabilities and motivation. On the other hand, Japanese management style slows the rate of development of managers who have strong skills in leadership or entrepreneurship. Future success will depend on merging Japanese and U.S. styles, so that leaders who are task oriented and provide innovative results and who have an entrepreneurial presence will also motivate and use everyone's capabilities [35] Most leading innovative firms in the United States have a participative culture and empower their employees to be creative.

32. Use a Problem-Solving Management Style.

Managers in innovative firms focus on problem solving. One of the worst things a manager can do is to harangue subordinates about failure. Good managers don't try to place blame; they want to solve problems and build trust. During the 1980s, for example, Frito-Lay gave all its managers training in creative problem solving so that they could work with their employees to find creative solutions to problems. The company estimates that over seven years the training paid off to the tune of $400 million.[36] Xerox has trained all of its employees in problem-solving techniques, and the results have been phenomenal.[37] Participation plays a major role in the problem-solving style, which requires that managers work jointly with subordinates to solve problems. In an organization whose managers favor empowerment, even more problem-solving authority is given to employees.

Comparing U.S. Firms with Japanese and European Firms

In the United States and much of Europe, managers assign blame. The philosophy of Japanese managers is "Fix the problem, not the blame."[38] In fact, in most Japanese firms finding problems is considered everyone's responsibility. When an employee joins a firm, he or she is taught that finding problems and making suggestions about how to solve them is part of the job. Employees are expected to help implement these solutions. In Japanese firms, unlike most U.S. and European firms, employees are taught how to solve problems. Finally, in Japan employees are always rewarded for solving problems, even if the reward is a small one.[39]

39. Use Transformational Leadership.

For proper management of innovation and creative human resources, a transformational leadership style is necessary. For example, successful idea champions exhibit transformational leadership characteristics.[40] The most common type of leadership activity is transactional. Leadership researcher Bernard Bass notes that transactional leaders "consider how to marginally improve and maintain the quantity and quality of performance, how to substitute one goal for another, how to reduce resistance to particular actions, and how to implement decisions."[41] This is typical of small-group leadership. However, Bass also notes that transformational leaders, "attempt and succeed in raising colleagues, subordinates, followers, clients, or constituencies to a greater awareness about the issues of consequence. This heightening of awareness requires a leader with vision, self-confidence, and inner strength to argue successfully for what he [or she] sees as right or good, not for what is popular or acceptable according to established norms."[42]

Bass notes that charisma is an important part of transformational leadership. He identifies Lee Iacocca as the premier example of a transformational leader with vision and charisma. He also argues that transformational leadership can occur not only at the top but throughout the organization, giving the example of a sergeant who transforms troops into extremely loyal followers.[43]

Innovate or Evaporate 9.4 describes how one top manager transformed his business through innovation.

TRANSFORMING THE ROGER SMITH HOTEL

When artist James Knowles took over the management of the Roger Smith Hotel in New York City in 1988, he was faced with a declining occupancy rate in a hotel that didn't really differentiate itself from others. Putting his artistic perspective to work, Knowles aimed to turn the Roger Smith into a work of art and a center for creative living that would also be a commercial success. His first actions were directed at changing the attitudes of the hotel's staff.

He began by creating a series of brightly colored flags to adorn the front of the hotel. Intended as a metaphor for the way Knowles wanted employees to think about the hotel, the flags' designs were positive, open, and friendly. This approach proved so successful that Knowles began designing new flags every few months so that new values could be integrated into the hotel's culture. The designs also appeared on the hotel's calling cards and on the back of workers' uniform shirts.

Knowles also created two life-size sculptures for the hotel entrance and placed several more throughout the hotel. He installed bronze relief panels in the lobby and on the front of the hotel, further enlivening its appearance. Architect Peter Woerner was hired to oversee the rest of the renovation of the hotel, and Steven Quinn was brought in to oversee the day-to-day operations. Knowles urged both men to set aside any preconceptions and view their work as a creative activity.

Knowles also initiated numerous art programs in the hotel. The Aurora Series features poetry reading, storytelling, plays, and musical performances. Media slumber parties with special en-

continued next page

INNOVATE OR EVAPORATE 9.4

46. Use Special Approaches in Managing Innovative Personnel.

Innovative companies recognize that very innovative personnel have to be treated differently from most other employees. Bernard L. Rosenbaum, president of Mohr Development Inc., reporting on an analysis of 300 technical managers from 19 different technology-based firms, lists five actions identified by those managers as necessary to manage creative personnel properly.[44] They are as follows:

1. Through coaching, the manager must align organizational and individual objectives and must also identify and solve performance problems.

2. Managers must run interference for creative employees, keeping other managers, especially upper management, from interfering with their efforts or sidetracking them.

3. Managers must orchestrate the professional development of these employees.

4. Teamwork should be used to increase productivity.

5. Managers need to encourage self-management by sharing information, delegating meaningful tasks, and encouraging upward communication.

Innovative employees require a degree of freedom that is not normally granted. They must be left alone to conduct their research. Merck & Company, voted the nation's most admired and best-managed corporation by top managers of U.S. firms for eight straight years, understood how to manage innovative people.[45] It gave them a degree of freedom that was unparalleled in U.S. industry. Edward M. Scolnick, Merck's head of research and development and a leading molecular biologist stated: "We tell people to control their own destiny. If you have bright, highly motivated people who feel responsible for their work, they will discover great things."[46] It should also be noted that Merck invested more heavily in R&D than did its competitors.

Unfortunately, the R&D well seems to be drying up at Merck. As is true for most pharmaceutical companies, its sales and profits are depressed as a result of the spread of managed health care programs. Critics claim, however, that Merck's problems are more fundamental: there aren't enough new products in the pipeline. Apparently Merck's bureaucratic structure slows the pace of new-product development. By the time a new product is approved, more flexible rivals have already introduced it to the market. Critics also contend that this lack of speed and the accompanying reduction in autonomy have caused many Merck researchers to seek jobs at other firms, further compounding the problem.[47]

Managers must recognize that it might take a while for results to become visible. For example, researchers at General Electric's plastics division toiled for more than a decade to develop Ultem, a heat-resistant plastic that can be used in everything from circuit boards to auto parts. They did so without either seeking or receiving the approval of corporate headquarters. They even built a $1 million plant to produce samples of the product before getting the go-ahead from headquarters. It paid off: sales of Ultem were estimated at $100 million in 1990.[48]

Most innovative companies also provide their researchers, scientists, and other innovative personnel with dual career ladders—a choice between the traditional management ladder and a separate ladder of laboratory-related titles, such as senior research associate or master researcher.[49]

Gary Day, former vice-chairman of the worldwide ad agency McCann-Erikson, comments, "Once you have done the editing on your people's effort you must back them totally. On the day of the presentation you must never move away from them and say I agree with you [the client], I didn't like it either."[50]

People are much more likely to perform well on a task that they believe they can do well. Research on ways of increasing creativity reveals that managers who enhance subordinates' confidence in their own creative ability are rewarded with higher levels of creative performance.[51]

Innovate or Evaporate 9.5 provides an additional insight into the appropriate leadership style for managing innovative people. As stated in Chapters 5 and 6, innovation often occurs in at least two ways—big bang and continuous improvement. The experience of Stranco, an innovative firm in the chlorination industry, suggests that the firms that practice these two types of innovation differ in certain ways and that each type requires different leadership style.

Fortune writer Alan Farnham interviewed numerous authorities on innovation and concluded that six simple rules, summarized in Exhibit 9.2, show how innovative people should be managed. Although they overlap with several of the Seven S's, it is worthwhile to review them here.

EXHIBIT 9.2 SIX RULES FOR MANAGING INNOVATIVE PEOPLE

Accommodate:

Creative individuals may require a greater personal investment, but the results justify the costs. Some are difficult to get along with, but if they are productive, don't make them do the budgets, or the progress reports if they don't want to.

Remember that creative people can't always control when ideas come to them. Microsoft software designer Sean Selitrennikoff says that he has only one complaint about being an idea person: You never know when ideas are coming. They pop up uninvited at night or while you're doing something else. So give creative people the chance to choose when they work and when they play.

Learn to listen to innovative people intently, be responsive, and never laugh at an idea. If there's room for only one ego in a conversation or meeting, let it be theirs.

Tolerate failure. Never punish mistakes, even in the slighest way.

STRANCO: INCREMENTAL VERSUS RADICAL INNOVATION

Stranco Incorporated was founded in 1970 to manufacture products for water chlorination. Its products incorporate new technologies created for this market by founder Frank Strand. To speed new-product development and growth, Strand encourages two types of innovative thinking: original thinking or radical innovation, and systematic creative thinking or incremental innovation. Major breakthroughs come from the original thinkers, while ongoing improvements come from the creative thinkers. The following table compares the two types of thinking.

Original Versus Creative Thinkers

Original	Creative
• More right-brained	• More left-brained
• Approach problems from new angles	• Systematic approach to problems
• Tend to be loners	• More sociable, competative
• Operate in messy environments	• Love results, progress, feedback
• Eccentric, extreme mood swings	• Neater, more methodical
• Well-developed sense of humor	• More stable personality

INNOVATE OR EVAPORATE 9.5

continued next page

STRANCO

Stranco has discovered that each type of thinking requires a distinct management style to make it most effective. Stanco's radical thinkers need a free rein. They don't like budgets or deadlines; they work best in a trusting, respecting environment. Conversely, the incremental thinkers respond to assignments and follow-ups. These employees can be managed through weekly technical meetings, problem definition, and milestone reviews. The following table compares the characteristics of the management style that Stranco has found to be best for each type of thinking.

Managing Radical and Incremental Thinkers

Radical	Incremental
• Stimulate through challenges and puzzles	• Set systematic goals and deadlines
• Remove budgetary and deadline constraints when possible	• Stimulate through competitive pressures
• Encourage technical education and exposure to customers	• Encourage technical education and exposure to customers
• Allow technical sharing and brainstorming sessions	• Hold weekly meetings that include key management and marketing staff
• Give personal attention - develop relationships of trust	• Delegate more responsibility
• Encourage praise from outside parties	• Set clear financial rewards for meeting goals and deadlines
• Have flexible funds for opportunities that arise	
• Reward with freedom and capital for new projects and interests	

Source: Harry S. Dent, Jr., "Growth Through New Product Development," *Small Business Reports* (November 1990), pp. 30-40.

EXHIBIT 9.2 CONT.

Stimulate:

Bring in artists, writers, and others who may stimulate creative thinking. Expose your people to new ideas.

Let innovative people create an office environment that makes them feel creative. Give them purple offices with eccentric (to you) furnishings, if that's what it takes.

Let creative people have their quiet times. John Cleese of Monty Python fame, who also produces training videos and Magnavox advertisements, says that one sure-fire way to stifle creativity is "to demand that people always be doing things."

Recognize and Reward—The Right Way:

The most powerful disincentive is a manager trying to monopolize the limelight or appropriate a creative person's ideas.

Positive incentives include contests; creative individuals enjoy recognition from their peers. Good execution of their ideas also helps.

Money is an incentive, but only if it is used correctly. Giving people room to create, giving them a challenge, and providing the autonomy they need to function are the strongest motivators. For example, Bob Christie, who developed Miracle Margarine for Kraft Foods, derives great pleasure from walking through a grocery store and seeing the impact of his work. Royalties, however, are becoming increasingly popular. They provide not only financial reward, but recognition of market impact.

Direct (Lightly) and Give Feedback:

Companies are a lot more focused on the applicability of products than they used to be. So it's necessary to review progress toward goals periodically. But this entails a delicate balance. Too much feedback upsets creative individuals.

Resources should be provided in the right amounts. In some instances resource deprivation can in fact actually stimulate creativity.

Protect Them:

You have to protect creative people from people who don't understand why they don't work normal hours, dress like everybody else, or clean up their desks every night before they go home.

Be Creative Yourself:

Each year about eighty executives participate in Hallmark's creative leadership course. They learn how to be creative and thus understand better what the firm's creative staff of 600 artists, designers, and writers must go through. For example, finance manager Ed Place was asked to create a new set of greeting cards during the course.

Source: Alan Farnham, "How to Nurture Creative Sparks," *Fortune* (January 10, 1994), pp. 94-100.

STRATEGIC AND OPERATIONAL PLANNING GUIDE

Style Question #	Where are we now? (Score)	Where do we want to be? (What are our objectives?)	
4. Create a vision for innovation			
11. Allow employees to make mistakes			
18. Suspend judgment on new ideas			
25. Empower subordinates to innovate			
32. Use a problem-solving management style			
39. Use transformational leadership			
46. Manage creative employees with special approaches			

How do we get there?		
What needs to be done?	**By whom?**	**By when?**

REFERENCES

1. Gary M. Yukl, *Leadership in Organizations*, 2nd. ed. (Englewood Cliffs, N.J.: Prentice-Hall, 1989), pp. 1-5.

2. James M. Higgins, *The Management Challenge: An Introduction to Management*, 2nd. ed. (New York: Macmillan Publishing Company, 1994), p. 8.

3. Ibid., p. 1.

4. Abraham Zaleznik, "Managers and Leaders: Are They Different?" *Harvard Business Review* (March-April 1990), pp. 126-135; Ted Levitt, "Command and Consent," *Harvard Business Review* (July-August 1988), p. 5; and John P. Kotter, *The Leadership Factor* (New York: Free Press, 1987).

5. John P. Kotter, "What Leaders Really Do," *Harvard Business Review* (May/June 1990), pp. 103-111.

6. Jack Falvey, "Before Spending $3 Million on Leadership, Read This," *Wall Street Journal* (October 3, 1988), p. A26.

7. Beverly Geber, "From Manager into Coach," *Training* (February 1992), pp. 25-31.

8. John P. Kotter, op. cit., p. 104.

9. Adapted from John P. Kotter, op. cit.

10. Noel M. Tichy and Mary Anne Devanna, *The Transformational Leader* (New York: Wiley, 1987).

11. Catherine Arnst, "Faith in a Stranger," *Business Week* (April 5, 1993), pp. 18-21.

12. Apple Computer Company, Inc., *Annual Report* (Cupertino, CA: Apple Computer Company, 1983), p. 2.

13. Discussion with Amgen Corporate Communications personnel May 23, 1994.

14. Brian Dumaine, "Closing the Innovation Gap," *Fortune* (December 2, 1991), p. 57.

15. *Challenge to America* with Hedrick Smith (Films for the Humanities & Sciences: Princeton, New Jersey, 1993)

16. Brian Dumaine, op. cit. p. 62.

17. Christopher Power, "At Johnson & Johnson, A Mistake Can Be A Badge of Honor," *Business Week* (September 26, 1988), pp. 126-128.

18. Amal Kumar Naj, "Creative Energy: GE's Latest Invention—A Way to Move Ideas From Lab to Market," *Wall Street Journal* (June 14, 1990), pp. A1, A9.

19. Karen Lowry Miller, "55 Miles Per Gallon: How Honda Did It," *Business Week* (September 23, 1991), pp. 82-83.

20. Alecia Swasy, "Kimberly-Clark, Bets, Wins on Innovation," *Wall Street Journal* (November 22, 1991), p. A5.

21. Brian Dumaine, op. cit., p. 62.

22. For a lengthy discussion on the empowerment of creative people, and in general, how to manage them, see Karl F. Gretz and Steven R. Drozdeck, *Empowering Innovative People* (Chicago: Probus Publishing Company, 1992).

23. Keith H. Hammonds, "Teaching Discipline to Six-Year-Old Lotus," *Business Week* (July 4, 1988), pp. 100-102.

24. Dawn Anfuso, "Soul-Searching Sustains Values at Lotus Development," *Personnel Journal* (June 1994), pp. 54-61.

25. Jay A. Conger, "Leadership: The Art of Empowering Others," *Academy of Management Executive* (February 1989), pp. 17-24.

26. Josef Frischer, "Empowering Management in New Product Development Units," *Journal of Product Innovation in Management* (November 1993), pp. 393-401.

27. "Companies Find That Quality Success Relies on Employee Empowerment," *Arizona Focus* (November 1993), p. 13.

28. Thomas F. O'Boyle, "Working Together: A Manufacturer Grows Efficient by Soliciting Ideas From Employees," *Wall Street Journal* (June 5, 1992), pp. A1, A4.

29. Alan Deutschman, "Bill Gates' Next Challenge," *Fortune* (December 28, 1992), pp. 30-41.

30. David Kirkpatrick, "Could AT&T Rule the World?" *Fortune* (May 17, 1993), pp. 54-66.

31. Jules Arbose, "How Perstorp Persuades Its Managers to Innovate," *International Management* (Europe Edition) (June 1987), pp. 41-47.

32. George D. Rodgers, "Strategic Planning and Sales Teams," *Journal of Business & Industrial Marketing* (Fall 1990), pp. 65-70.

33. Thomas A. Stewart, "GE Keeps Those Ideas Coming," *Fortune* (August 12, 1991), pp. 41-49.

34. Alan Deutschman, "How H-P Continues to Grow and Grow," *Fortune* (May 2, 1994), pp. 90-100.

35. Akira Totoki, "Management Style for Tomorrow's Needs," *Journal of Business Logistics* (#2, 1990), pp. 1-4.

36. Marc Hequet, "Creativity Training Gets Creative," *Training* (February 1992), p. 42; Bennett Davis, "Working the Imagination," *USAIR* (September 1988), pp. 18-27.

37. Ibid.

38. John E. Rehfeld, "What Working for a Japanese Company Taught Me," *Harvard Business Review* (November/December 1990), pp. 167-176.

39. Min Basadur, "Managing Creativity: A Japanese Model," *Academy of Management Executive* (May 1992), pp. 29-42.

40. Jane M. Howell, "Champions of Technological Innovation," *Administrative Science Quarterly* (June 1990), pp. 317-341.

41. Bernard M. Bass, "From Transactional to Transformational Leadership: Learning to Share the Vision," *Organizational Dynamics* (Winter 1990), pp. 19-31. Also see Bernard M. Bass, *Leadership and Performance Beyond Expectations* (New York: Free Press, 1985); and Bernard M. Bass, J. Avolio, and Laurie Goodheim, "Biography and the Assessment of Transformational Leadership at the World Class Level," *Journal of Management* (Spring 1987), pp. 7-19.

42. Ibid., p. 17.

43. Bernard M. Bass, "Leadership: Good, Better, Best," *Organizational Dynamics* (Winter 1985), pp. 26-40.

44. "The Art of Handling Technical Workers," *Electrical World* (February 1990), pp. 29-30.

45. Alan Farnham, "America's Most Admired Company," *Fortune* (Feburary 7, 1994), p. 50.

46. John A. Byrne, "The Miracle Company," *Business Week* (October 19, 1987), p. 90.

47. Joseph Weber, "Merck is Showing It's Age," *Business Week* (August 23, 1994), pp. 72-74.

48. Kenneth Labich, "The Innovators," *Fortune* (June 6, 1988), p. 52.

49. Walter Kitchell, III, "Managing Innovators," *Fortune* (March 4, 1985), p. 182.

50. Ibid.

51. Matthew R. Redmond, Michael D. Mumford, and Richard Teach, "Putting Creativity to Work: Effects of Leader Behavior on Subordinates," *Organizational Behavior and Human Decision Processes* (June 1993), pp. 120-151.

CHAPTER 10

Nobody manages creativity. People are what gets managed.

Horst Stormer
Director of Physical Research
Bell Labs

If you want to work magic, just remember that its real name is creativity. And creativity is PEOPLE.

Dennis F. Hightower
President of Disney Consumer
Products, Europe and the Middle East

We already know that successful companies use innovation strategies to create a strategic competitive advantage (that is, relatively high differentiation and/or relatively low cost). We have also recognized that other elements must be in place—structure, systems, and style. But it is people who make it happen. Thus, human resource management is essential to innovation.[1]

Staff, as used here, refers to organizational demographics. To be innovative, the firm must employ people with the right skills at the right place, at the right time.[2] This doesn't mean that only certain types of people should be hired, although for strictly R&D positions that may be necessary. Rather, it means that those who are hired must learn to behave in certain ways. They must learn to have ideas (and be allowed and encouraged to have them). They must be trained in creativity and innovation skills and must be able to get their ideas adopted by the organization.

Knowledge workers are the workers of the future.[3] Since intellectual capital will build tomorrow's industries, human resource management (HRM) practices must be directed at finding and developing knowledge workers. HRM practices, whether they are part of an individual manager's staffing activities or performed by the HRM department, are of two principal types: those concerned with placing the employee in the job and those concerned with the relationship between the job holder and the organization. Placement practices occur sequentially; the second type occur continuously.

In placing an employee, the company begins by developing a human resource strategy based on its corporate strategy. Job analysis and design follow. The firm then recruits, selects, orients, and trains and develops new personnel. Once employees are in place, the firm will simultaneously provide compensation and benefits, continue developing employees, provide for employee health and safety, manage employee relations, evaluate and control employees, and manage human resources in accordance with corporate strategy. Key issues include managing organizational culture, improving productivity and quality, managing personnel at locations throughout the world, and managing innovation.[4]

Several activities are essential for the proper management of innovation. Among them are: viewing human resources as a strategic weapon, recruiting the right people, providing the means to push an innovation through the company's evaluation system, training people to become creative, using techniques that can increase creativity, providing time for reflection, and providing physical facilities conducive to innovation.

THE CHARACTERISTICS

Exhibit 10.1 lists the characteristics of innovative firms in relation to staff.

EXHIBIT 10.1 CHARACTERISTICS OF INNOVATIVE
ORGANIZATIONS RELATED TO STAFF

To what extent does your organization:

5. Treat people as a vital resource for building a competitive advantage.

12. Recruit people who can generate ideas.

19. Have idea/innovation champions.

26. Train people to be creative.

33. Use creativity processes such as brainstorming, verbal checklists, mind mapping, storyboarding, and lotus blossom.

40. Encourage and provide time for reflection.

47. Provide physical facilities that are conducive to the exchange of ideas and creative thinking.

5. Treat People as a Vital Resource for Building a Competitive Advantage.

More than ever before, an organization's strategic success depends on its human resources,[5] especially with regard to innovation.[6] Improving productivity through product and process innovation depends not just on automation, computers, and robots but also on people. Yet never has the task of managing people been more difficult. The work force is more diverse than ever before, with expectations, needs, and demands that are very different from those of its predecessors. And as often as not, members of the work force come ill prepared to cope with rapidly changing technology and the pace of business life. Demographic studies suggest that at least half of the scientists and engineers needed in this country between now and the year 2000 will be foreign born.[7] Moreover, the need to turn companies into learning organizations demands a new view of human resources, their capabilities, and what can be done to improve them.

Comparing U.S. Firms with Japanese and European Firms

Japanese firms are ahead in their approach to people. This means that U.S. and European employers must make significant capital investments in human resources. They must learn to treat human resources as a vital source of competitive advantage, especially those involved in product and process innovation. These resources must first be acquired, then managed appropriately (see Chapter 9) and invested in continually to improve their capabilities. Few firms in the United States invest more heavily in their human resources than Motorola. *Innovate or Evaporate 10.1* reviews some of the ways in which Motorola is investing in its human resources.

12. Recruit People Who Can Generate Ideas.

Bell Labs recruits great thinkers, great idea people. So do 3M, Apple Computer, Intel, General Electric, Microsoft, Sony, Toshiba, Philips, Thomson SA, and others. *Innovate or Evaporate 10.2* discusses how Microsoft recruits idea people.

Sony's engineers are the most prolific innovators in the world. They turn out four new products a day, every day, every year—not an easy task in the highly competitive consumer electronics industry. How do they do it? For starters, Sony recruits generalists and manages them in such a way that they remain generalists. Sony looks for engineers who are *neyaka*—optimistic and open-minded, with a wide range of interests. And Sony encourages its employees to move around among product groups, both to broaden their interests and to bring a fresh eye to problems in other areas of the company. Sony's success can be attributed to much more than its recruitment policies, but it begins with them.[8] (See *Innovate or Evaporate 2.2*).

M. J. Kirton, director of the Occupation Research Center at Hatfield Polytech in St. Albens, Derbyshire, England, suggests that there are two basic types of creative people: adaptors and innovators. The adaptor is interested in change for the good of the organization; the innovator is more concerned with change for its own sake. In a typical organization each type needs the other. Innovators need adaptors to be able to get their ideas applied.[9]

MOTOROLA INVESTS IN ITS FUTURE

Recognizing the various strategic challenges it faces between now and the turn of the century, Motorola has decided that "the most crucial weapons will be responsiveness, adaptability, and creativity." To acquire these organizational skills, Motorola has initiated a lifelong-learning program for its employees. The program, established by former chairman Robert W. Galvin, is designed to provide training and development for every employee, from the shop floor to the top echelons.

The financial commitment to the program is significant, not only in terms of the cost of training and development, but also in terms of time lost from work. Motorola already gives every employee at least forty hours of training and development a year, spending an amount equal to 4 percent of sales a year on training and development. It expects to quadruple those levels by the year 2000. The expected cost is $600 million a year—about the cost of a new chip factory. CEO Gary L Tooker comments "If knowledge is becoming antiquated at a faster rate, we have no choice but to spend on education. How can that not be a competitive weapon?"

continued next page

MOTOROLA

Much of the company's willingness to invest in education comes from its past successes with training and development. Motorola University, headquartered in Schaumburg, Illinois, has fourteen branches in locations from Tokyo to Honolulu, and a budget of more than $120 million. Courses are designed by "instructional engineers" and cover such diverse topics as critical thinking and problem-solving management, robotics and computers, and remedial English. Courses are specifically designed for each geographic area so that cultural references are relevant. Motorola also works closely with its suppliers to train them in ways that benefit both parties—for example, by providing training in problem solving and total quality management.

One of the key areas for improvement in the future is innovation and the creativity that leads to it. Some of the corporate skills that have made Motorola a world-class competitor also make it rather inflexible and thus unable to innovate well. In particular, the degree of regimentation required if a firm is to be a high-quality, low-cost competitor tends to stifle innovation. Fortunately, Motorola has a culture that encourages conflict and leads to continual improvement. Moreover, Motorola's culture encourages the pursuit of neglected technologies and uses teams to help it innovate and anticipate change. It is among the top ten U.S. firms in absolute annual spending on R&D.

Motorola, now the global leader in cellular phones, pagers, two-way radios, and microchips (used to control devices other than computers), recognizes that to remain on top of tomorrow's business situation it needs to make some changes. It has already begun to develop in its employees the independent thinking that is vital to innovation. Yet much remains to be done.

Sources: Kevin Kelly and Peter Burrows, "Motorola: Training for the Millennium," *Business Week* (March 28, 1994), pp. 158-163; G. Christian Hill and Ken Yamada, "Staying Power: Motorola Illustrates How an Aged Giant Can Remain Vibrant," *Wall Street Journal* (December 9, 1992), pp. A1, A18.

HOW MICROSOFT RECRUITS

Bill Gates, founder, CEO, and chairman of Microsoft, describes how his firm hires the best creative talent:

"We try to look for a certain level of intelligence—that's key. Then, we take on each person's résumé. Usually, there is a project that they have worked on for a long time. We ask them questions about it. For example, if they worked on one piece of a project, did they understand the whole thing? Can they explain it? Can they draw a diagram? If they're just dull or say, 'I didn't work on that part,' or if you bring up something that's somewhat related and they can't reply to it—you can see their minds are not really that sharp after all.

About 90 percent of the people we hire are right out of college or graduate school. The amount of time we spend on recruiting is incredible. A lot of companies send nontechnical people to campuses. We don't, we send developers. They tell students what we're doing, ask them the tricky questions. Our personnel people set up the databases and are in charge of the other administrative work back here. But the heart of the recruiting is done by software developers themselves."

Source: Anne R. Field, "Managing Creative People," *Success* (October 1988), p. 87.

INNOVATE OR EVAPORATE 10.2

Roger VonOech, a noted creativity consultant, identifies four types of roles that successful creative people must fill. The first is the **explorer**, who seeks out situations and ideas. The second is the **artist**, who creates ideas. The third is the **judge**, who evaluates ideas, and the fourth is the **warrior**, who carries ideas to the rest of the organization to get them adopted.[10] The explorer and the artist are similar to Kirton's innovator; the judge and the warrior are similar to his adaptor. Clearly, the organization must provide not only a place for idea people to work but a way in which their ideas can be adopted by the organization. Systematic methods for rewarding ideas and encouraging creativity in the organization help do this. Normally, no one person performs all these functions in a large organization; typically there are several people who help innovators carry their ideas forward.

Comparing U.S. Firms with Japanese and European Firms

All employees in Japanese firms, to a much greater extent than employees in U.S. and European firms, are expected to be "idea people," at least in the area of continuous improvement in processes and products. Japanese systems for idea management are designed to elicit suggestions from all members of the organization rather than just a few.[11] Until recently, U.S. firms tended to put all their eggs in one basket—the R&D department. Today their approach is changing.

19. Have Idea/Innovation Champions.

It is not enough to have idea people; there must also be a group of idea/innovation champions who are willing to wade through the organization's bureaucracy to make ideas work and get them to market. An **idea champion** is someone who generates an idea, believes in it, and supports it as it overcomes the myriad obstacles it will face in progressing through the organization.[12] A champion is someone with the passion and/or power to drive the idea through the organization. Gifford Pinchot, best known for his writing and consulting in the area of intrapreneurship (see Chapter 7), surveyed 200 firms and found that while plenty of new product ideas were generated, few ever reached the market. He concluded that the primary reason for this lack of success was the absence of a champion. Pinchot comments that, "often there is no one person within the company willing to work to drive the idea through the inevitable corporate barriers."[13] Often an inventor is his or her own idea champion, as seen in *Innovate or Evaporate 10.3* .

A champion must have vision, persistence, enthusiasm, technical competence, analytical skill, persuasiveness, selling ability, motivation, and political astuteness.[14] Don Frey, who spent forty years making new products happen, first at Ford Motor Company and later as CEO of Bell & Howell, cautions champions that financial controllers are often unable to grasp the softer side of business—for example, the revolutionary implications of product innovation and the energizing power of a company's most talented employees.[15] That's one reason why the skills mentioned earlier are so important.

Sometimes a whole hierarchy of champions may exist. Above the idea person, a **sponsor**, a middle manager who recognizes the importance of the idea, will help fund and implement it. Above that, the **orchestrator**, an upper-level manager, will articulate the need for innovation, fund it, create incentives for sponsors, and protect people.[16] Amoco Chemicals Corporation, for example, fosters an innovative atmosphere and a tolerance for failure by using "connectors," people who assist the company's inventors in developing their ideas into reality.[17] The idea champion concept has been a major part of product development at many other firms as well.[18]

Comparing U.S. Firms with Japanese and European Firms

In Japan major ideas are moved forward through quality (or creativity) groups or with the aid of a sponsor. The supervisor usually acts as the champion of minor ideas although sometimes the worker may be his or her own champion.[19]

26. Train People to be Creative.

According to Tony Buzan, developer of the creativity technique called mind mapping, business executives spend 20 percent of their

Staff

Chapter 10

time solving problems and thinking creatively, yet over 90 percent of executives have no training in these areas.[20] Thus, training executives and other personnel in creativity and innovation is essential to an organization's success. Most creativity training programs focus on teaching the basic of creative problem solving (CPS) and the use of various creativity techniques such as brainstorming, mind mapping, storyboarding, metaphors, and excursion .[21]

Interest in creativity training has increased in recent years. A survey of firms with 100 or more employees shows that the proportion of such firms offering creativity training doubled in five years from 16 percent in 1985 to 32 percent in 1990. A survey of 2600 firms by the Conference Board showed that 32 percent offered creativity training in 1990, up from 22 percent a year earlier. There has also been a significant increase in the number of middle and top managers attending such programs.[22] A 1993 survey of 2500 U.S. firms with 100 or more employees conducted by *Training* magazine indicates that 42 percent offer at least some training in creativity.[23]

Norfolk Southern Railways may be the most innovative firm in its industry. Numerous innovations have come not only in service delivery and processes but in marketing and management as well. The image of the lone black stallion dominating his environment is an example of the company's innovative marketing program, which probably evolved from its "target innovation" program in which all the firm's managers attended a five-day program on creative problem-solving processes such as brainstorming and the excursion technique. Participants reported marked improvement in their ability to solve problems both individually and in groups. Additional benefits included increased openness in communication and more participation in problem solving.[24] (See *Innovate or Evaporate 2.3*.)

Many other examples can be cited. Over a period of twenty years, Xerox sent more than 100,000 of its employees through creativity training sessions at the Creative Education Foundation in Buffalo, New York. Frito-Lay also sent many of its employees to this and other programs. Frito executives estimate that from 1982 to 1988 the company saved over $400 million as a result of the problem-solving techniques learned, and used, by employees who had attended such programs.[25] Texas Utili-

ART FRY, CHAMPION OF POST-IT NOTES, AND BELL ATLANTIC'S CHAMPION PROGRAM

Post-It Notes can be found in almost any office in the United States today, and they are a $200 million a year success for 3M. But it wasn't easy getting them there. The idea originated with Art Fry, a 3M employee who used bits of paper to mark hymns when he sang in his church choir. These markers kept falling out of the hymn books. He decided that he needed an adhesive-backed paper that would stick as long as necessary but could be removed easily, and soon found what he wanted in the 3M laboratory.

Fry saw the market potential of his invention but others did not. Market survey results were negative; major office supply distributors were skeptical. Fry therefore began giving samples to 3M executives and their secretaries. Once they actually used the little notepads, they were hooked. Having sold 3M on the project, Fry used the same approach with other executives throughout the United States. He mailed samples to the secretaries and CEOs of Fortune 500 firms. They soon became hooked too. Twelve years after Fry conceived the idea, Post-It Notes has become a huge financial success. In this case Art Fry was not only the innovator of an idea but its champion as well.

continued next page

ART FRY

In contrast, Bell Atlantic's Champion Program was specifically designed to stimulate new ideas. Any employee who is judged to have a good idea is allowed to leave his or her job to turn the idea into a marketable product or service. The employee receives full pay and benefits, as well as training in skills such as writing a business plan, and organizing and scheduling a development project. Funding is provided as needed. The employee can invest up to 10 percent of his or her salary in the project and trade his or her bonus for up to 5 percent of the revenues generated by the product or service (subject to certain limits) if it is marketed. In two years the Champion Program has generated two patents, with eleven more pending.

Sources: Brian Dumaine, "Closing the Innovation Gap," *Fortune* (December 2, 1991), pp. 56-62; Thomas J. Peters and Nancy Austin, *A Passion for Excellence* (New York: Random House, 1985), p. 108.

ties trained its top 400 executives to use a variety of techniques and more recently began offering similar instruction to other employees. Corning has trained nearly 20,000 employees in several countries. Exxon has trained nearly 7,000 employees in its sales, exploration, and chemicals divisions since 1988.[26]

As part of its declared innovation strategy, Avco Financial Services trains its employees extensively in using multi-task Windows environments, encouraging them to use their knowledge to develop new work processes and even create new services. Most of the focus is on enabling employees to design their own techniques to improve work flows. As employees faced frequent interruptions and constant change it became apparent that a favorable PC environment was important to the firm's success. The company spent substantial sums to train employees in lifelike situations, showing them (rather than just telling them) how they could improve their jobs. The company encourages its employees to devise new ways of using their PCs as well. A substantial improvement in productivity has resulted.[27] *Innovate or Evaporate 10.4* describes how Bell Labs teaches people how to be more creative and innovative in a somewhat different way than most firms do.

HOW BELL LABS TURNS AVERAGE EMPLOYEES INTO STAR PERFORMERS

An oft-cited axiom about researchers is that the top 10 percent produce most of the results. Bell Labs decided to find out why. A team of consultants examined the behavior of the lab's top performers and compared them to that of average, less productive performers. They identified nine work strategies that made the top performers successful: taking initiative, networking, self-management, teamwork, effectiveness, leadership, followership, perspective, show-and-tell, and organizational savvy (see chart).

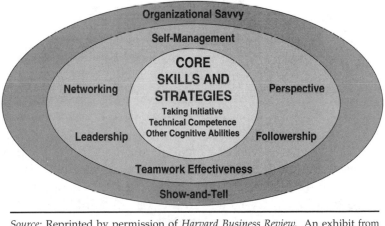

Source: Reprinted by permission of *Harvard Business Review.* An exhibit from "How Bell Labs Creates Star Performers," by Robert Kelley and Janet Caplan (July-August 1993), p. 131. Copyright © 1993 by the President and Fellows of Harvard College; all rights reserved.

INNOVATE OR EVAPORATE 10.4

continued next page

BELL LABS

The Nine Work Strategies

Taking initiative: accepting responsibility above and beyond your stated job, volunteering for additional activities, and promoting new ideas.

Networking: getting direct and immediate access to coworkers with technical expertise and sharing your own knowledge with those who need it.

Self-management: regulating your own work commitments, time, performance level, and career growth.

Teamwork effectiveness: assuming joint responsibility for work activities, coordinating efforts, and accomplishing shared goals with coworkers.

Leadership: formulating, stating, and building consensus on common goals and working to accomplish them.

Followership: helping the leader accomplish the organization's goals and thinking for yourself rather than relying solely on managerial direction.

Perspective: seeing your job in its larger context and taking on other viewpoints such as those of the customer, manager, and work team.

Show-and-tell: presenting your ideas persuasively in written or oral form.

Organization savvy: navigating the competing interests in an organization, be they individual or group, to promote cooperation, address conflicts, and get things done.

Of these nine strategies, taking initiative was viewed as the most important. Six other skills—self-management, perspective, followership, teamwork effectiveness, leadership, and networking—were next in importance. Organization savvy and show-and-tell were considered icing on the cake.

Source: Robert Kelly and Janet Caplan, "How Bell Labs Creates Star Performers," *Harvard Business Review* (July-August 1993), pp. 128-139.

Comparing U.S. Firms with Japanese and European Firms

While U.S. firms are currently increasing their investment in programs to develop innovation skills in their employees, many European firms have been doing so for years. This is especially true of Scandinavian, German, and British-based firms. Japanese firms have also trained their employees in basic processes such as brainstorming. Now they are using cultural change training to try to get employees to think more freely and creatively. Typical of such training is the approach in *Innovate or Evaporate 10.5*. Notice how Shiseido built on its Far Eastern culture to accomplish its goals.

INNOVATE
OR
EVAPORATE

PART II

SHISEIDO MEDITATES FOR CREATIVITY

At the heart and soul of Japanese organizations is their consensus approach to management. It works well when they are pursuing continuous improvement in processes and products, but not so well when it comes to creating new products, markets, and whole new businesses—activities that will be vital to corporate success in the twenty-first century. Thus, Japanese organizations are attempting to make their cultures more receptive to bold new ideas. A few, such as Hitachi (See *Innovate or Evaporate 1.1*) and Sony (see *Innovate or Evaporate 2.2*), have always been receptive to new ideas; but most have not.

Japanese firms are trying different approaches to develop creativity. Omron Corporation, a manufacturer of electronic controls, holds a monthly *juku*, or cram school. In a process is designed to stimulate creativity, middle-level managers take on various roles, such as a nineteenth-century warlord, Formula One race-car driver, or private detective. They then tackle problems, thinking and planning as one would in those roles.

At Fuji Film, senior managers are asked to study offbeat subjects such as the history of Venice or the sociology of apes. Useful insights into business problems may occur as a consequence of the new perspectives gained in this manner. Similarly, employees at Shimizu Corporation, Japan's largest construction firm, spend several days each year at company retreats, playing games that force them to tackle "impossible" problems such as getting back from the moon in a damaged spacecraft.

Shiseido, Japan's largest cosmetics maker, recently undertook a series of four-day seminars at resorts on the snowy shoulders of Mount Fuji. It was an ambitious attempt to use philosophical

continued next page

INNOVATE OR EVAPORATE 10.5

SHISEIDO

introspection to change corporate culture. The seminars were undertaken despite the company's continued financial success during a period of recession. The firm's president, Yoshiharu Fukuhara, expressed his concern this way: "Our company cannot be like a military troop where the president gives an order and then everyone rushes to do it. Companies like that will not survive in the next era." His aim is to create a company in which individuals set their own goals and find ways to achieve them. This is a revolutionary approach for a Japanese firm.

The four seminars were titled "Time and Space," "Expression and Language," "Body and Soul," and "Beauty and Truth." They consisted of a mixture of lecture, discussion, self-disclosure, introspection, and exercises. For example, "Body and Soul" began with a lecture on the words "human being." It was presented by Seigo Matsuoka, an independent consultant who viewed his role as one of bridging the worlds of technology, business, and culture. Next there was an open discussion of progress toward solving personal problems that had been revealed at the previous seminar. This process was not easy for men who had spent their entire lives stifling their personal feelings for the good of the company. The next day, discussions of personal vulnerability continued, followed by a lecture on the organization as a living system, delivered by Hiroski Shimizu, a professor of pharmacy at Tokyo University. In the evening the group studied goldfish in a bowl and drew parallels to the firm in its environment. On day three President Fukuhara addressed the group. After showing a video of his favorite Kabuki actor and a film of an economist talking about the intricacies of corporate culture, he disclosed some of his own vulnerabilities and presented his philosophy for the company.

After lunch the participants listed the physical quirks of other members of the group. These were then discussed in a session led by Seiko Ito, a psychologist. Then body language became the focus of the discussion. Three men were asked to act like Americans. They did so by moving about in an exaggerated fashion, flailing their arms. Another leader provided exercises related to body and motion. For example, participants were asked to balance an egg on end (About half succeeded in doing so.)

SHISEIDO

The fourth day began just before dawn with a meditation led by Zen master Ryomin Akizuki. Reflective discussion followed. After lunch the group was asked by consultant Matsuoka to summarize what they had learned. Most acknowledged that they had achieved a different perspective, but it was hard for them to list any actions they would take to make specific changes in their lives.

This firm's experience is typical of that of many firms, in the United States and Europe as well as the Pacific Rim, in introducing more creativity into their cultures. The process often involves trial and error when you approach it from a philosophical perspective. Shiseido's program may not work elsewhere— different approaches have to be used in different cultures. As a human resources manager at Fuji Film puts it, "You can't just tell your employees, 'Be creative.'" Firms have to create an environment that is conducive to greater individualism, something that most haven't done in the past.

Source: Emily Thornton, "Japan's Struggle to Be Creative," *Fortune* (April 19, 1993), pp. 129-134.

33. Use Creativity Processes Such as Brainstorming, Verbal Checklists, Mind Mapping, Storyboarding, and Lotus Blossom.

"Employing creative people is necessary in today's competitive world, but absolutely not sufficient," says Sheldon Buckler, vice chairman of Polaroid. "You also need an environment that values and encourages what employees do, and they need tools to help them to keep renewing creativity. That is what creativity techniques do."[28]

There are more than 100 creativity techniques that can be used in CPS. I have described them in *101 Creative Problem Solving Techniques: The Handbook of New Ideas for Business*.[29] There are four primary types of creativity techniques: **fluency techniques**, which help stimulate the generation of ideas; **excursion techniques**, which push the mind to grope for illumination; **pattern breakers**, which free thinkers to relate problems

Staff

Chapter 10

in novel ways; and **shake-up techniques**, which help wake up groups and make them more receptive to new and unusual ideas.[30] Few firms train employees in all of these techniques. Rather, they pick several that fit their needs and use these most of the time.

Frito-Lay, Xerox, Norfolk Southern Railways, Kodak, Corning, Exxon, and Mitsubishi are among the increasing number of firms that have trained their employees in creative processes and encourage their use. At Mazda's U.S. plant, for example, new hires receive extensive training in interpersonal relations, brainstorming, and quality control. They are expected to use these techniques in solving day-to-day problems.[31] Corning has trained 26,000 employees in these techniques and Exxon, 7,000.[32] At Frito-Lay, before its formal CPS program was abandoned in favor of an empowerment program, many of these techniques had become part of the everyday problem-solving process.[33]

DuPont trains all its employees in the use of five techniques: lateral thinking, metaphoric thinking, positive thinking, association trigger, and capturing and interpreting dreams.[34] Use of these techniques has been very profitable. For example, DuPont researchers were trying to figure out a way to dye Nomex fibers, which had proved to be impervious to dyes. Using the metaphor of a mine shaft, one researcher realized that timbers (metaphorically speaking) were needed to hold the fibers apart so that the dye could take effect. He then found a chemical agent that acted in much the same way that a timber would in a mine shaft—holding the hole open until dyes could take effect.[35]

Sometimes various groups of employees respond to certain processes better than others. For example, Amoco Chemical has found that its researchers prefer brainwriting (writing ideas on slips of paper for modification by others) over brainstorming because it helps cut down on self-censorship.[36]

General Motors has an automated brainwriting facility that uses networked PCs. Allstate Business Insurance, GE, and Bell Atlantic all use versions of storyboarding (a structured but flexible version of brainstorming used for complex problems).

Companies such as First Chicago Bank have used role playing, complete with customers, to stimulate new perspectives. Kodak even has a humor room stocked with games, creativity books, and Monty Python videos. Polaroid's creativity specialist, Suzanne Merritt, working with managers seeking better ways to mesh functional areas together, used paintings as idea triggers. Managers had to force-fit the problem to the pictures and see what ideas evolved. A picture of fish provided an insight into how difficult it was for researchers to talk to other people. The fish (researchers) couldn't talk to the birds (marketers) in the picture. As a result, members of various functional departments now meet periodically to learn how to talk to one another.[37]

Comparing U.S. Firms with Japanese and European Firms

Japanese firms have used creativity techniques much more extensively than their global counterparts. Much of this is due to the group problem-solving orientation predominant in Japan. In addition, collections of creativity techniques have been available for a longer time in Japan than in the United States.[38]

40. Encourage and Provide Time for Reflection.

Michele McCormick, a public relations consultant, says, "We're too busy for ideas." She notes that people need to take time to reflect.[39] Really good ideas often come when people have had time to reflect on what they are doing, when they have thought through a problem and have let their minds wander, rather than straining for a solution. Studies of the brain show that reflection tends to produce more ideas than rational problem solving. The left hemisphere becomes inactive and the more intuitive right hemisphere takes control. Quiet time, time for reflection, often helps increase levels of intuition and creativity.[40] At Hewlett-Packard and Texas Instruments, select groups of employees are expected to spend some time each day reflecting, thinking about how to improve the firm, and creating.[41] At 3M, certain employees are allowed to spend 15 percent of their time each week on anything they want, as long as it is related to new-product development.[42]

Staff

Chapter 10

47. Provide Physical Facilities That are Conducive to the Exchange of Ideas and Creative Thinking.

One of the goals set for the designers of GTE Telephone Operation's world headquarters in Irving, Texas, was to create a work environment that supported productivity, promoted creativity, and encouraged open communication. Expert observers say that the completed facility is unrivaled in terms of size, efficiency of design, construction techniques, and human design features.[43]

When he was director of HP Labs, Frank Carrubba created a neighborhood atmosphere at the labs to foster the exchange of information among employees. In the midst of office cubicles he created casual meeting areas furnished with easy chairs, tables, and desks. These areas serve as "neighborhood" gathering places for exchanging ideas.[44] In the center of Ricoh Corporation's R&D Center near Yokohama, Japan, an open area contains an eight-spoked "tree-of-imagination." The spokes are of various lengths and are shaped like split logs. Employees are free to come and go, mingle, discuss ideas and solve problems, while sitting at these log benches on log stools.[45]

Sometimes unusual facilities can provide unique opportunities for corporate innovation. When Nokia Group, a Finnish consumer electronics and telecommunications conglomerate, acquired Technophone Ltd., a British pioneer in digital cellular handsets, the engineers from the two firms' product-development groups didn't always see eye to eye. But the British engineers decided to "melt away" cultural differences; they followed the Finns into the saunas located near the R&D department. Informal brainstorming in the sauna led to many satisfactory solutions.[46] *Innovate or Evaporate 10.6* discusses the facilities of two competitors—Steelcase and Herman Miller.

An important means of accommodating creativity is the design and construction of groupware facilities, which incorporate multiple PCs or work stations and group problem-solving software enabling groups to use brainstorming and other techniques.[47]

STEELCASE AND HERMAN MILLER: PROVIDING FACILITIES THAT FACILITATE INNOVATION

Steelcase Company, the nation's largest maker of office furniture, has invested heavily in the concept of managing space for the purpose of improving innovation. Steelcase's new corporate development center just outside Grand Rapids, Michigan, is housed in a pyramid-shaped office structure rising 128 feet above the Michigan prairie. Long known for high-quality but boring office furniture, and seeking to compete more effectively with innovative rivals like Herman Miller and others, Steelcase decided to put more emphasis on innovation.

Architect Donald J. Koster didn't start out to design a pyramid, but he found that a pyramidal structure best suited Steelcase's desire for a light, airy, ethereal environment. The building has other features that are conducive to creativity, including one-person think-tank areas called caves, "neighborhoods" of people working on the same product lines, and a central atrium. "We're trying to get people to connect. We're trying to maximize the serendipitous," comments Wayne Veneklasen, an organizational psychologist at Steelcase.

continued next page

FACILITIES

Additional features include a 71-foot stainless-steel pendulum in the middle of the central atrium. The pendulum, which moves according to the movement of the sun, symbolizes the company's quest for change. Manager's offices look out on the atrium and the offices of their subordinates, instead of having panoramic outside views. The building was designed not to provide places for creativity but to *inspire* creativity.

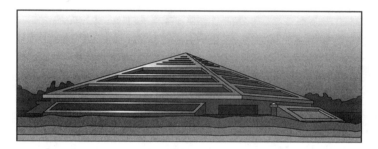

Herman Miller, Inc., one of the most innovative office furniture-design companies in the country, seeks to elicit creativity in its employees by eliminating stress and inconveniences from their daily work routine so that they can concentrate on being creative. Several techniques are used to achieve this goal:

1. Providing informal meeting places. Scattered throughout Herman Miller's buildings are niches and alcoves with chairs and sofas. These give people a place to sit and chat.

2. Locating the research department away from the main office. This lets new-product pioneers develop plans without the pressures often imposed by marketing and advertising departments.

3. Letting employees design their own offices. Different people need different work places. When employees are involved in the layout and furnishing of their offices they are more comfortable—and more creative.

FACILITIES

Max DuPree, chairman and CEO of Herman Miller, advises: "If you want the best things to happen in corporate life, you have to find ways to be hospitable to the unusual person. You don't get innovation as a democratic process. You almost get it as an anti-democratic process. Certainly you get it as an antithetical process, so you have to have an environment where the body of people are really amenable to change and can deal with the conflicts that arise out of change and innovation."

Sources: Joani Nelson-Horchler, "The Magic of Herman Miller," *Industry Week* (February 18, 1991), pp. 11-17; Gregory Witcher, "Steelcase Hopes Innovation Flourishes Under Pyramid," *Wall Street Journal* (May 26, 1989), p. B1; George Melloan, "Herman Miller's Secrets of Corporate Creativity," *Wall Street Journal* (May 3, 1988), p. 18; "Eureka! New Ideas on Boosting Creativity," *Success* (December 1985), p. 27.

STRATEGIC AND OPERATIONAL PLANNING GUIDE

Staff Question #	Where are we now? (Score)	Where do we want to be? (What are our objectives?)	
5. Treat employees as a vital resource for competitive edge			
12. Recruit idea people			
19. Have idea/innovation champions			
26. Train employees to be creative			
33. Use a variety of creative processes to stimulate ideas			
40. Encourage and provide time for reflection			
47. Provide physical facilities that stimulate creativity			

How do we get there?		
What needs to be done?	**By whom?**	**By when?**

REFERENCES

1. Ashok K. Gupta and Arvind Singhad, "Managing Human Resources for Innovation and Creativity," *Research and Technology Management* (May/June 1993), pp. 41-48; and Dave Ulrich and Dale Lake, "Organizational Capability: Creating Competitive Advantage," *Academy of Management Executive* (February 1991), pp. 77-92.

2. For a lengthy discussion of how to manage innovative people see Karl F. Gretz and Steven R. Drozdeck, *Empowering Innovative People* (Chicago: Probus Publishing Company, 1992).

3. Kathryn Rudie Harrigan and Gaurov Dalmia, "Knowledge Workers: The Last Bastion of Competive Advantage," *Planning Review* (November/December 1991), pp. 4-9, 48.

4. James M. Higgins, *The Management Challenge*, 2ed (New York: Macmillan, 1994), pp. 419-457.

5. Randall S. Schuler, Strategic Human Resources Management: Linking the People with the Strategic Needs of the Business," *Organizational Dynamics* (Summer 1992), pp. 18-32; J. E. Butler, G. R. Ferris, and N. K. Napier, *Strategy and Human Resource Management* (Cincinnati: Southwestern, 1992).

6. Ashok K. Gupta and Arvind Singhad, loc. cit.; Dave Ulrich and Dale Lake, loc. cit.

7. William B. Johnston and Arnold H. Packer, *Workforce 2000: Work and Workers for the 21st Century* (Indianapolis, Ind: Hudson Institute, 1987).

8. Brenton R. Schlender, "How Sony Keeps the Magic Going," *Fortune* (February 22, 1992), pp. 76-84.

9. M.J. Kirton, "Adaptors and Innovators — Why Do Initiatives Get Blocked?" *Long Range Planning* (April 1984), pp. 137-143.

10. Roger VonOech, *A Kick in the Seat of the Pants* (New York: Perennial Books, 1986).

11. Min Badasur, "Managing Creativity: A Japanese Model," *Academy of Management Executive* (May 1992), pp. 29-42.

12. Kathryn M. Bartol and David C. Martin, *Management* (New York: McGraw-Hill, 1991), p. 26.

13. Source unknown

14. Carol A. Beatty and John R. M. Gordon, "Preaching the Gospel: The Evangelists of New Technology," *California Management Review* (Spring 1991), pp. 73-94.

15. Don Frey, "Learning the Ropes: My Life as a Product Champion," *Harvard Business Review* (September/October 1991), pp. 46-56.

16. Kathryn Bartol and David C. Martin, op. cit., pp. 26, 27.

17. Sophie Wilkinson, "Insight into In-House Innovation," *Chemical Week* (December 20, 27, 1989), pp. 56, 58.

18. Christopher Byron, "Bell Labs: Imagination, Inc.," *Time* (January 25, 1982), pp. 56-57.

19. Min Badasur, loc. cit.

20. Tony Buzan, "Mind Mapping," *Executive Excellence* (August 1991), pp. 3-4.

21. See James M. Higgins, *101 Creative Problem Solving Techniques: The Handbook of New Ideas for Business* (Winter Park, Florida: The New Management Publishing Co., 1994) for a discussion of creativity processes.

22. Marc Hequet, "Making Creativity Training Creative," *Training* (February 1992), p. 41.

23. "Industry Report," *Training* (October 1993), p. 63.

24. 1990 interview with C. Thomas Hughes and Joe Gelmini, developers of the Nor-folk-Southern program.

25. Bennett Davis, "Working the Imagination," *USAIR* (September, 1988), pp. 18-27.

26. Thomas Kiely, "The Idea Makers," *Technology Review* (January 1993), p. 33.

27. C. Eric (Rick) Clay, "Innovation: As Easy as Using a Pencil," *Credit Magazine* (May/June 1990), pp. 19-21.

28. Thomas Kiely, "The Idea Makers," *Technology Review* (January 1993), p. 32.

29. James M. Higgins, loc. cit.

30. Thomas Keily, op. cit., p. 34.

31. Thomas Keily, loc. cit.

32. Frito-Lay's new CEO abandoned a formal CPS program in 1991, in favor of an empowerment program. Source: discussion with Frito-Lay's corporate staff in Fall of 1993.

33. David Tanner, "Innovative and Creative Change," *Executive Excellence* (June 1992), pp. 15-16.

34. Thomas Kiely, op. cit., p. 34.

35. Ibid., p. 35.

36. Ibid., pp. 34-35.

37. Sheridan M. Tatsuno, *Created in Japan: From Imitators to World Class Innovators*, (New York: Harper & Row: Bellinger Division, 1990), pp. 104-115.

38. Michele McCormick, "We're Too Busy For Ideas," *Newsweek* (March 29, 1993), p. 10.

39. For a representative discussion see Jacquelyn Wonder and Priscilla Donovan, *Whole Brain Thinking* (New York: Ballantine Books, 1984).

40. Thomas Keily, op. cit., p. 40,

41. Russell Mitchell, "Masters of Innovation," *Business Week* (April 10, 1989), pp. 58-63.

42. Holly Sraeel, "GTE Pushes Technology and Design to the Limit," *Facilities Design & Management* (December 1992), pp. 32-37.

43. Gene Bylinsky, "Turning R&D Into Real Products," op. cit. p. 74. Carubba ac-cepted a position with Philips of the Netherlands in late 1993 to be in total control of Philips R&D operations, a position with unprecedented authority. See Jonathan B. Levine, "Has Philips Found Its Wizard?" *Business Week* (Sep-tember 6, 1993), pp. 82-84.

44. Akira Okamoto, "Creative and Innovative Research at Ricoh," *Long Range Plan-ning* (October 1991), p. 169.

45. Barbara N. Berkman, "Brainstorming in the Sauna: Inside the Nokia-Technophone Merger," *Electronic Business* (November 18, 1991), pp. 71-75.

46. David Kirkpatrick, "Groupware Goes Boom," *Fortune* (December 27, 1993), pp. 99-106.

Staff

Chapter 10

293

SHARED VALUES

CHAPTER 11

Creating a culture of innovation is the best competitive tool a company can have today, and the best weapon American business has in the increasingly global marketplace.

Lewis W. Lehr,
then CEO of 3M

Organizational culture is the pattern of shared values that distinguishes an organization from all others.[1] If you review the McKinsey Seven S's framework presented in Figure 11.1, you'll notice that shared values are at the core of that framework. Strategy, structure, systems, style, and staff are not enough by themselves to achieve organizational skills. Shared values influence, and are influenced by, all of the other six S's.

Organizational culture must be understood at two levels: the mythical level and the normative level. The mythical level includes the organization's myths, stories, heroes, symbols, slogans, and ceremonies. A story telling how Stan Starr had the

Shared
Values

Chapter 11

flash of brilliance that led to the creation of the Mickey Mouse hot air balloon that daily soars over Walt Disney World in Florida, would be an example of the mythical level.[2] The normative level is "the way we do things around here"[3]—that is, the set of values that are formally sanctioned by the organization and consist of culture as indicated in strategy, structure, systems, style, staffing, and skills, as well as in rules, procedures, and policies. The fact that all members of the cast (employees) at Disney theme parks must be well groomed, including short hair cuts for men and women, is an example of the normative level. Every manager, whether a department manager or the CEO, must learn how to manage both levels of the organization's culture.

FIGURE 11.1 THE SEVEN S'S FRAMEWORK

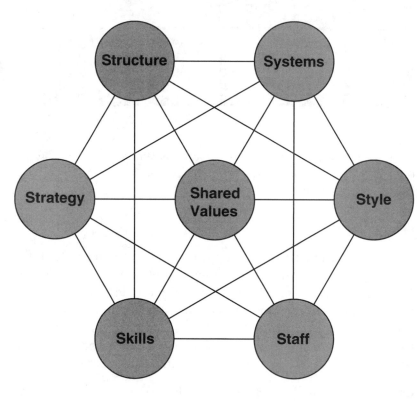

An organization's **shared values** provide direction, meaning, and energy for its members. Managing culture involves defining the organization's values, instilling those values in employees and integrating them into the organization through cultural artifacts such as myths and stories, controlling organizational climate, and changing the organization's values if necessary.

As noted earlier, the Seven S's are highly interdependent. For example, if strategy is changed, culture must be changed also. Corporate and business strategies are major influences on corporate culture. Conversely, organizational culture affects a firm's strategy and must support that strategy if it is to succeed.

Many large U.S. and Japanese firms have succeeded in managing their organizational cultures so as to increase productivity and become more competitive.[4] Not all such efforts have been successful, however, especially when they have involved transferring an organizational culture from one society to another. European firms have found that assimilation of different cultures must occur on a country-by-country basis.[5] For example, because French managers tend to be elitist and authoritarian, it would not be easy to use Japanese participative management techniques in France. Many English firms, in contrast, have incorporated many of these techniques into their more egalitarian structures.

The effective manager assesses the organization's existing culture and its impact on strategy, structure, systems, style, staff, and skills. He or she then determines whether that culture is appropriate and changes it if it is not. Creating a corporate culture that stimulates innovation is essential if an organization is to succeed.

Multiple Cultures

The management of organizational culture is further complicated by variations in the environment within which it operates. There is usually a widely shared or mainstream culture as well as a set of subcultures, often with varying degrees of acceptance or rejection of the key values of the mainstream culture.[6] A culture that stresses innovation may be the organization's mainstream culture or a subculture. Such fac-

tors as the personality of a particular manager or group of managers, a particular set of environmental circumstances or corporate pressures, disagreement with company policies and procedures, and differing interpretations of values can lead to different behaviors within the organization.

Organizations that are made up of people of different races, ethnicities, nationalities, genders, and ages, are characterized by cultural diversity. Multiple cultures may also exist as the result of a merger of two companies; a change in top management in which the new management team tries to install a new culture on top of an older one or to eliminate the older culture altogether; multinational operations or alliances; and cultural differences between different functional areas, product groups, or strategic business units.

The culture of the organization embodies the other six S's, and some of the related cultural phenomenon have been examined in other chapters of this book. In fact, most of the questions in the four questionnaires presented in Chapter 4 are related in one way or another to issues that help define organizational culture. This chapter therefore examines the firm's underlying values, and its efforts to manage them.[7]

An organization's culture either encourages or discourages innovation to some degree.[8] Keeping people focused on innovation is therefore an important cultural management skill. In attempting to create an innovative culture, we are looking for the set of values that helps make a company innovative. *Innovate or Evaporate 11.1* describes how Xerox has managed its corporate culture to become a highly innovative firm in a very competitive industry.

XEROX: DUPLICATING ITS PAST SUCCESSES

In its heyday, around 1970, Xerox controlled 95 percent of the U.S. copier market. In 1982, however, it had only a 13-percent market share. Its top executives had fallen asleep at the switch. In the late 1980s CEO David Kearns wrested control of Xerox's culture and turned it into what many considered to be an American samurai. Kearns directed the effort that enabled Xerox to win Japan's Deming Award, the United State's Baldrige Award, and the European Quality Award. Xerox is the only firm ever to have captured all three of these awards.

But quality wasn't the only problem; innovation was another major issue. Xerox's brilliant scientists were turning out good ideas, but the corporation wasn't taking those ideas to market. Although in the early 1980s Xerox had invented the user-friendly PC as we know it today and the PC mouse, its management decided to make higher-priced copiers instead. Critics note that Xerox missed one opportunity after another.

Kearns's leadership brought Xerox to the point where it could compete on the basis of both quality and price in all but the low-end market. Kearns made Xerox's core business competitive again. His successor, Paul Allaire, has formulated a strategy aimed at positioning Xerox for a world that is changing from analog to digital information gathering, storage, retrieval, and exchange. Allaire comments, "We expect to be the preeminent company in the document field." He wants Xerox to be "The Document Company." A critical component in the implementation of this strategy will be innovation, especially product innovation.

INNOVATE OR EVAPORATE 11.1

continued next page

XEROX

To achieve his strategy Allaire has moved to align Xerox's Seven S's so as to achieve the company's goals. Although it hasn't been easy, financial analysts agree that the arrows are all pointing in the same direction (see Chapter 4). Allaire points out that "A lot of times people will just change the structure and reporting relationships. But if you want to change a company, you'd better change more than that. There's the formal structure and then there's the way the company really works. You have to change the way it really works." Among the many actions he has taken to achieve this goal are the following:

- Increasing the number of strategic alliances in which Xerox participates, recognizing that the company cannot do everything by itself.

- Switching from a functional to a business unit structure, with each semiautonomous unit based on the final customer. Each business unit is accountable for its profits and losses, and each has its own manufacturing and sales group, as well as allocated research and service teams.

- Developing a closer relationship between Xerox's renowned research and development unit, PARC (Palo Alto Research

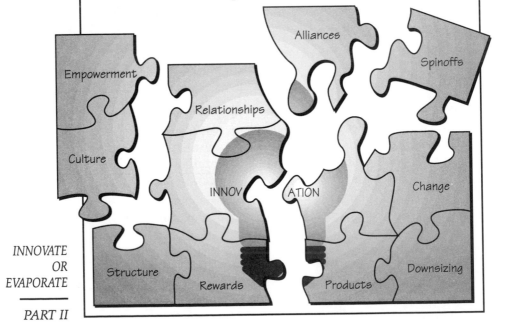

XEROX

Center), headed by Chief Scientist John Seely Brown, and its marketing and manufacturing functions.

- Creating a bonus system based on individual, unit and corporate performance, thus tying each employee's future more tightly to the company's performance.

- Empowering employees.

- Downsizing.

- Changing the corporate culture to focus not only on quality and cost but also on innovation.

- Creating new-venture spinoffs when business units do not feel that a specific research result matches their product lines.

- Embracing change. Allaire asserts, "We will need to change Xerox more in the next five years than we have in the past ten."

- Introducing several major products. One of these, DocuTech, is extremely versatile—it can scan, copy, print, and even bind and staple small booklets. Using DocuTech, Blue Cross/Blue Shield of North Carolina found that it could put together benefits booklets in two to three days; this activity formerly required six to nine weeks. DocuSP is a software architecture that works with DocuTech. Introduced in April 1994, it allows for data from all types of PC's located anywhere in the world to be input into a document capture machine. It then provides common frameworks for text, art, and graphics, which can be printed by a DocuTech system.

Peter van Cuylenberg, the executive vice-president responsible for Xerox's new emphasis on digital processes, describes what the company has accomplished: "What is new here is that we've looked at the whole document pipeline, from creation to use, and provided all of the software and hardware to build the whole infrastructure. No one has been able to integrate the system we're talking about because the components didn't exist until now."

Source: Subrata N. Chakravarty, "Back in Focus," *Forbes* (June 6, 1994), pp. 72-76; Tim Smart, "Can Xerox Duplicate Its Glory Days?" *Business Week* (October 4, 1993), pp. 56-58.

Shared Values

Chapter 11

The Characteristics

Exhibit 11.1 lists the seven summary questions related to the characteristics of shared values examined in the questionnaires in Chapter 4.

EXHIBIT 11.1 CHARACTERISTICS OF INNOVATIVE ORGANIZATIONS RELATED TO SHARED VALUES

To what extent does your organization:

6. Hold creative people and their contributions in high esteem.

13. Encourage new ideas and risk taking.

20. Value and practice openness.

27. Possess a shared value that this is an innovative organization.

34. Manage organizational culture to make it more innovative.

41. Place a high value on change and make it part of the organization's culture.

48. Require nonmanagerial employees to have objectives for product, process, marketing, and management innovation, and evaluate their performance in relation to those objectives.

---

6. Hold Creative People and Their Contributions in High Esteem.

As discussed in Chapter 9, special approaches are needed to manage creative people. The entire organization, not just management, must appreciate the importance of creative people. Some firms fail to recognize the importance of creative people or accept them fully. Their odd hours and sometimes quirky behavior may be misunderstood. This is often the case in smaller firms. Other employees may want to know why they don't punch a time clock, or why they don't have to wear coats and ties, or why they can get up and walk outside anytime they want to. Firms that don't resolve such issues will experience morale problems. Often the solution may be to separate creative individuals from the rest of the company. For example, the Kirchman Corporation, a large bank software firm, has a separate building for its programmers and systems designers located several miles away from its headquarters building, where its sales and service employees work.

Some managers are willing to go the extra mile to accommodate the needs of creative employees. Sidney Green, president of Terra Tek in Salt Lake City, provides this revealing insight: "We have a scientist who doesn't like to be bothered with budgets. We'll set benchmarks related to technical accomplishments and then have someone else translate them into financial data."[9]

The success of Bell Labs over the years has been due in part to its very special culture. Bell respects creative people even if their ideas might never help the company directly. In the mid-1960s Arno Penzias and another Bell scientist, Robert Wilson, detected faint echos of the "big bang" that is believed to have formed the universe.[10] For this achievement, which will not affect the telephone industry very much, they were awarded the Nobel Prize in 1978. In describing the culture at Bell Labs, Penzias states: "Unless it can be demonstrated that you are really wasting your time and our money, people leave you alone. This place demands work but also demands that you think, and while Bell Labs aims towards practical products that AT&T can put in the marketplace, beyond that very broad guideline its employees can let their minds roam." In recent years Bell Labs has focused more on products, but it still recognizes the importance of ideas. Ironically, it is Penzias as head of Bell Labs, who is leading this product focus.[11]

Comparing U.S. Firms with Japanese and European Firms

Innovative U.S., Japanese, and European firms all hold creative individuals and their contributions in high esteem. However, in Japanese firms creative people are often viewed as members of a team and are not allowed much individual freedom. However, basic research scientists are only beginning to be given the freedom they need and to be less stiffled by bureaucratic procedures than they were in the past. In some European firms, in contrast, one's social status is often more important than one's position in the company. In some countries in Europe, such as Germany, researchers are having to become more applications oriented.

Shared Values

Chapter 11

13. Encourage New Ideas and Risk Taking.

Innovative firms actively promote risk taking and the pursuit of new ideas. They don't squelch ideas or punish risk taking.[12] Rather, the organization's culture, its myths, policies, and procedures, convey the message that having new ideas and taking risks are desired behaviors. Royal Dutch Shell has achieved its preeminent position by taking calculated risks, such as stockpiling oil before the shortages in the 70s and 80s which only they forecasted. It encourages its employees to do the same.[13] Rubbermaid, which now dominates a market once owned by Tupperware, encourages its employees to develop new-product ideas.[14] Innovation means taking risks and making mistakes. At Johnson & Johnson, a mistake can be a badge of honor.[15] *Innovate or Evaporate 11.2* describes how Johnson & Johnson views these issues.

In today's rapidly changing environment, decision makers can't wait until they have complete information or have evaluated every alternative. They have to take risks; otherwise they will miss opportunities or fail to solve problems.[16] Among the numerous values associated with risk taking are the following:

- freedom to try things and fail
- acceptance of mistakes
- freedom to discuss "dumb" ideas
- absence of punishment for failure
- ability to challenge the status quo
- lack of attention to the past
- willingness not to focus on the short term
- the expectation that innovation is part of the job
- a positive attitude toward change
- a drive to improve[17]

The key is to **manage** risk.[18] Once firms define a particular risk, they can assess it in terms of the three basic categories: strategic, market, and internal. They can then use actions such as soliciting customer inputs, using a proven product-development process, and employing creative compensation programs to reduce the level of risk they face and make it manageable.[19]

JOHNSON & JOHNSON RECOGNIZES THAT MISTAKES OFTEN ACCOMPANY INNOVATION

Johnson & Johnson is a highly decentralized firm comprising more than 160 separate businesses. It is the model for firms seeking to run autonomous business units in order to become more customer-focused and innovative. Johnson & Johnson continually evaluates the role of corporate headquarters relative to its autonomous units and has recently centralized certain functions to save money. Although it has had its share of problems and unsuccessful products, it has an enviable record of sustained new-product success. Approximately 22 percent of its revenues come from products that are less than five years old.

Johnson & Johnson has consciously developed a culture in which innovation and risk taking are encouraged and mistakes are recognized as part of the price of such actions. Former CEO Jim Burke is a perfect example of how the J&J culture works. His first major product launch was a flop. But chairman Robert Wood Johnson congratulated him on taking a risk, demonstrating that at J&J a mistake can be a badge of honor. Burke went on to achieve several major successes and two more failures, one of which occurred while he was CEO. Burke may be best known for his handling of the Tylenol poisonings. His proactive

continued next page

INNOVATE OR EVAPORATE 11.2

JOHNSON & JOHNSON

response to the situation, recalling all the products on the shelves and forthrightly explaining the problem to the public, is widely viewed as the "how to" of crisis management.

Not all of J&J's divisions are run by risk takers; some are run by risk-averse managers who want to keep their good records intact. Burke and his successor, Ralph S. Larsen, continually encouraged innovation and risk taking, and developed reward systems for those who took these actions. They also stepped up spending on research in order to push the firm forward not only in new products but in product enhancements as well.

Sources: Ralph S. Larsen, "The Challenge of Change: Building a New Competitive Spirit for the 21st Century," *Executive Speeches* (December 1992-January 1993), pp. 19-22; Joseph Weber, "A Big Company That Works," *Business Week* (May 4, 1992), pp 124-132; Christopher Power, "At Johnson & Johnson, a Mistake Can Be a Badge of Honor," *Business Week* (September 26, 1988), pp. 126-128.

20. Value and Practice Openness.

Innovative organizations value and practice **openness**—that is, information is shared; doors are open; communication moves in all directions; and managers are accessible. Innovative organizations share the following values related to openness:

- open communication and sharing of information
- ability to listen
- open access to management
- bright people with strong egos
- scanning, broad thinking
- exposure of employees to ideas outside the company
- frequent moves between functions, departments, or divisions

- encouragment of **lateral thinking**

  (**Lateral thinking** is defined as "seeking to solve problems by unorthodox or apparently illogical methods." With lateral thinking, "we move sideways to try different perceptions, different concepts, different points of entry." [You dig lots of holes instead of digging the same hole deeper.])[20]

- willingness to adopt the customer's perspective

- acceptance of criticism

- avoidance of excessive sensitivity to criticism

- continuous training

- emphasis on intellectual honesty

- expectation and acceptance of conflict

- willingness to consult others[21]

Chapter 8 examined the importance of open communication and sharing of information. Levi-Strauss and Kao Corporation were discussed in terms of their policy of giving employees access to needed information. Chapter 10 described the openness of physical facilities such as those at Microsoft and Hewlett-Packard. Underlying these measures is a belief in the value of openness in communication. Employees are not afraid to speak out. In firms like GE, Microsoft, and Nucor Steel, they are even expected to voice any disagreement with management's actions.

Firms with open communication use several approaches to develop this atmosphere.[22] They may use attitude surveys to determine employee, customer, and supplier satisfaction. They may hold periodic meetings with employees, communicate via TV networks or newsletters, develop open-door policies, distribute handbooks, and/or provide counseling to employees. In short, they create a climate of understanding and openness.

Shared Values

Chapter 11

27. Possess a Shared Value that This Is an Innovative Organization.

Employees in innovative firms believe strongly in their firm's innovativeness. Recognizing the need to instill an "I think I can, therefore I can" attitude, innovative firms actively advertise this quality to their employees and others. At TRW, for example, employees believe that creativity is their business. TRW has gone to great lengths to convey this message internally and has also spent several million dollars on a television advertising campaign—"It Was Just An Idea"— to convey the message externally as well.[23] In this series of ads, an idea was depicted as a drop of water in a pond. As the ripples caused by the idea expanded throughout the pond, it led to many other ideas.

At Apple Computer, the story of how the Macintosh was developed is constantly retold. Innovators are glorified in such stories. Conference rooms are named after great inventors. Developers announce new products. In short, the company's vision, mission, and values focus on innovation.

At Eaton Corporation, front-line workers view themselves as creative problem solvers.[24] At Microsoft, Bill Gates's vision inspires employees to follow in the footsteps of earlier innovators. The stories of how Windows and other programs were created glorify innovators. The Innovator's Hall of Fame at Milliken, as well as the Carleton Society at 3M, were mentioned earlier; 3M also gives "Golden Step" Awards to innovators. All such actions are aimed at creating a culture of innovation.

Comparing U.S. Firms with Japanese and European Firms

Japanese organizations are characterized by confidence, including confidence about being innovative. For example, Sharp Electronics believes in innovation and believes in itself as an innovator. As can be seen in *Innovate or Evaporate 11.3*, it is staking its future on that belief.

In contrast, many European firms have lost confidence in their ability to innovate. For example, Lothar Spaeth, a leading German political figure, and Herbert A. Henzler, chairman of

INNOVATE
OR
EVAPORATE
———
PART II

SHARP'S FLAIR FOR INNOVATION

Sharp, a diversified electronics company, has rivals that are four or five times its size: Toshiba, Hitachi, Matsushita, and Sony. But it has a not-so-secret weapon that it hopes will quadruple its sales by the year 2000. That weapon is a well-established penchant for innovation.

Sharp has introduced an impressive array of optoelectronics—devices that combine optics and electronics. Among its innovations are lightweight, energy-efficient liquid-crystal displays (LCD's) on laptop computers, semiconductor lasers that "read" compact disks, and the electroluminescent computer screens on the space shuttle. The company now hopes to apply its optoelectronic savvy in such areas as filing systems based on erasable optical disks and high-definition video products.

Sharp's 1970 gamble on LCD's put it in position for its current dominance of that market, an industry that is growing at a rate of 37 percent per year and had total sales of $1.6 billion

continued next page

SHARP

in 1991. LCD's are likely to replace bulky cathode-ray tubes in many televisions and computer systems as screen quality improves and prices fall. The latest technology, active-matrix LCD's, achieves a level of color and clarity nearly equal to that of picture tubes—and Sharp makes 40 percent of the world's supply. By 1994 the company will have spent $740 million on new LCD facilities, more than any other company. Sharp introduced an LCD camcorder in 1993, that uses a small LCD screen instead of a viewfinder, thereby differentiating its product from the also-rans.

Laser diodes are another optoelectronic gamble that has paid off for Sharp. Long before Sony and Philips developed the compact disk player, Sharp developed and commercialized technology to create laser diodes—tiny semiconductor crystals that release a beam of laser light when stimulated by an electric current. Sharp now makes nearly half of these diodes, which are used in optical disk drives for computers, laser printers, CD players, and videodisk players. Its engineers hope to leapfrog rivals like Canon, which dominates the laser printer market, with new products that combine the functions of laser printers, fax machines, and optical recording systems.

Sources: David P. Hamilton, "Sharp Gets Set to Ride Hottest Trends in Electronics," *Wall Street Journal* (October 4, 1993), p. B4; Neil Gross, "Sharp's Long Range Gamble on Its Innovation Machine," *Business Week* (April 29, 1991), pp. 84-85.

McKinsey & Company, Germany, have written a book titled *Can the Germans Still be Saved?* that reviews German industry's recent failures in high technology. Their book not only chronicles Germany's failures but points to a scientific malaise and a feeling of hopelessness among German managers. They cite computer chips and genetic engineering as two especially unsuccessful areas. Germany's Minister of Economics, Guenter Rexrodt, has called for *Innovationskrise,* an "innovation offensive."[25]

34. Manage Organizational Culture to Make It More Innovative.

Managing organizational culture means managing both the mythical level and the normative level. Many companies do a good job of managing the normative level. For example, when Dana Corporation became concerned about its lack of quality and innovation, it created a culture characterized by minimal hierarchy, enriched jobs, management by wandering around, rules of behavior, well-defined corporate goals, trust in management, a team-oriented environment, and a focus on change. These were normative actions. It also went about making certain that its rituals, stories, and symbols supported its normative efforts.[26]

Dunlop Tire Corporation employs benchmarking to compare its management of creativity and innovation with that of competitors. In addition to improved processes and products, this approach leads to a common vision throughout the organization.[27]

At General Electric, productivity growth is believed to be the ultimate competitive advantage. As described in *Innovate or Evaporate 5.4*, GE set up process mapping, workouts, and best practices programs to increase employee creativity and productivity. The programs focus on faster new-product development, greater market penetration, and improved product quality and customer service by reducing complexity.[28] While process mapping and best practices focus on the normative, the stories that are told about workouts help to mythically reinforce the normative aspects. Furthermore, the firm makes a concentrated effort to change the language of success; for example, when CEO Jack Welch speaks of empowerment to management development classes at GE's management development center in Orisino, New York. And the firm constantly tells other parts of the firm how another division solved its problems, again using stories to reinforce normative behavior. One such story focused on the success of the Canadian appliance subsidiary in process mapping its operations resulting in huge productivity gains. A team of executives from this plant then toured other GE facilities spreading the story of their success.[29]

Shared Values

Chapter 11

Innovate or Evaporate 11.4 describes the management of organizational culture at Microsoft. This example reveals how shared values from the various Seven S's enter into the firm's culture. *Innovate or Evaporate 11.5* describes the changes taking place at Europe's Rhône-Poulenc as it tries to transform its culture into a more innovative one.

Comparing U.S. Firms with Japanese and European Firms

U.S. and European firms learned to manage their cultures by observing Japanese firms. U.S. firms are ahead of European firms in this regard. Japanese firms must now learn how to change the culture of their firms to adjust to rapidly changing environments.

41. Place a High Value on Change and Make It Part of the Organization's Culture.

Innovative firms place a high value on change. They see change as an opportunity to innovate, not as a threat.[30] Managing properly under chaotic conditions leads to new ideas that become new products, services, and/or processes. Innovative organizations focus on and even embrace change. For example, Steelcase, the nation's largest business furniture maker, uses a giant pendulum in the center of its R&D facility to symbolize its quest for change.[31]

Innovative firms are willing to make whatever changes are necessary to accommodate new competitive situations, adapt to new environments, and become more innovative. DuPont changed the structure of its product development division five times in six decades before adopting (in 1985) the collaborative model it now uses.[32] Hewlett-Packard consistently cannibalizes its own products in order to develop newer ones before someone else does.[33]

But change isn't easy, as Machiavelli suggested in *The Prince* as long ago as 1532.

MICROSOFT'S INNOVATION CULTURE

Microsoft became the world's leading software producer through a lot of hard work, astute technological and business acumen, and careful management of organizational culture. Microsoft's founder and CEO, Bill Gates, based the firm's culture on the principle of empowerment, a shared value about leadership and structure. Managers delegate power to the developers, who write and design software. The firm is managed in such a way that managers interact as little as possible with the developers, although they do provide mentors for newly recruited developers to help them understand the firm's culture.

This concept of user friendliness permeates the company, which itself is user (employee) friendly. The company's physical layout facilitates creativity and innovation. Corporate headquarters resembles a college campus, with playing fields, an outdoor eating area, and a basketball court. Almost every office has a window, and almost every door is open. Employees work hard (80-hour weeks) and play hard (parties, pranks, picnics, sports, and good-natured fun).

A great deal of effort goes into recruitment. Interviewers grill prospective staffers about their job knowledge and capabilities to determine what the candidate really knows and how he or she may be able to apply it at Microsoft.

Although everyone at Microsoft believes in the firm's innovative capacity, employees are also well aware of the competitive market in which it operates. "It's etched in our brains: don't get complacent," says Jeff Raikes, head of U.S. sales. Gates has an ambitious ten- to twenty-year vision, "Information at Your Fingertips." In his words, "Any piece of information you want should be available to you." He wants users to be able to ask

INNOVATE OR EVAPORATE 11.4

continued next page

"...it ought to be remembered that there is nothing more diffcult to take in hand, more perilous to conduct, or more uncertain in its success, than to take the lead in the introduction of a new order of things. Because the innovator has for enemies all those who have done well under the old conditions, and lukewarm defenders in those who may do well under the new."

Innovate or Evaporate 7.5 reviewed the actions taken by IBM's management to change the company's structure so that it would be more consistent with its business strategy, which is based largely on its focus on innovation and the customer. But as pointed out earlier, strategy and structure do not operate in isolation. There must also be appropriate systems, style, staff, and shared values if the necessary skills are to be obtained. *Innovate or Evaporate 11.6* examines the actions taken by CEO Lou Gerstner to overcome what he perceives as a culture of arrogance and lethargy, a culture that is not conducive to innovation.

Comparing U.S. Firms with Japanese and European Firms

Japanese firms, like their U.S. counterparts, vary in their receptivity to change. Although firms such as Toshiba and Sony are exceptionally receptive to change, others have been bound by tradition. In fact, one of the major criticisms of Japanese management is its inability to react quickly to change. Another is its inability to change itself.[34] Most European firms have historically resisted change, but since the 1992 initiative, they have been immersed in a sea of change, with little choice but to adapt or perish.

INNOVATE OR EVAPORATE

PART II

THE DRIVE FOR INNOVATION AT RHÔNE-POULENC

In April 1993 Jean-Réné Fourtou, chairman and CEO of the French chemical/pharmaceutical giant Rhône-Poulenc, was awarded the Palladium Medal by the American Section of the Société de Chimie Industrielle for his efforts to transform his company from a national to a global competitor. Much of that globalization came through acquisitions, especially two major ones in the United States: pharmaceuticals producer Rorer and vaccine-producer Connaught. Wishing to concentrate on the firm's strengths, Fourtou also trimmed the number of businesses it operated from 110 to 45.

With most of the portfolio management activities completed, Fourtou shifted his focus to growth through innovation. He observed that the company faces two constant challenges: maintaining the appropriate organizational culture and stimulating innovation. He comments, "It is our main business now to progress in innovation, organization, and day-to-day performance. We are in businesses where science is very important. We are evaluating [new products and new technologies] very quickly these years, and have never before had so many innovations in the pipeline." He also wants to change the firm's culture to support innovation and quality. This is no easy task in a company with 87,000 employees, of whom only 37,000 are French, and with operations on every continent.

Peter J. Neff, CEO of Rhône-Poulenc Inc., the company's North American operation, echoes Fourtou's views on innovation. In a

INNOVATE OR EVAPORATE 11.5

continued next page

RHÔNE-POULENC

speech to the 1993 annual meeting of the Chemical Management & Resources Association, he reviewed some of the actions the firm has taken to make innovation part of its culture. First, Fourtou has established innovation as the firm's number one priority. This goal is emphasized in the firm's internal and external communications and reinforced by all levels of management throughout the world. It is supported by long-term commitments of human and financial resources to research. Cross-functional and cross-divisional research, as well as shared research by units in different countries, are encouraged. Employees compete for an annual innovation prize and several annual research prizes. Total quality management (TQM) is being used to help everyone in the company focus on the customer. Management, especially top management, is setting the example of innovative behavior.

Neff suggests that a firm's managers can get an idea of their firm's IQ (Innovation Quotient) by asking themselves five questions:

1. Who gets promoted in your organization? The people who preserve the status quo or those whose initiative might sometimes cause waves that rock the boat a bit?

2. What was the last good innovation you can think of in your organization, and how was it recognized or rewarded?

3. How much of an obstacle is the bureaucracy in your organization? How many approval hoops does someone with an innovative idea have to jump through before it's approved?

4. How good are the schools and how vital and creative are the communities that surround your facilities and are the sources of your future employees?

5. How do *you* react when confronted with a new idea or an alternative solution to one that you've suggested?

Both Fourtou and Neff recognize that, while much has been accomplished, still more remains to be done to create a culture of innovation that can give Rhône-Poulenc a strategic advantage through innovation.

Sources: Peter J. Neff, "Innovation: A Key to Competitive Advantage," speech to the annual meeting of the Chemical Management & Resources Association, Boston, May 4, 1993; Patricia Layman, "France's Rhône-Poulenc Looks to Innovation for Growth," *Chemical & Engineering News* (May 3, 1993), pp. 27-28.

IBM CHANGES ITS CULTURE IN ORDER TO REINVENT ITSELF

When Lou Gerstner became CEO of IBM, he quickly shelved the three "basic beliefs" that had guided the firm for decades: pursue excellence; provide the best customer service; and above all, show respect for the individual. In their stead he proposed the following guidelines:

1. The marketplace is the driving force behind everything we do.

2. At our core, we are a technology company with an overriding commitment to quality.

3. Our primary measures of success are customer satisfaction and shareholder value.

4. We operate as an entrepreneurial organization with a minimum of bureaucracy and a never-ending focus on productivity.

5. We never lose sight of our strategic vision.

6. We think and act with a sense of urgency.

7. Outstanding, dedicated people make it all happen, particularly when they work together as a team.

8. We are sensitive to the needs of all employees and to the communities in which we operate.

Longtime IBM employees and managers were shocked and dismayed. Thomas J. Watson, Jr., the son of IBM's founder, had been preaching the three basic beliefs for decades. They were ingrained, practically a mantra to be recited by every member

INNOVATE OR EVAPORATE 11.6

continued next page

IBM

of the company. Watson had said that everything at IBM could be changed except these basic beliefs. Most galling was the relegation of respect for employees to the last place on the list.

Gerstner also expected IBM employees to act like owners. Lee Conrad, a dissident at an IBM plant in Endicott, New York, retorted in a newsletter to colleagues, "Nice words, Lou, but it's hard to think as an owner when we're treated like hired hands." Gerstner thus experienced at first hand the difficulty of changing an organizational culture that has been firmly entrenched for seventy years.

The first thing Gerstner did when he came to IBM, was to attack the firm's financial weaknesses. In July 1993 he took a $8.9 billion pretax charge and announced cuts of 35,000 jobs. In March 1994 he announced his new strategy. Next he has to tackle the heart and soul of the firm, its culture. Impatient with IBM's culture of arrogance and lethargy, he has informed employees that they should not feel entitled to their jobs. He balks at the "uniform" of blue suit and white shirt and dislikes the overhead transparencies that have traditionally been used for presentations. He holds town meetings during which he answers employee's questions. He has initiated new personnel policies and a new performance appraisal system and has completely changed the IBM training program, giving it a clearer focus on customers and quality. He is revamping the sales force to make its members business problem solvers, not just salespeople. Through various symbolic gestures and public statements, he has let it be known that research and development are still essential to IBM. But perhaps most important, through firings and resignations of those who opposed him, he has made it clear that he won't accept anything less than full compliance with his goals.

Sources: Ira Sager, "The Few, the True, the Blue,"*Business Week* (May 30, 1994), pp. 124-126; Peter Coy, "Is Big Blue Still Big on Research? You Bet." *Business Week* (May 16, 1994), pp. 89-90; Laurie Hays, "Blue Period: Gerstner Is Struggling as He Tries to Change Ingrained IBM Culture," *Wall Street Journal* (May 13, 1994), pp. A1, A8.

*INNOVATE
OR
EVAPORATE*

PART II

48. Require Nonmanagerial Employees to Have Objectives for Product, Process, Marketing, and Management Innovation and Evaluate Their Performance in Relation to Those Objectives.

This point could have been discussed in the strategy chapter, but it is placed here because it reveals the extent to which the drive for innovation has spread throughout the organization. Motorola, for example, forms teams whose objectives are to improve quality, increase production efficiency, develop innovative products, and improve profits.[35] At Eaton Corporation, teams are the focus of the company's innovation and quality efforts.[36] At Hewlett-Packard, innovation objectives are assigned to employees at all levels. At 3M, employees are expected to contribute to the firm's overall level of productivity by being innovative. Ford Motor Company has established a new suggestion program in an effort to get all its employees involved in innovation.

Comparing U.S. Firms with Japanese and European Firms

In most U.S. firms front-line employees have been left to carry out basic day-to-day maintenance operations with no thought  of innovation.[37] That is changing, however, as firms begin using autonomous work teams, reengineering, new-product development teams, and other innovative structural mechanisms. In Japanese firms front-line employees are expected to engage in *Kaizen*, or continuous improvement. Employees in many functional areas, not just R&D, may even create big bang innovations.[38] In Europe, most employees in most firms are discouraged from innovating.

STRATEGIC AND OPERATIONAL PLANNING GUIDE

Shared Values Question #	Where are we now? (Score)	Where do we want to be? (What are our objectives?)	
6. Hold creative people and their contributions in high esteem			
13. Encourage new ideas and risk taking			
20. Value and practice openness			
27. Possess a shared value that this is an innovative firm			
34. Manage organizational culture to make it more innovative			
41. Place a high value on change and make it part of the culture			
48. Require non-managerial employees to have objectives for innovation			

How do we get there?		
What needs to be done?	**By whom?**	**By when?**

REFERENCES

1. Ralph H. Kilmann, Mary Jane Saxton, and Roy Serpa, "Issues in Understanding and Changing Culture," *California Management Review* (Winter 1986), pp. 87-94; and Robert H. Waterman, Jr., "The Seven Elements of Strategic Fit," *Journal of Business Strategy* (Winter 1982), pp 69-73.

2. Author's personal knowledge of this event.

3. Dr. David Boles, senior vice-president, the Hay Group, Los Angeles. Quoted in "Tailoring Culture to Fit the Times," *Electric World* (February 1987), p. 29.

4. Brian Dumaine, "Creating a New Company Culture," *Fortune* (January 15, 1990), pp. 127-131; William G. Ouchi, *Theory Z: How American Business Can Meet the Japanese Challenge* (Reading, Mass.: Addison-Wesley, 1981); and Richard T. Pascale and Anthony Athos, *The Art of Japanese Management* (New York: Warner Books, 1981).

5. Shawn Tully, "Europe 1992: More Unity Than You Think," *Fortune* (August 24, 1992), pp. 136-142; Chris Brewster and Frank Bournois, "Human Resource Management: A European Perspective," *Personnel Review* (1991, no. 6), pp. 4-13; and Barry Louis Ribin, "Europeans Value Diversity," *HR Magazine* (January 1991), pp. 38-41,78.

6. W. Jack Duncan, "Organizational Culture: 'Getting a Fix' On an Elusive Concept," *Academy of Management Executive* (August 1989), pp. 229-236; K. L. Gregory, "Native-View Paradigms: Multiple Cultures and Culture Conflicts in Organizations," *Administrative Science Quarterly* (September 1983), pp. 359-376.

7. Charles O'Reilly, "Corporations, Culture, and Commitment," *California Management Review* (Summer 1989), pp. 9-25.

8. Fred F. Jespersen, "Corporate Culture is the Real Key to Creativity," *Business Month* (May 1989), pp. 73-75.

9. "Creative People Can Meet Deadlines," *Inc.* (December 1981), pp. 97-98.

10. Brian Christopher, "Bell Labs: Imagination, Inc.," *Time* (January 25, 1982), pp. 56-57.

11. Gene Bylinsky, "The New Look at America's Top Lab," *Fortune* (February 1, 1988), pp. 60-64.

12. Briane Dumaine, "Closing the Innovation Gap," *Fortune* (December 2, 1991), p. 59; Karen Fitzgerald, "Encouraging Risk-Taking, Sanctioning Failures are Helping Spur Creativity," *IEEE Spectrum* (October 1990), pp. 67-69.

13. Christopher Knowlton, "Shell Gets Rich by Beating Risk," *Fortune* (August 26, 1991), pp. 79-82.

14. Brian Dumaine, "Closing the Innovation Gap," loc. cit.

15. Christopher Power, "At Johnson & Johnson, a Mistake Can Be a Badge of Honor," *Business Week* (September 26, 1988), pp. 126-128.

16. Donald R. Gamache, "Infusing Creativity," *Executive Excellence* (September 1993), pp. 12-13.

17. Charles O'Reilly, "Corporations, Culture, and Commitment: Motivation and Social Control in Organizations," *California Management Review* (Summer 1989), p. 15.

18. Thomas D. Kuczmarski and Arthur G. Middlebrooks, "Innovation Risk and Reward," *Sales & Marketing Management* (February 1993), pp. 44-50.

19. Ibid.

20. Edward DeBono, *Serious Creativity* (New York: Harper Collins, 1992), pp. 52-53.

21. Ibid.

22. James M. Higgins, *The Management Challenge*, 2nd. ed. (New York: Macmillan, 1994), pp. 638-643.

23. Ed Fitch, "TRW Image Campaign Frees Wise Ideas," *Advertising Age* (November 29, 1984), pp. 50-51.

24. Thomas F. O'Boyle, "Working Together: A Manufacturer Grows Efficient by Soliciting Ideas From Employees," *Wall Street Journal* (June 5, 1992), pp. A1, A4.

25. Daniel Benjamin, "The Trailing Edge: Some Germans Fear They're Falling Behind in High-Tech Fields," *Wall Street Journal* (April 27, 1994), pp. A1, A6.

26. Discussion with Dana Corporation Public Relations personnel June 21, 1994 and June 28, 1994.

27. David Wilkerson, Andres I. Delgado, and Jefferson Kellogg, "Experience with Cultural Benchmarking at Dunlop," *Employment Relations Today* (Summer 1993), pp. 159-166.

28. Thomas A. Stewart, "GE Keeps Those Ideas Coming," *Fortune* (August 12, 1991), pp. 41-49.

29. Mike Belanger, Dick Hilbert, and Murray Wilson, "Putting the 'Best' in Best Practices," presentation at the Strategic Management Society Annual Meeting (Toronto, Canada, October 24, 1991).

30. W. Harvey Hegarty, "Organizational Survival Means Embracing Change," *Business Horizons* (November-December 1993), pp. 1-4.

31. Gregory Witcher, "Steelcase Hopes Innovation Flourishes Under Pyramid," *Wall Street Journal* (May 26, 1989), pp. D1, D8.

32. Gene Bylinsky, "Turning R&D Into Real Products," *Fortune* (July 2, 1990), p. 74.

33. Alan Deutschman, "How HP Continues to Grow and Grow," *Fortune* (May 2, 1994), pp. 90-100.

34. Aaron M. Cohen, "Japan in Transit: Remodelling the Japanese Corporation," *Management Japan* (Autumn 1993), pp. 25-31; "What's Killing Japanese Business? 'Japanese-Style Management'" *Tokyo Business Today* (July 1993), pp. 24-26.

35. Geoffrey Brewer, "Employee Motivation: On With the Show," *Incentive* (May 1992), pp. 30-34.

36. Thomas P. O'Boyle, loc. cit.

37. William Lareau, *American Samurai* (Warner Books: New York, 1992).

38. Ibid; Min Basadur, "Managing Creativity: A Japanese Model," *Academy of Management Executive* (May 1992), pp. 29-42.

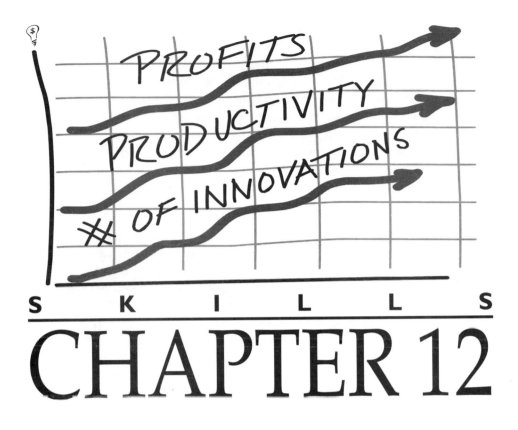

S K I L L S

CHAPTER 12

The key to competive advantage isn't reacting to chaos; it's producing that chaos.

Ed McCracken
CEO, Silicon Graphics

If to this point, appropriate innovation strategy, structure, systems, style, staff, and shared values are in place, then the organization will possess innovation skills that it would not otherwise have. **Skills** as defined here are synergistic in nature, and would not exist except for the interaction of the other six S's. Skills are corporate wide. Skills are not related to what one individual or group has as skills, but rather what the entire organization has in the way of skills. Organizations may possess different sets of skills. Rubbermaid, 3M, Hewlett-Packard, Apple Computer, Federal Express, Sony, Toyota, and "Today's" Chrysler Corporation are all known for their skills at innovation. BIC, Gillette, UPS, and Nucor Steel are all very efficient. Motorola, United States Automobile Association, and Mercedes have strong quality-management skills. These three skills are not mutually exclusive, however. Hewlett-Packard and Apple are very efficient and produce high quality products, and Motorola is also very innovative and efficient, for example. In fact, one typically finds that these three corporate skills—efficiency, innovation, and quality often appear together. An important point to remember is that if a firm's Seven S's are not all pointing in the same direction, sought skills will fail to emerge. Thus if strategy seeks innovation but structure accomodates only efficiency, and systems are designed only for quality, none of these three skills may be obtained.

As the opening quote for this chapter suggests, being able to create chaos leads to the ability to compete. Innovation is how you create chaos. Apple Computer has caused two major chaos' in the personal computer industry. They developed the first consumer targeted PC with Apple II, and they developed the first user friendly PC with the Macintosh. They are trying to create a third with the Power Mac, introduced in March of 1994.[1] 3M and Sony continually launch new products that revolutionize and cause chaos: Scotch Tape, Post-It Notes, Walkman, and the 8mm camcorder, for example. Research by Gary Hamel and C. K. Prahalad, authors, consultants, and professors, strongly suggests that the successful companies in the 1990s are creating new products and new markets that didn't already exist and that these will be based on a firm's **core competencies**—what the firm does especially well.[2] One key competency for successful firms is innovation: *Innovate or evaporate.*

THE CHARACTERISTICS

Exhibit 12.1 lists the seven summary questions related to the characteristics of skills examined in the questionnaires in Chapter 4. Questions 7, 14, and 21 identify the end results expected. The other four questions are skill indicators as well, but of behaviors that lead to results, not of the results themselves.

To what extent does your organization:

7.   Proactively create new opportunities and respond to change.

14. Continuously create new products and services; enhance old ones; continuously develop process, marketing, and management innovations.

21. Successfully practice continuous as well as big bang innovation.

28. Engage in knowledge management—identifying knowledge assets, sharing information, tapping innate knowledge of individuals.

35. Practice organizational learning—learn from experience and knowledge.

42. Leverage resources to achieve seemingly unobtainable objectives.

49. Invest heavily and appropriately in R & D.

---

7. Proactively Create New Opportunities and Respond to Change.

The environment in which business operates is full of change. Much of that change results in chaos for many firms, but as senior *Fortune* writer Thomas A. Stewart observes, "Change means opportunity as well as danger."[3] Some companies embrace change; others try to kill it—and often do.[4] Thomas J. Peters, in *Thriving on Chaos*, sets the stage for the need for innovation by declaring, "There are no excellent companies. The old saw, 'If it ain't broke, don't fix it' needs revision. I propose: 'If it ain't broke, you just haven't looked hard enough.' Fix it anyway."[5] He then proclaims innovation as one of the keys to thriving on chaos that characterizes the rapidly changing business environment.[6] However, a firm not only wants to be able to respond to change, but it must also be able to create it. Since change is going to happen anyway, the firm might as well make sure it happens in a way that's beneficial to the firm. This means then that firms must be dually prepared for change—to create it, and to respond to it.

Skills

Chapter 12

327

Silicon Graphics, the California-based computer graphics firm, shook up the entire computer industry with its 3-D graphics. Its alliances with Nintendo, Time Warner, and Kodak are helping revolutionize the computer game, home video, and film industries respectively. Nucor Steel (See *Innovate or Evaporate 12.1*) first made the mini-mill successful, forever changing the U.S. steel industry by making U.S. steel cost-competitive on a global basis. Then it developed a flat-rolled steel process that is revolutionizing the steel industry for a second time. American Airlines set the industry standard for reservation systems with its Sabre system. This system totally changed the way the industry booked seats and gave American Airlines a tremendous strategic advantage. American Airlines also created the "frequent flyer" program, another first in the industry. Chrysler reintroduced the convertible to the American consumer; it created the mini-van; and most recently, it developed the "cab forward" design. All of these wreaked havoc on its competitors. These examples of creating change reveal just how critical innovation is to achieving competitive advantage. In every case, strategic advantage accrued to the innovator. *Innovate or Evaporate 12.1* describes in more detail how Nucor Steel created chaos in its industry. Not all firms can create change, but most must react to it. Thousands of firms do so every day. *Innovate or Evaporate 12.2* describes how one firm took advantage of a changing environment that it did not create.

Comparing U.S. Firms with Japanese and European Firms

Major Japanese firms continually scan their environments, searching for new opportunities and seeking to identify problems. Nippon Steel, for example, includes "forward looking" among its principles of innovation management. The firm continually searches for new opportunities and sees them in environmental changes. But Nippon Steel also creates change. Another of its principles is **technology fusion**—that is, creating a new technology from two existing technologies. Such actions usually result in chaos for competitors.[7] Similarly, 3M is always examining two areas of potential innovation: customer needs and market trends. It also continually develops

*INNOVATE
OR
EVAPORATE*
—
PART II

NUCOR STEEL CHANGES THE RULES OF THE GAME

One of the capabilities of innovative firms is to change the industry of which they are a member. The innovative firm can create chaos for the others. Nucor Steel is a firm that has done just that in the steel industry. The firm's primary innovations in recent years have been in the development of new technologies. Historically, the firm has also been innovative in process design, management practices, organizational structure, and human resource management practices.

When Ken Iverson, the firm's Chairman and CEO took over in 1965, he saw steel as a commodity with relatively little differentiation. He therefore initiated a low-cost strategy, using technology and increased employee productivity to reduce costs. Other firms thought he was crazy. But today, Nucor is the sixth-largest U.S. producer of steel, and other firms are emulating its approach.

Nucor achieved $1.6 billion in sales in 1992 with only four layers of management: foremen, department heads, general managers, and top management. The corporate staff consists of only twenty-one individuals, including secretaries and clerical personnel. The firm empowers its general managers (of profit divisions) to make the decisions necessary to run their businesses.

The company shares information with its employees so that they can make better decisions and understand the firm's operations more fully. Employees are encouraged to ask managers why they made a particular decision and even to tell them when they think a decision is ill-advised. The firm doesn't want its managers to continue making bad decisions, and front-line workers often know the most about what should be done in a particular situation.

INNOVATE OR EVAPORATE 12.1

continued next page

NUCOR STEEL

A significant part of employee compensation is based on the company's financial success. All bonuses are based on written guidelines for exceeding standards. There are no discretionary bonuses. The front-line employee's group-based bonus is paid weekly so that it has a motivational impact. The company is nonunionized, and the average mill employee was paid $40,000 in 1992, about twice the going rate for people doing the same work in the same geographic areas. Everyone shares the pain of a bad year, but the impact is greater on managers, whose compensation packages are reduced progressively at higher levels of the hierarchy.

The firm has always used the latest technology, much of it internally derived. It was one of the first mini-mill companies, and it entered the flat-rolled steel business in direct competition with large integrated companies by creating a new flat-rolled process that gave it a cost advantage. In the late 1980s the firm had created new manufacturing processes for ball bearings, entering a mature market with the aim of being a low-cost producer. It had also entered into a joint venture with a Japanese company, Yamato Kogyo, Ltd., to make large structural steel items using mini-mill technologies, something no one had tried before.

Nucor's results have been impressive. For example, the firm can make steel in its Connorsville, Indiana, plant with only $40 a ton in labor costs, about the same as the cost of shipping it from Korea, Japan, or Brazil. Such cost advantages allowed Nucor to make $87 million in 1992 while most major steelmakers were losing money. The company has not shown a quarterly loss in 25 years, and dividends have increased in each of the last twenty years.

The firm does have some problems. Iverson is about to retire, and as noted earlier, imitators have begun to follow the mini-mill strategy. Moreover, Nucor's flat-rolled mills depend on scrap steel, which has doubled in price recently. But true to its strategy, the firm is already looking for low-cost alternatives.

Sources: Timothy Aeppel, "Nucor Corporation Steels Itself for Battle of the Look-a-likes," *Wall Street Journal* (December 9, 1993), p. B2; F. Kenneth Iverson, "Changing the Rules of the Game," *Planning Review* (September-October 1993), pp. 9-12; Frank Barnes, "A Nucor Commitment," in James M. Higgins and Julian W. Vincze, *Strategic Management: Text and Cases,* 5th ed. (Ft. Worth: Dryden Press, 1993), pp. 816-843.

BANDAG REINVENTS ITS EUROPEAN OPERATION

In the mid-1980s, Bandag Inc., a tire retreading firm based in Iowa, was experiencing a decline in its European operations. Important patents were running out, and Europe was slowly but surely moving toward a single economy. Although the firm had been operating in Europe since 1950, its distribution operations were characterized by high prices and little concern for volume. When Martin G. Carver took over the business, one of his major goals was to increase Bandag's share of the European market.

To do so, he reinvented the company's distribution scheme, turning the firm into the European McDonald's of the retreading business. He began by using aggressive franchising ($150,000 apiece). More important, in a radical departure from the way other retreading firms operate in Europe, franchisees were expected to do much of their business at the customer's location rather than having the customer bring trucks to the shop. Tires are carried to the customer's location and mounted on the spot, enabling truckers to drive their rigs all day and not lose shipping time for tire changes.

This innovative strategy has been extremely successful. Bandag's market share in Europe's retread market jumped from 5 percent in the early 1980s to 20 percent in 1992.

Source: Patrick Oster, "Breaking Into European Markets by Breaking the Rules," *Business Week* (January 20, 1992), pp. 88-89.

INNOVATE OR EVAPORATE 12.2

new technologies and applications.[8] (Nippon Steel and 3M are discussed further in Chapter 13.) Hewlett-Packard cannibalizes its own products by introducing new ones in order to preempt competitors.[9] Among the major European firms, Ikea and Philips are the most likely to create chaos for others. Ikea has revolutionized the furniture industry by redefining the role of the customer (see *Innovate or Evaporate 3.3*). Philips is working hard on new multimedia products and is a market leader in that area.[10] (See *Innovate or Evaporate 9.1*.)

14. Continually Create New Products and Services and Enhance Old Ones; Continually Develop Process, Marketing, and Management Innovations.

Throughout this book we have described numerous firms that are innovative—firms that have produced new products and services and developed new processes. U.S.-based firms such as Merck, 3M, Kodak, Johnson & Johnson, General Electric, Corning, Procter & Gamble, Xerox, Federal Express, and UPS are successfully competing against global competitors like Sony, Toyota, Toshiba, Ikea, and Philips by developing hundreds of new products.[11] In 1991, 50 percent of Hewlett-Packard's total sales were contributed by products that didn't exist three years previously.[12] By 1993, this proportion had risen to nearly 70 percent.[13] A study of 69 strategic business units of *Fortune* 500 manufacturing firms revealed that, on average, 25 percent of total sales were contributed by new products.[14]

U.S.-based firms are also meeting global competition through process innovations that cut costs.[15] Cooper Tire Company (see *Innovate or Evaporate 1.2*) relies heavily on a product innovation strategy based on customer needs supported by a company-wide process-innovation strategy. In a mature industry with little prospect of furthur growth, Cooper's strategy has succeeded in spurring substantial growth in revenues and profits. Heavy emphasis is placed on customer service and innovative customer service operations.[16]

Many of the firms mentioned in this book have advertising programs based on innovation skills. Lockheed, for example, focused major ads on the theme of its innovation. TRW has used the "It was just an idea," theme; while GE "brings new things to life."

Firms such as GE (see discussion of question #38 in Chapter 8 and *Innovate or Evaporate 5.4 and 8.5*) actively seek innovative improvements in management. Through programs such as work outs, process mapping, and best practices, GE has started a management revolution.[17] Ray Stata, chairman of Boston-based Analog Devices, Inc., believes that management innovation is absolutely necessary to the future success of U.S. firms. He cites Japan as the first nation to make major economic breakthroughs as a result of management innovation. Improved management practices were the focal point of his rejuvenation of Analog Devices.[18]

Comparing U.S. Firms with Japanese and European Firms

Business Week teamed up with CHI Research, Inc. to perform **innovation bibliometrics**, a type of statistical analysis that scans patents and scientific papers. Together they have produced a ranking of the technological power of firms throughout the world. Toshiba ranks first, followed by three other Japanese firms. In fifth place is Eastman Kodak. Europe's highest scorer is Philips Electronics, in eleventh place.[19] Japanese firms also have high levels of skill in continuous improvement. U.S. and European firms are moving rapidly to catch up.

21. Practice Continuous Improvement as Well as Big Bang Innovation.

Chapter 6 discussed the need for firms to engage in two forms of innovation: big bang and continuous improvement. The following firms, all of which have been discussed in this book, are successful at both: General Electric, Chrysler, Johnson & Johnson, Ford, Toyota, Norfolk Southern, McDonalds, AT&T, Nippon Steel, Xerox, Nucor Steel, 3M, Honda, Merck, Hewlett-Packard, Apple Computer, parts of IBM, Toro, Texaco, Motorola, Sony, Intel, Hitachi, Eastman Chemical, Philips, Steelcase,

Herman Miller, BMW, Mazda, and Samsung. Other firms that have had some success in these endeavors include SGS-Thomsen, some divisions of General Motors, Boeing, Kodak, Amoco Chemical, Acer, Black & Decker, UPS, USAA, Federal Express, Frito-Lay, Anheuser Busch, Cincinnati Milacron, Procter & Gamble, Ciba-Geigy, and Silicon Graphics. Most of these firms, good as they are, still have room for improvement.

Comparing U.S. Firms with Japanese and European Firms

U.S. firms have historically been excellent big bang innovators, particularly in the new-product arena, while Japanese firms excel at continuous improvement of both product and process. U. S. firms tend to pursue dramatic innovations, while Japanese firms have settled for smaller innovations, especially in processes. Today, however, the Japanese are learning how to create big bang innovation while U.S. firms are learning about continuous improvement and process innovation. The United States is even inching ahead in management innovation with reengineering. European firms are, on average, a distant third in both types of skills.

28. Engage in Knowledge Management—Identifying Knowledge Assets, Sharing Information, Tapping the Innate Knowledge of Individuals.

Recall from Chapter 1 that *knowledge* as used in this book means "patents, processes, management skills, technologies, information about customers and suppliers, and old-fashioned experience."[20] It is becoming increasingly clear that successful innovative organizations engage in **knowledge management**. This means identifying knowledge resources, creating new knowledge, and disseminating knowledge throughout the organization. It also means taking the tacit knowledge of each employee about how to do his or her job and turning it into explicit knowledge that others may use.[21] Treating the organization as a depository for intellectual capital requires a new perspective for most U.S. organizations and their managers, who are used to thinking in terms of tangible rather than intangible assets.[22]

Comparing U.S. Firms with Japanese and European Firms

Japanese firms understand better than U.S. firms that knowledge and knowledge management are key ingredients in successful innovation, although many U.S. firms are moving in this direction. As Ikujiro Nonoka, a professor of business who has conducted research on Japanese management practices, observes, "The centerpiece of the Japanese approach is the recognition that creating new knowledge is not simply a matter of 'processing' objective information. Rather, it depends on tapping the tacit and often highly subjective insights, intuitions, and hunches of individual employees and making those insights available for testing and use by the company as a whole."[23] U.S. firms that manage knowledge successfully for the purpose of becoming more innovative have focused primarily on disseminating information and knowledge throughout the firm. GE, for example, holds seminars in which a division explains to others the results of best practices surveys or the knowledge gained through workouts or process mapping.[24] Another U.S. firm that is coming to grips with knowledge management is Hewlett-Packard. *Innovate or Evaporate 12.3* reviews part of HP's approach to knowledge management.

35. Practice Organizational Learning—Learn From Experience and Knowledge.

Innovation requires a commitment to organizational learning. A **learning organization** "is an organization skilled at creating, acquiring, and transferring knowledge, and at modifying its behavior to reflect new knowledge and insights."[25] Practitioners and researchers alike recognize that organizational learning is a key factor in innovation strategy.[26] "Learning organizations are skilled at five main activities: systematic problem solving, experimentation with new approaches, learning from their own experiences and past history, learning from the experience and best practices of others, and transferring knowledge quickly and efficiently throughout the organization. Each is accompanied by a distinctive mind-set, tool kit, and pattern of behavior."[27] Innovation can occur in all five skill areas but is most likely to be used in systematic problem solving and to be the objective of experiments with new approaches. One of the key skills organizations

Skills

Chapter 12

can learn is how to innovate.[28] One organization that is skilled at organizational learning is Xerox. *Innovate or Evaporate 12.4* reviews Xerox's approach to applying the systematic problem-solving skills necessary for organizational learning.

From the standpoint of innovation, there are two principal types of learning: single-loop and double-loop. **Single-loop learning** "emphasizes the type of association building that results from repetition and routine. The organization is open to its environment but only in ways consistent with its guiding norms and the capabilities of its existing technology."[29] **Double-loop learning** "involves changing 'what the organization is doing' in terms of its underlying norms and technologies."[30] A third type of learning enters the picture at the corporate level. While single-loop and double-loop learning deal with particular projects, products, or processes, **institutional learning** deals with the overall corporate effort "to learn to improve the effectiveness of future innovation projects based on experience with previous product innovations, successful and unsuccessful."[31]

If we match types of learning with types of innovation, we find that continuous improvement or incremental innovation is associated with singe-loop learning whereas discontinuous or big bang innovation is associated with double-loop learning.[32] Single-loop and double-loop learning are related to the "S" curves described in Chapter 6, as can be seen in Figure 12.1.

FIGURE 12.1 INNOVATION-BASED LEARNING RELATIONSHIPS

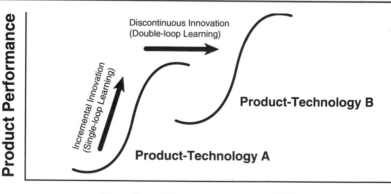

HEWLETT-PACKARD'S KANBAN APPROACH TO EMPLOYEE EDUCATION

An important trend in knowledge management is analogous to the Kanban approach to inventory management. The Kanban approach is named after the Kanban cards used in Toyota's production lines. In this system, when a team of workers needs a specific part it sends a Kanban card to internal suppliers requesting that part. Because it sends the card only when it needs parts, supply is based directly on demand and there is no need to hold more inventory than is needed at a particular time. A similar shift to just-in-time delivery of knowledge to employees is occurring in several companies. The basic idea is to do away with classrooms and put education on line, on demand. Hewlett-Packard is leading the way to improved educational services at a small percentage of previous costs.

As discussed in *Innovate or Evaporate 4.1*, at HP innovation is a corporate strategy. In human resources, for example, the firm has adopted a Kanban approach to training. "We're constantly pushing to blur the lines between learning and doing the job," says Susan Burnett, manager of worldwide sales force development.

A few years ago HP found that virtually all of its sales training was done in the classroom. Sales reps were spending three weeks a year in classrooms rather than with customers. Moreover, of

continued next page

HEWLETT PACKARD

the time spent with customers, about three-fourths was spent transferring catalogs and reports from the central office to the customers' offices. Compounding problems for the sales force was a shrinking product life cycle from eighteen months to as little as six months. At the same time, the technological complexity, specs, and applications of products were growing by leaps and bounds. Finally, administrative overhead was being cut just when all this information was approaching overload levels.

The solution was the Hewlett-Packard Interactive Network (HPIN) that Tom Wilkins, R&D manager for media technologies, helped create. The network has been so cost-effective that it has become a profit center. Before 1990, whenever HP rolled out a major new product, it would bring its 950 sales reps to a conference center for a day or two of training, at a cost of about $5 million. The use of HPIN has reduced that cost to $80,000, a reduction of more than 98 percent, with no loss in effectiveness.

Sources: Lewis J. Perelman, "Kanban to Kanbrain," *Forbes ASAP* (June 6, 1994), pp. 85-95.

Comparing U.S. Firms with Japanese and European Firms

Japanese firms are especially adept at organizational learning, partly because Japanese managers think organizationally rather than individually or functionally, and partly because they emphasize continuous improvement. Typical is the Japanese pharmaceutical industry. Japanese firms first learned how to make drugs under licenses from foreign firms, borrowing or buying knowledge from others. Now they are on the leading edge as innovators of pharmaceutical products.[33]

XEROX'S SYSTEMATIC PROBLEM-SOLVING PROCESS

Systematic problem-solving in most firms draws heavily upon the philosophy and methods of the quality movement. Real learning demands hard facts to support problem solving; otherwise it cannot take place. Thus, firms that practice organizational learning use the following techniques:

- The scientific method, as opposed to guesswork, for recognizing and identifying problems (what Deming referred to as the "Plan, Do, Check, Act" cycle and others call hypothesis-generation, hypothesis-testing techniques).

- Data, rather than assumptions, for solving problems. This is referred to as "fact-based management."

- Simple statistical tools (histograms, Pareto charts, correlations, cause-and-effect diagrams) to organize data and draw inferences.

- Simple idea generation techniques, such as brainstorming, for generating alternative solutions.

In 1983 Xerox launched its Leadership Through Quality initiative. Since then virtually all Xerox employees have been trained in small-group dynamics and problem-solving techniques. They follow the six-step problem-solving process shown in the accompanying table.

Employees have been provided with problem-solving tools in four areas: collecting information and generating ideas (interviewing, surveying, and brainstorming); reaching consensus (rating forms, list reduction, weighted voting); analyzing and displaying data (force-field analysis and cause-and-effect diagrams); and planning actions (Gantt charts and flow charts). The result has been a consistent, scientific approach to problem solving. Employees are expected to use these techniques in all meet-

continued next page

INNOVATE OR EVAPORATE 12.4

339

XEROX

ings, and no topic is off limits. CEO Paul Allaire states that when a group was formed to review the firm's organization structure and suggest alternatives, it used the same process.

To determine the effectiveness of what Xerox has done, look at its track record since it became a quality learning organization. It has recaptured market share, raised its quality to high levels, created many new products, and cut its costs.

Sources: David A. Garvin, "Building a Learning Organization," *Harvard Business Review* (July-August 1993), pp. 81-82; Robert Howard, "The CEO as Organizational Architect: An Interview with Xerox's Paul Allaire," *Harvard Business Review* (September-October 1992), p. 106.

XEROX's PROBLEM SOLVING PROCESS

Step	Question to Be Answered	Expansion/ Divergence	Contraction/ Convergence	What's Needed to Go to the Next Step
1. Identify and select problem	What do we want to change?	Lots of problems for consideration	One problem statement, one "desired state" agreed upon	Identification of the gap "desired state" described in observable terms
2. Analyze problem	What's preventing us from reaching the "desired state"?	Lots of potential causes identified	Key cause(s) identified and verified	Key cause(s) documented and ranked
3. Generate potential solutions	How could we make the change?	Lots of ideas on how to solve the problem	Potential solutions clarified	Solution list
4. Select and plan the solution	What's the best way to do it?	Lots of criteria for evaluating potential solutions Lots of ideas on how to implement and evaluate the selected solution	Criteria to use for evaluating solution agreed upon Implementation and evaluation plans agreed upon	Plan for making and monitoring the change Measurement criteria to evaluate effectiveness of solution
5. Implement the solution	Are we following the plan?		Implementation of agreed upon contingency plans (if necessary)	Solution in place
6. Evaluate the solution	How well did it work?		Effectiveness of solution agreed upon Continuing problems (if any) identified	Verification that the problem is solved, or Agreement to address continuing problems

There are four types of organizational learning in Japanese organizations:[34]

1.   Maintenance learning, with the emphasis on incremental changes.

2.   Adaptive learning, in which new procedures are established.

3.   Transitional learning, through radical environmental changes.

4.   Creative learning, in which objectives, procedures, structures, and systems undergo a complete overhaul.

U.S. and European firms are behind in organizational learning and would do well to base their learning efforts on this model.

42. Leverage Resources to Achieve Seemingly Unobtainable Objectives.

Strategy researchers Gary Hamel and C. K. Prahalad have identified two distinct perspectives on how to implement the basic model of strategic management. The **strategic fit** model suggests that the firm should adjust its strategy according to the fit between its strengths and weaknesses and the threats and opportunities in its external environment. In this model, ambitions should be trimmed to match available resources. The **leveraging resources** approach, in contrast, suggests that resources should be leveraged to achieve seemingly unreachable goals, as embodied in the term **strategic intent**.

Strategic intent encompasses not only unfettered ambition but a management process that includes "focusing the organization's attention on winning; motivating people by communicating the value of the target; leaving room for individual and team contributions; sustaining enthusiasm by providing new operational definitions as circumstances change; and using intent consistently to guide resource allocations."[35] By leveraging its resources the firm increases its strengths or looks for ways to use them to overcome weaknesses and threats and take advantage of opportunities. (See discussion at beginning of chapter 5.)

In short, strategic fit is a conservative interpretation of strategic management, whereas, leveraging resources is an aggressive interpretation. The strategic fit model appears to be more popular in western firms, while the leveraging resources model is more popular in Japan.

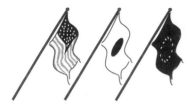

Comparing U.S. Firms with Japanese and European Firms

Examination of Japanese firms such as Komatsu, Toyota, Honda, and Canon suggests that under the strategic fit model they would never have become such powerful players in their respective industries. Rather, they would have been satisfied simply to be niche players. It was their focus on strategic intent that made them powerful. Meanwhile, the strategic fit strategies of Western firms have caused them to decline because of the diminished ambitions resulting from their efforts to fit themselves to their environments. For example, U.S. firms stopped manufacturing television sets and most other consumer electronic products. U.S. firms also forfeited large market shares in steel, automobiles, and textiles. European firms are giving up significant market shares in consumer electronics, and as the EEC lowers its trade barriers they will forfeit a major share in autos as well. In Germany, for instance, where free trade exists, Japan already has 30 percent of the auto market.[36] One U.S. firm that pursues innovation by leveraging its resources and is a leading competitor in its industry is Whirlpool, which is highlighted in *Innovate or Evaporate 12.5.*

49. Invest Heavily and Appropriately in R&D.

This is *almost* a trick question. The key word is appropriately. R&D managers and others who manage innovation suggest that providing limited resources for innovators (product innovators in this case) actually motivates them. In such situations, "less is more." When there's too much money, people are less likely to stretch; less money causes innovators to stretch.[37] However, a survey of R&D managers reports that the single greatest perceived obstacle to successful product innovation is lack of resources.[38]

WHIRLPOOL LEVERAGES ITS RESOURCES TO BECOME A WORLD-CLASS COMPETITOR

When David Whitwam became CEO of Whirlpool in 1987, the firm was mired in a war of attrition in the U.S. market, a war in which cost and quality were the only weapons and declining margins the only prize. Whitwam recognized, however, that the firm had to be a global competitor and that this would require leveraging global capabilities and eliminating regional fiefdoms and inadequate ways of satisfying customers.

In 1989 in a daring move, he purchased N.V. Philips's floundering European appliance business, a move that catapulted Whirlpool into the number one position in the worldwide appliance industry. Then he chose to transform the two firms into a unified, customer-driven organization that could use its combined talents to create chaos in the global marketplace. As a result, Whirlpool has set the standard for the industry in terms of new-product innovation and industry price structure.

Whitwam asserts, "The only way to gain lasting competitive advantage is to leverage your capabilities around the world so that the company as a whole is greater than the sum of its parts. Being an international company—selling globally, having global brands or operations in different countries isn't enough....To me, 'competitive advantage' means having the best technologies and processes for designing, manufacturing, selling, and

continued next page

INNOVATE OR EVAPORATE 12.5

WHIRLPOOL

servicing your products at the lowest possible costs. Our vision of Whirlpool is to integrate our geographical businesses wherever possible....We want to be able to take the best capabilities we have and leverage them in all of our operations worldwide."

To achieve these goals, he adds, "You must create an organization whose people are adept at exchanging ideas, processes, and systems across borders, people who are absolutely free of the 'not-invented-here' syndrome, people who are constantly working together to identify the best global opportunities and the biggest global problems facing the organization."

"Our strategy is based on the premise that world-class cost and quality are merely the ante—the price of being in the game at all. We have to provide a compelling reason other than price for consumers to buy Whirlpool-built products. We can do that only by understanding the consumer better than anyone else does and then translating our understanding into clearly superior product designs, features, and after-sales support." His goal is for consumers to prefer the Whirlpool brand because it offers greater overall value than competing products. He believes that achieving that goal requires taking a giant step back from the business and rethinking who their customers are and what their needs are. He suggests that to many this may not sound earth-shattering, but it is because it means rethinking the very nature of the business.

He continues, "all of us in this industry have been telling ourselves that we're in 'the refrigerator business,' 'the washing-machine business,' or 'the range business.' None of us saw a great deal of room for product innovation, which is undoubtedly why there hasn't been radical innovation in thirty years, apart from the microwave oven and the trash compactor. If you want to open the door to imagination and innovation, isn't it more useful to think of 'the fabric-care business,' and 'the food-preservation business'?"

He believes that the starting point isn't the existing product but the function consumers buy products to accomplish. "When you return to first principles, the design issues dramatically

WHIRLPOOL

change. The microwave couldn't have been invented by someone who assumed he or she was in the business of designing a range. Such a design breakthrough required seeing that the opportunity is 'easier, quicker food preparation,' not 'a better range.'"

Whirlpool is applying these broader definitions in very direct ways. For example, organizationally, they have created what they call an advanced product-development capability to serve markets around the world. Its mission is to look beyond traditional product definitions to the consumer processes for which products of the future will have to provide clear benefits.

He adds, "take 'the fabric-care business,' which we used to call the 'washing-machine business.' We're now studying consumer behavior from the time people take off their dirty clothes at night until they've been cleaned and ironed and hung in the closet. What are we looking for? The worst part of the process is not the washing and drying. The hard part is when you take your clothes out of the dryer and you have to do something with them—iron, fold, hang them up. Whoever comes up with a product to make this part of the process easier, simpler, or quicker is going to create an incredible market."

the innovatively correct term for me is
"Food Preservation Device"

Source: Regina Fazio Maruca, "The Right Way to Go Global: An Interview with Whirlpool CEO David Whitwam," *Harvard Business Review* (March-April 1994), pp. 134-145.

Skills

Chapter 12

Comparing U.S. Firms with Japanese and European Firms

On average, Japanese firms spend the equivalent of about 3 percent of GDP on R&D, while the proportion for U.S. firms is about 1.9 percent.[39] And the Japanese get more bang for their buck: more new products and processes for the funds invested.[40] Failure to provide adequate R&D funding can have unfortunate results. For example, American Home Products Corporation, a health care/pharmaceutical company, got caught up in the cost-cutting craze of the 1980s, slashing R&D as well as other costs. As a result, profits began to slip; there simply weren't any new products in the pipeline. In 1990, therefore, the firm spent an amount equal to 11 percent of sales on R&D,[41] a record for the firm and a substantial amount compared not only to the industry average but also to the meager 2.5 percent of sales spent by U.S. industry on average in 1990.[42]

Some U.S. firms invest heavily in R&D, but most do not. Over the years U.S. firms in textiles, steel, consumer electronics, and automobiles have fallen behind in the innovation race. Now the same thing is happening to U.S.-based construction firms. Their Japanese counterparts are investing significantly more in R&D and gaining major competitive advantages over their U.S. counterparts. *Innovate or Evaporate 12.6* reviews the plight of the U.S. construction industry.

THE U.S. CONSTRUCTION INDUSTRY TRAILS JAPAN IN R&D

The U.S. construction industry has been mired in a recession since the mid-1980s. Overbuilding has left the industry with a ten-year oversupply of office buildings in some cities. And while members rightfully complain that they are locked out of Japan's construction industry, they now have a growing problem at home. Japanese firms are increasingly entering the global markets, including the United States, with superior technology. Because of its relatively low cost and reduced construction time, that technology gives those firms a tremendous competitive advantage. The new Salt Lake Arena, for example, was built for $86 million by a Japanese joint venture firm. The Japanese firm took one year less to complete the project than a typical American firm would have taken, and at a lower cost. Part of the cost and time differential resulted from superior technology. For instance, the Japanese placed the entire roof on the arena at once rather than hoist it piece by piece by cranes as American firms would have done.

U.S. firms' share of the global market dropped from 37 percent in 1982 to 34 percent in 1989. The collective share of firms from the five biggest competing countries rose to 52.5 percent from 38.5 percent over the same period. Japanese firms' share of construction outside of Japan rose from 8 percent to 11.5 percent.

Japanese construction firms gross about $500 billion annually, U.S. contractors about $400 billion. But Japanese firms spend $2 billion annually on R&D compared to only $400 million for U.S. firms. Japan has at least thirty major construction labora-

continued next page

INNOVATE OR EVAPORATE 12.6

CONSTRUCTION

tories; the United States has only five. And on average the Japanese employ about 300 people in their labs; in contrast, the five U.S. labs employ only about a half dozen people. U.S. firms are mired in age-old, antiquated processes, at least partly owing to a competitive bidding process that emphasizes cost and discourages innovation. Japanese firms have emphasized innovation and technology for the past forty years. As a result, they have invented such things as construction robots, earthquake-proof building foundations, and specialized tunneling devices. They have also adopted modern management practices and use sophisticated information systems to a much greater extent than their U.S. counterparts.

Source: Jim Carlton, "U.S. Contractors Trail Japan in R&D," *The Wall Street Journal* (August 6, 1991), p. A2.

STRATEGIC AND OPERATIONAL PLANNING GUIDE

Skills Question #	Where are we now? (Score)	Where do we want to be? (What are our objectives?)	
7. Proactively create new opportunities and respond to change			
14. Continuously create new ideas			
21. Practice "big bang" & continuous inno-vation			
28. Engage in know-ledge management for innovation			
35. Practice organiza-tional learning			
42. Leverage resources to achieve difficult objectives			
49. Invest heavily and appropriately in R&D			

How do we get there?		
What needs to be done?	By whom?	By when?

REFERENCES

1. Kathy Rebello, "A Juicy New Apple?" *Business Week* (March 7, 1994), pp. 88-90.

2. Gary Hamel and C. K. Prahalad, "Strategy as Stretch and Leverage," *Harvard Business Review* (March/April 1993), pp. 75-84; C. K. Prahalad and Gary Hamel, "The Core Competence of the Corporation," *Harvard Business Review* (May/June 1990), pp. 79-91.

3. Thomas A. Stewart, "Welcome to the Revolution," *Fortune* (December 13, 1993), p. 66.

4. Thomas A. Stewart, "Rate Your Readiness to Change," *Fortune* (February 7, 1994), pp. 106-110.

5. Thomas J. Peters, *Thriving on Chaos* (New York: Knopf, 1987), p. 3.

6. Ibid, pp. 191-279.

7. B. Bowonder and T. Miyake, "Management of Corporate Innovation: A Case Study From the Nippon Steel Corporation," *Creativity and Innovation Management* (June 1992), pp. 75-85.

8. Ronald A. Mitsch, "Three Roads to Innovation," *Journal of Business Strategy* (September/October 1990), pp. 18-21.

9. Alan Deutschman, "How Hewlett-Packard Continues to Grow and Grow," *Fortune* (May 2, 1994), pp. 90-100.

10. Gail Edmondson, "Philips Needs Laser Speed," *Business Week* (June 6, 1994), pp. 46-47.

11. Kenneth Labich, "The Innovators," *Fortune* (June 6, 1988), pp. 51-64; "These Innovators Discover New Products—New Profits," *Money* (April 1991), pp. 57-62.

12. Robert D. Hof, "Suddenly Hewlett-Packard is Doing Everything Right," *Business Week* (March 23, 1992), pp. 55-56.

13. Alan Deutschman, op. cit., p. 90.

14. Vijay Mahajan and Jerry Wind, "New Product Models: Practice, Shortcomings and Desired Improvements," *Journal of Product Innovation Management* (June 1992), pp. 128-139.

15. Kenneth Labich, "The Innovators," loc. cit.

16. Carol Hymowitz and Thomas F. O'Boyle, "A Way That Works: Two Disparate Firms Find Keys to Success in Troubled Industries," *Wall Street Journal* (May 29, 1991), pp. A1, A7; Ivan Gorr, "Cooper Tires: Successful Adaptation in a Changing Industry," *Journal of Business Strategy* (Winter 1987), pp. 83-86.

17. Thomas A. Stewart, "GE Keeps those Ideas Coming," *Fortune* (August 12, 1991), pp. 41-49.

18. Ray Stata, "Organizational Learning—The Key to Management Innovation," *Sloan Management Review* (Spring 1989), pp. 41-49.

19. Robert Buderi, "Global Innovation: Who's in the Lead?" *Business Week* (August 3, 1992), pp. 68-73.

20. Thomas A. Stewart, "Brainpower," *Fortune* (June 3, 1991), p. 44.

21. Ikujiro Nonaka, "The Knowledge-Creating Company," *Harvard Business Review* (November/December 1991), p. 97.

22. Thomas A. Stewart, "Brainpower," op. cit., pp. 44-57.

23. Ikujiro Nonaka, op. cit., pp. 97-98.

INNOVATE
OR
EVAPORATE
———
PART II

24. Mike Belanger, Dick Hilbert, and Murray Wilson, "Putting the 'Best' in Best Practices," presentation at the Strategic Management Society Annual Meeting (Toronto, Canada, October 24, 1991).

25. David A. Garvin, "Building a Learning Organization," *Harvard Business Review* (July/August 1993), p. 78.

26. Daryl McKee, "An Organizational Learning Approach to Product Innovation," *Journal of Product Innovation Management* (September 1992), pp. 232-245.

27. David A. Garvin, op. cit., p. 81.

28. Daryl McKee, op. cit., p. 232.

29. Ibid., p. 236.

30. Ibid.

31. Ibid., p. 237.

32. Ibid., p. 235.

33. "Japan's Medicine Men Take Aim," *Economist* (March 2, 1991), pp. 61-62.

34. B. Bowonder and T. Miyake, op. cit., p. 81; P. W. Meyers, "Non-Linear Learning in Large Technological Firms," *Research Policy* (1985), pp. 97-115.

35. Gary Hamel and C. K. Prahalad, "Strategic Intent," *Harvard Business Review* (May/June 1989), pp. 64-65.

36. Shawn Tully, "Europe Hits the Brakes on 1992," *Fortune* (December 17, 1990), p. 137.

37. A representative discussion can be found in Alan Farnham, "How to Nurture Creative Sparks," *Fortune* (January 10, 1994), p. 100.

38. David H. Gobeli and Daniel J. Brown, "Improving the Process of Product Innovation," *Research-Technology Management* (March/April 1993), pp. 38-44.

39. "U.S. Patents: Big Blue Tops Japanese Firms, *U.S. News & World Report* (March 28, 1994), p. 16; Brian Dumaine, "Closing the Innovation Gap," *Fortune* (December 2, 1991), pp. 57-59; Robert Buderi, "The Brakes Go On in R&D," *Business Week* (July 1, 1991), pp. 24-26.

40. Brian Dumaine, Ibid.; Robert Buderi, Ibid.

41. Bruce Hager, "Learning to Spend at American Home," *Business Week* (June 11, 1990), pp. 80-81.

42. Frederick Shaw Myers, "Japan: Putting The 'R' in R & D," *Chemical Engineering* (February 1990), pp. 30-33, 48; Bruce C. P. Rayner, "The Rising Price of Technological Leadership," *Electronic Business* (March 18, 1991), pp. 52-56; Fumiaki Kitamura, "Japan's R & D Budget Second Largest in World," *Business Japan* (November 1990), pp. 35-47.

CHAPTER 13

"The best companies see innovation as a function that needs managing."
Brian Dumaine,
"Closing the Innovation Gap"
Fortune

The forty-nine characteristics presented in the questionnaires in Chapter Four are used to identify innovation strengths and weaknesses in organizations. Chapters 5-12 help firms take the actions that are necessary to make those characteristics part of their organizational skill set. Some of the characteristics identified in the questionnaires may be more important than others, depending on a firm's unique situation. But clearly, the more of them a firm possesses, the more likely it is to be innovative—and, therefore, the more likely it is to be highly competitive and highly profitable. *Innovation is not a guarantee of competitiveness, but a firm can not be competitive without it.*

ORGANIZATIONAL ROLE MODELS

3M is one of the few companies that possesses virtually all of these characteristics. If a firm wants a role model to follow, it could hardly do better than 3M. And if a firm wants a model for managing innovation appropriately, it could hardly do better than Nippon Steel Company.

Both of these firms are instructive for their prowess in innovation, and each is instructive in other ways. 3M found its innovation machine stalled as it hit the nineties. It had been guilty of creating a bureaucracy that was stifling creativity. It was slow in getting new products to market. It was focusing too much on basic research without achieving the accompanying products that basic research is supposed to spawn. In short, its innovation quotient was slipping. CEO L. D. DeSimone took corrective actions, and the innovation machine is now functioning well again.[1] 3M is instructive in this situation because it shows that even innovative firms can loose focus. Such lapses occur even in the best of firms, and therefore, we must guard against them.

I am often asked if innovation guarantees competitive success. The answer is of course, no. It is necessary but not sufficient. Good decisions in running the business are necessary throughout the firm as Nippon Steel attests. Nippon has been suffering financially despite having the absolutely most innovative products and processes. The reason, it misestimated the demand for steel. It built a $350 million plant which has sat idle for two years now, draining corporate resources.

This chapter now examines 3M from the viewpoint of the forty-nine characteristics; and examines the Nippon Steel Company from the perspective of its approach to managing innovation.

3M:
THE
MASTERS OF
INNOVATION

While a number of firms, including Hitachi, Merck, Toyota, Banc One, Sony, AT&T, Milliken, Kodak, Barnett Banks, Hewlett-Packard, Intel, Johnson & Johnson, and Rubbermaid, have been highlighted in this book as being very creative, 3M has been mentioned more than any other firm. Indeed, 3M could have been used as the example for each of the forty-nine characteristics of innovative organizations. Most authorities consider it the most innovative firm in the United States, not only in product innovation—it has over 60,000 items in its product lines—but also in process, marketing, and management innovation. Why is 3M so successful? Because it has paid attention to innovation and has created a culture that fosters it. Following is a list of examples of actions taken by 3M to promote innovation as related to each question of the questionnaire. There is a mixture of types of innovation but most are product and process related. Many more could be cited.

3M:

1. Has a stated and working strategy of product and process innovation.

2. Constantly spins out new business units with the innovator in a key position.

3. Ties salaries and promotions to innovation. It even rewards other companies for innovation. For example, in conjunction with The Healthcare Forum, it presents an annual innovation award to the most innovative healthcare organization.

4. Focuses the entire company on innovation.

continued next page

INNOVATE OR EVAPORATE 13.1

3M

5. Has people who generate ideas. It seeks inquisitive, creative people as employees.

6. Celebrates extremely creative people and their accomplishments, for example, through the Carleton Society and the Golden Step Award.

7. Proactively creates new opportunities and responds to change.

8. Encourages employees to spend part of each day figuring out ways to improve products from the customer's perspective. Researchers, marketers, and managers routinely visit customers, and customers often sit in on brainstorming and other product development sessions. Both TQM and innovation programs start with a focus on the customer.

9. Uses cross-functional new-product teams and process-redesign teams. For example, cross-functional "action" (speed) teams were used to develop a new respirator in record time.

10. Celebrates creative successes through various media, including promotional videotapes.

11. Allows people to make mistakes; it looks for a good batting average rather than a home run every time at bat.

12. Has a large staff devoted to R&D. Has encouraged everyone to be an idea person.

13. Encourages risk taking through various programs, including financial investment in new ideas (project Genesis).

14. Continually creates new products or services and/or enhances old ones. Its corporate objectives state that 30 percent of its sales are to come from products that did not exist four years previously. 3M has innovation requirements for all product divisions and for process as well as product innovation. Virtually everyone at 3M is involved in innovation and is given the time and direction to be innovative. Products and services are marketed innovatively. For example, 3M sales personnel use floppy disk sales materials, which replace bulky paper catalogs. Technical information is delivered in the same way. Innovative management is practiced. For example, TQM and innovation are treated as

partners in creating customer satisfaction. 3M has learned that these two forces work well together to create a competitive advantage.

15. Has objectives for its managers for product and process innovation. One of the firm's major objectives is that 30 percent of sales must come from products that did not exist four years previously.

16. Has three different layers of product research centers.

17. Has information management systems that scan the environment for new opportunities, track competitors' actions, conduct benchmarking analyses, keep abreast of new technologies, and exchange information internally. For example, when Dow Chemical chose not to market a unique nonstick coating, 3M licensed the concept from Dow.

18. Suspends judgment on new ideas through a formal process in which new ideas are presented to various groups at various levels of the organization.

19. Uses idea/innovation champions to move ideas through formal processes. For example, Art Fry championed Post-It Notes.

20. Does all it can to separate politics and other factors from the evaluation of ideas. Ideas are reviewed on their merit by several different groups.

21. Seeks continuous, incremental process innovation, but also goes for the big bang in new-product development.

22. Puts every product on trial for its life every five years (or sooner).

23. Stresses maintaining open communication, including positive forms of conflict.

24. Has a formal idea-assessment system for product, process, marketing, and management innovation that, among other things, separates creation from evaluation.

25. Delegates large amounts of authority to division managers, who in turn delegate to their subordinates. Objectives are clearly stated, but how to achieve them is up to the manag-

*The
High-IQ
Organization*

ers and/or subordinates. There are relatively few company policies and little bureaucracy.

26. Trains its people in the use of creativity techniques to generate new ideas.

27. Believes in a creativity ethic: that it has always won or lost through innovation and that unfettered creativity pays off in the end.

28. Engages in knowledge management—identifying knowledge assets, sharing information, and tapping the innate knowledge of individuals. Actively uses information-sharing programs to search for knowledge both outside and inside the firm. 3M encourages its employees to look everywhere for ideas—including competitors, customers, suppliers, and scientific sources outside the company.

29. Makes commercialization or utilization of new processes a priority.

30. Keeps business units small (usually under $200 million in sales), giving them flexibility and the authority to pursue any opportunities they see.

31. Sets financial hurdles for new products, but as only one of several criteria. 3M looks past the numbers to other issues, such as market share.

32. Has a very trusting management style in which employees are encouraged to self-manage and solve problems.

33. Employees use various creative problem-solving techniques.

34. Began managing its culture to make it creative and innovative more than seventy years ago, long before the concept of managing organizational culture became popular. (3M has been in business for over 100 years.)

35. Practices organizational learning through knowledge-sharing sessions.

36. Uses speed strategies and/or almost unobtainable objectives for product, process, marketing, and management innovation.

3M

37. Uses alliances to obtain product, process, marketing, and management innovations; for example, 3M has an alliance with two leading companies of the Sumitomo Group in Japan.

38. Has formal information-distribution systems that require sharing of knowledge among divisions, and encourages informal exchange networks.

39. Uses transformational leadership.

40. Allows selected employees to spend 15 percent of their time every week for reflection on innovative new products or processes.

41. Insists on constant change if it improves the firm.

42. Leverages resources to achieve seemingly unobtainable objectives.

43. Knows when to lead the customer to new products or services, reduce costs through improved processes, take advantage of new-product opportunities through marketing, and reduce costs through innovative management.

44. Has an effective and efficient structure for evaluating product design, process improvement, and marketing or management innovation.

45. Has effective employee suggestion programs.

46. Manages innovative personnel with special approaches, including a hands-off management style, dual career ladders, a penchant for innovation, and removal of political barriers.

47. Provides physical facilities that are conducive to creative thinking and the exchange of ideas.

48. Requires nonmanagerial employees to have stated objectives for product, process, marketing, and/or management innovation.

49. Invests heavily and appropriately in R&D. (In 1992 the company spent $1 billion on R&D, an amount equivalent to 7.3 percent of sales.)

The High-IQ Organization

Chapter 13

3M

Sources: Kevin Kelly, "The Drought is Over at 3M," *Business Week* (November 7, 1994), pp. 140-141; James J. Thompson, "Quality and Innovation at 3M: A Partnership for Customer Satisfaction," *Tapping the Network Journal* (Winter 1993-1994), pp. 2-5; Chris Rauber, "21st Century Vision," *Healthcare Forum* (January-February 1994), pp. 75-78; "Computerized Sales Tools Give Instant Information," *Adhesives Age* (April 1994), pp. 37-38; Philip E. Ross, "Teflon Deja Vu?" *Forbes* (April 11, 1994), p. 130; George M. Allen, "Succeeding in Japan," *Vital Speeches of the Day* (May 1, 1994), pp. 429-432; Gregory E. David, "Minnesota Mining & Manufacturing," *Financial World* (September 28, 1993), p. 58; Michael K. Allio, "3M's Sophisticated Formula for Teamwork," *Planning Review* (November-December 1993), pp. 19-21; "3M Backgrounds: 30 Percent Challenge," internal corporate document, 1993; Steve Blount, "Test Marketing: It's Just a Matter of Time," *Sales and Marketing Management* (March 1992), pp. 32-43; Tom Eskstein, "Reader's Report— 3M's Creativity Takes a Lot of Practice," *Business Week* (May 15, 1989), p. 6; Russell Mitchell, "The Masters of Innovation," *Business Week* (April 10, 1989), pp. 58-64; Lewis W. Lehr, "A Hunger for the New," *Success* (September 1988), p. 12; Alicia Johnson, "3M Organized to Innovate," *Management Review* (July 1986), pp. 38-39; Kevin Kelly, "3M Run Scared? Forget About It," *Business Week* (Industrial/Technology Edition, September 16, 1991), pp. 59, 62; Ray Kubinski, Sam Bookhart, Anita Callahan, Marvin L. Isles, Charles Porter, Anthony T. Liotti, and Margie Tomczak, "Managers Forum Focuses on Competitive Strategies and Continuous Improvement," *Industrial Engineering* (February 1992), pp. 30-32.

NIPPON STEEL CORPORATION: HOW TO MANAGE INNOVATION

The steel industry faces many challenges. It is a mature industry with more capacity than demand, and its products are being replaced by plastics and other synthetics. As a result of competition from other heavy industries and a downturn in the economy, many steel producers have gone out of business. Despite this unfavorable environment, Nippon Steel of Japan has persevered. Its competitiveness stems from its ability to innovate.

The following discussion explores Nippon's success from four perspectives: the challenges the company faces, its approach to technological innovation, its emphasis on innovation management, and the lessons that can be learned from its experience.

According to Nippon Steel's management, several major challenges result from the current business environment. They are:

1. The need to introduce new products and improve manufacturing processes.

2. The need to integrate economic functions, such as marketing, design, and operations, so as to speed product and process innovation.

3. The need to scan the environment for future opportunities and threats, and to use new technologies before others do.

4. The need to introduce entirely new technologies.

continued next page

NIPPON STEEL

5. The need to develop new management systems to cope with rapid change.

6. The need to change organizational structure and information management systems, and to speed up the CPS process because of the shortening cycle time between design and manufacturing .

7. The need for specialization as well as integration.

8. The need to recover R&D costs.

9. The need for continuous skill development to match new innovations.

In its efforts to deal with these challenges, Nippon Steel considers innovation the most critical aspect of its strategy.

At the center of Nippon Steel's innovation strategy is technological innovation. The company has grouped its technological innovations into seven categories:

1. Integrating different steps of a process in order to reduce processing delays or waste, or drastically reduce processing time.

Example: linking continuous casting and direct rolling into an integrated process.

2. Developing new products based on market demand.

Example: fire-resistant structural steel.

3. Developing new processes and instruments to increase quality, improve a process, or make monitoring systems more effective.

Example: artificial intelligence controls for blast furnaces.

4. Assimilating acquired technology and transferring it horizontally into new fields.

Example: gold bonding wires.

NIPPON STEEL

5. Developing new construction or fabrication methods.

Example: air-inflated double-membrane stainless-steel roof.

6. Creating new technologies by fusing two diverse technologies.

Example: laser neural network to detect defects in rolling.

7. Using joint ventures to develop new technologies and integrate competencies in diverse fields.

Example: satellite broadcasting receiver system.

Innovation management at Nippon Steel is typical of that found in many Japanese firms. It consists of the following elements:

1. **Forward looking**—to identify new business areas.

2. **Organizational intelligence**—about competitors, new technologies, and other environmental factors.

3. **Four types of organizational learning**—maintenance, adaptive, transitional, and creative.

4. **Technology fusion**—merging of two technologies to form a new technology.

5. **Concurrent engineering.**

6. **Competence building**—through joint ventures.

7. **Horizontal information flow**—using a structure specifically created to promote functional integration.

8. **Intensive skill development in all areas**—reinforced by organizational learning and horizontal information flow.

Nippon Steel's innovation strategy is set forth in the following statement by B. Bowonder and T. Miyake:

"Organizational changes are needed for responding to market changes in its place. New information and communication technology systems have to be implemented, which can facilitate

NIPPON STEEL

organizational communication for coping with the dynamic changes in the environment. Implementing new information and communication systems can simultaneously support a greater degree of centralization and coordination, and at the same time promote flexibility. New information and communication technologies will stimulate innovations through a variety of modes such as:

a) Integrated organizational intelligence made possible by rapid communication and data exchange.

b) Rapid decision making facilitated by information networking and functional integration.

c) Computer graphics, computer aided design and engineering, facilitating design and engineering sharpening the skills.

d) Technical decision support systems, expert systems, and supercomputers, permitting knowledge-based real-time controls and competence fusion.

e) Real-time information exchange through high-quality facsimile system through digital transmission.

f) On-line technical information support system for getting ideas.

Nippon Steel Corporation, as a creative integrator and as an innovative supplier, is expanding its business into new technologies, coupling its own assets with external strengths through original development, establishment of new firms, and capital participation in or business ties with other firms. This is the essence of innovation strategy at Nippon Steel Corporation.

The strategy adopted by Nippon Steel Corporation indicates that 'time' is the most crucial determinant of innovativeness. Through joint ventures, concurrent engineering, strategic alliances, networking, multifunctional new development teams, and new-product subsidiaries Nippon Steel has been able to bring out innovative product/process changes rapidly. Functional integration, together with a decentralized operation, is

TURNING YOURS INTO A HIGH IQ ORGANIZATION

You now know your organization's IQ, and you've developed a set of action plans to help overcome the weaknesses you've uncovered. Your firm is well on its way to becoming a high-IQ organization. So where do you start?

Everything in business must start with strategy. Your organization's innovation strategy reflects the demands of its future environment, and how the organization plans on reacting to or changing that environment to meet its needs. Strategy leads to everything else. The other Seven S's must be pointed in the same direction as strategy.

Shared values must be closely coordinated with strategy. It is highly recommended that the necessary shared values begin to be established during the strategic planning sessions used to formulate innovation strategy. Strategy determines what the shared values should be. Existing shared values should never determine strategy but often do. Strategy is the result of looking at the future, both the internal and external environments, and determining what the organization must do to survive and

The
High-IQ
Organization

Chapter 13

prosper. If organizational shared values are not in alignment with the shared values necessary to accomplish these ends, then they must be changed. Organizational buy-in in terms of shared values is critical to the success of any strategy. Once top management agrees to the new set of values, the rest of the organization must be educated and must participate in embracing the new values and changing the old values.

Changing an organization's shared values takes many months to several years depending on the size of the organization and the extent to which the existing culture is ingrained. Existing and potential organizational catastrophes have a way of moving the organization forward to change its culture more rapidly. For example, a year or two of significant financial losses will make the organization much more likely to change than if it muddles through and makes some money. General Motors is a good example of this. Only when it lost $4.5 billion in 1991, did the motivation develop to make the really significant changes necessary to enable the firm to become a global competitor.

From this point forward, immediately after strategy is determined and work has begun on creating the proper shared values, the organization needs to begin to develop the right structure, the right systems, the right style, and the right staff. To the extent that the items contained in these four S's are simple to do and are low in cost, they can be begun immediately. To the extent that they require comprehensive revision of current organizational practices, work may begin immediately but it may take a long time to complete the necessary changes. Performance Evaluation Review Technique (PERT) charts or Gantt Charts can be used to schedule changes in these four S's in a timely fashion that is coordinated with changes in strategy and shared values. As can be seen in Figure 13.1, which is a Gantt Chart of the typical schedule of activity among the Seven S's, strategy occurs before the others but is overlapped with shared values. Shared values then overlaps each of the other five of the Seven S's.

While three of the measures for skills are essentially results of activity performed in the other Seven S's, to the extent that building a learning organization and managing knowledge require change in the organization, these must be begun fairly early on in the process as indicated in Figure 13.1. To the extent that investing significantly and appropriately in R&D requires change and new levels of organizational commitment, then this work must be begun early on as well. And to the extent that the organization must learn to leverage its resources and achieve the seemingly unobtainable goals relative to innovation, then these practices too must be begun early in the commitment of organizational resources.

FIGURE 13.1 GANTT CHART OF A REPRESENTATIVE SCHEDULE FOR SEVEN S'S ACTIONS

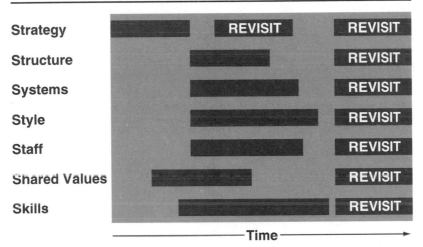

THE STEPS TO BECOMING A HIGH IQ ORGANIZATION

The following paragraphs provide more detail on the actions suggested by Figure 13.1. These actions are divided into three steps. These steps follow in the order necessary for achieving organizational skills, the overall objective of Seven S's actions. Most activity occurs in step 3. The whole process starts with strategy and culture management. Activities within steps can occur simultaneously. However, each firm and manager will want to prioritize these actions as need be.

The High-IQ Organization

Chapter 13

The steps are subdivided by the Seven S's categories relevant to each step. Under each of these categories the numbers of the related questions from the IQI are provided, along with a description of what actions are necessary to satisfy each question. Most of the descriptions assume that the firm has a score of zero for that activity. Thus the terms "establish, develop, begin, and learn" are often used to direct organizational action. If the firm has a score greater than zero, then you should substitute terms such as "improve, and strengthen" to describe desired actions.

STEP I

STRATEGY

1   Establish a stated and working strategy of innovation.

15,42   Establish strategic purposes built around innovation-vision/strategic intent, mission, goals, objectives. Strategic intent requires a strategy of leveraging resources to reach seemingly unobtainable goals.

STYLE/STRATEGY

4   Top management especially, but other managers as well, should create the vision/strategic intent for the firm and for the particular group of employees being managed.

CULTURE

34   At this point, even as you develop strategic purposes and related strategies, using groupware, you may begin to manage the organization's culture to make it more innovation oriented. The new culture can be embraced by those involved in the purposes and strategies formulation sessions. This new culture can then be transferred to the rest of the organization through change management programs aimed at the culture. Typically education and employee participation in sessions aimed at working out the specifics of the new culture are important keys to successful change.

STEP 2

First:

15   Distribute innovation performance objectives to managers. As soon as possible begin to evaluate performance relative to these objectives.

Then:

8   Develop a market orientation.

22   Put each and every product, process, marketing and management practice on trial for its life every eighteen months or sooner.

29   Make commercialization of new ideas a priority.

36   Use speed strategies and/or stretch objectives or deadlines.

43   Learn when and how to lead the customer.

CULTURE

First:

48   Require nonmanagerial employees to have innovation performance objectives. As soon as possible begin to evaluate performance relative to these objectives.

Then:

6   Develop the attitude and behavior of holding creative employees and their contributions in high esteem.

13   Begin to encourage new ideas and the taking of risks.

20   Develop the valuing and practicing of openness.

27   Spread the word that this is an innovative organization and reinforce that value.

41   Place a high value on change and make this part of the organization's culture.

*The
High-IQ
Organization*

Chapter 13

371

STEP 3

STRUCTURE

2	Begin to develop structural mechanisms for innovation.
9	Begin using cross-functional development teams.
16	Institute innovation programs, centers.
23	Develop open communication between innovation centers, programs, teams, and the rest of the company.
30	Change the organization's structure so that it is sufficiently flexible to seize opportunities.
37	Begin building alliances to obtain innovation.
44	Develop an effective and efficient structure for evaluating ideas.

SYSTEMS

3	Develop a system for rewarding creativity and innovation.
17	Develop an innovation management information system.
10	Establish various types of celebrations for creativity and innovation performance.
24	Develop formal product idea assessment systems that separate creation from evaluation and look beyond simple financial analysis.
31	Develop a system for getting products from lab to market place, and a system for implementing process, marketing, and management innovations.
38	Develop both formal and informal programs for information exchange within the company.
45	Develop an effective suggestion program.

11   Develop the attitude in the company, among managers and others, that its acceptable to make mistakes when you innovate (as long as you don't make too many, of course).

18   Develop in managers the behavior of suspending judgment on ideas.

25   Begin a meaningful empowerment program.

32   Teach managers to use a problem solving style for managing.

39   Teach managers how to be transformational leaders, then have them use these skills in moving the organization forward.

46   Teach managers to use the required special skills when managing creative and innovative people.

STAFF

5   Establish the attitude and the related behaviors that show that employees are viewed as vital resources in the achievement of strategy and competitive advantage.

12   Establish a program for recruiting idea people.

19   Develop an idea/innovation champion program.

26   Train employees in creative problem solving, including creativity techniques.

33   Require that employees use the creativity techniques that they have been taught.

40   Begin to provide time for reflection, creativity.

47   Change physical facilities as needed so that they are conducive to idea exchange and creative thinking.

7   Proactively create new opportunities, and respond to change as needed with new products and processes.

14   Continuously create new products or services, and processes, and enhance old ones.

21   Successfully practice big bang and continuous innovation.

28   Begin a knowledge management program.

35   Develop the organization's learning capabilities.

42   The organizationleverages its resources to achieve seemingly unobtainable goals.

49   Begin investing heavily and appropriately in R&D.

ACT NOW

A recent study by Jeff Mauzy of The Synectics Corportion found that eighty percent of U.S. company executives feel that innovation is critical to their companies' survival but only four percent feel that their companies are superior at making innovation happen. The study, which surveyed 750 executives at 150 U.S. companies, found that innovative companies experienced growth rates that were twice as great as those for non-innovative companies, with an even more significant difference in profit rates.[2]

Everyday that you delay, your competition gets further and further ahead. You know your position; your strengths and weaknesses. You have plans of action. The time to move forward is now. So what are you waiting for?

Innovate or Evaporate!

REFERENCES

1.   Kevin Kelly, "The Drought is Over at 3M," *Business Week* (November 7, 1994), pp. 140-141.

2.   Jeff Mauzy, *Succeeding in Innovation: The Synectics Report on Creativity & Innovation in U.S. Corporations* (The Synectics Corporation: Cambridge, MA, 1993).

INDEX

C̄

Index

Finn, David 256
First Chicago Bank 285
Fisher, George M. C. 176
Fitch, Ed 323
Fitzgerald, Karen 200, 322
Flexibility 187
Flexible system 188
Flores, Fernando 139
Flow 179
Flow International Corporation 177
Fluency techniques 283
Ford Motor Company:
            suggestion program 233
Ford Motor Company 4, 8, 155, 185, 210, 245, 319
Ford's Skunk Works 185
Forward looking 365
Foster, Richard N. 23-24, 146, 169
Four types of organizational learning 365
Four Ps of Creativity & Innovation 13
Four Types of Innovation 17
Fourtou, Jean-Rene 125, 315
Frederickson, James W. 198
Freedman, George 140
French managers 297
Frey, Don 237, 275, 292
Frische, Josef R. 264
Frito-Lay 146, 253, 276, 284
Fry, Art 206, 277
Fukuhara, Yoshiharu 282
Functional strategy 48
Funk, Jeffery L. 198
Future Shock 5

G

Gain sharing 206
Galbraith, Jay R. 95
Gallup Organization 231
Galvin, Robert W. 271
Gamache, Donald R. 322
Gantt Chart 339, 368
Garvin, David A. 340, 353
Gates, Bill 273, 313
Gates, Michael 236, 238
Gates, Richard 110
Gault, Stanley 109
GE and new product success 125
Geber, Beverly 264
Geffi, Craig A. 138
Gelmini, Joe 293
General Electric 3, 8, 108, 123-125, 227, 229, 248, 257, 284, 311, 333, 335
General Magic 22

General Motors 155, 192, 240, 284, 368
Gerlinger, Karl H. 151
Geroski, Paul 200
Gerstner, Louis 192, 194, 314, 317
Ghoshal, Sumantra 219
Gifford, Sharon 138
Global Competition 27
Global competitiveness 25
Globalization of Business Competition 5
Globalization of business 64
Goals 104, 121
Gobeli, David H. 353
Goddard, Robert W. 23
Golden Step Award 308, 357
Gomory, Ralph E. 46, 168
Goode, David 39
Goodheim, Laurie 265
Goodyear Tire & Rubber Company 210
Gordon, John R. M. 292
Gorr, Ivan 21, 352
Govoni, Stephen J. 63
Graven, Kathryn 22
Green, Robert T. 23
Green, Sidney 303
Greenberg, Daniel 46
Greskovich, Charles 248
Gretz, Karl F. 264, 292
Griffin, Ricky W. 95
Groffman, Steven E. 238
Gross, Neil 12, 44-45, 140, 169-170, 310
Group creativity 15-16
Groupware facilities 286
Grove, Andrew 47
Gryskiewicz, S. S. 95
GTE Telephone 286
Guenter Rexrodt: Germany's Minister of Economics 310
Guiltinan, Joseph 237
Gupta, Ashok K. 140, 236, 292
Guyon, Janet 22
GVO 128, 156

H

Habib, Mohammed H. 198
Hage, David 41
Hager, Bruce 353
Hall, Robert 128, 156
Hall, William K. 46, 48-49, 66
Halliday, Karen Kahler 189
Hallmark Cards 231
Hall's Competitiveness Model 48-49
Hamel, Gary 23, 141, 326, 341, 352-353
Hamilton, David P. 310

Index

Index

Index

383

INNOVATE
OR
EVAPORATE

Y

Z

BOOK ORDER FORM

Customer Information: Date: _____

Name: _____

Address: _____

City/State/Zip: _____

Item #	Description	Unit Price	Qty	Subtotal
101	*101 Creative Problem Solving Techniques: The Handbook of New Ideas for Business*	$17.95		
102	*Innovate or Evaporate: Test & Improve Your Organization's IQ – Its Innovation Quotient*	$23.95		
103	*Escape From the Maze: Increasing Personal and Group Creativity*	$15.95		

Comments:	**Sub.**	
Discounts are available for volume orders	**S & H***	
Shipping and handling is single book orders*		
Sales tax in Florida is 6%	**Tax**	
If payment is by check, please pay in <u>U.S. dollars only</u>	**Total**	

CREDIT CARD INFORMATION: VISA ☐   MASTER CARD ☐   AMEX ☐

Exact Account Name _____

Card Number _____ Expiration Date _____

Signature _____

*101 Creative Problem Solving Techniques *and* Escape From the Maze *ship at $3.00 each in the U.S. and Canada.* Innovate or Evaporate *will ship at $4.00 each to the U.S. and Canada. Shipping to other countries will be on a cost basis.*

THE NEW MANAGEMENT PUBLISHING COMPANY

400 North New York Avenue, Suite #215, Winter Park, Fl 32789
407-647-5344 or 800-266-8283/fax: 407-647-5575

SURVEY

As an author, I like feedback on my books. Please take the time
to fill out the three questions below and send them to me. As
this book is revised for reprinting, I will review my readers
suggestion and do changes as necessary. Thank you for taking
the time to help do improvements.

What did you like about the book?

_____

_____

_____

_____

_____

What would you like to see added?

_____

_____

_____

_____

_____

What changes should be made and why?

_____

_____

_____

_____

_____

Please mail this to:

New Management Publishing Company, Inc.
ATTN: Innovate or Evaporate Survey
400 North New York Avenue, #215
Winter Park, FL 32789